SCOTTISH
GOLD AND SILVER
WORK

"But others, which would fain catch their owne shaddowes, may not nor will not be perswaded that any goodnes can be produced out of Scotts ground, and are doubtfull whether the sonne and moone and starres shine there or not; for, say they, gold and silver engenders with the heate of the sonne and moone and alsoe, where such riches be, the people of that countrey cannot be poore nor beggarly, as the Scots be."

STEPHEN ATKINSON

The Discoverie and Historie of the Gold Mynes in Scotland (1619)

SCOTTISH GOLD AND SILVER WORK

IAN FINLAY

REVISED AND EDITED

by

Henry Fothringham

THE STRONG OAK PRESS

ISBN: 1-871048-04-4

Publishing History:
This work was first published in 1956. It has been out of print for
many years and is scarce and much sought-after. This new edition
incorporates the greater part of the original text and illustrations.
Chapter 15 has been rewritten and expanded by Henry Steuart Fothringham,
who is a Fellow of the Royal Society of Arts (FRSA) and a member of The
Incorporation of the Goldsmiths of the City of Edinburgh. There are
many new illustrations as well as new chapter notes, bibliography and
index.

Published by

The Strong Oak Press
SPA Books Ltd
PO Box 47
Stevenage
Herts SG2 8UH
United Kingdom

The publishers acknowledge subsidy from the Scottish
Arts Council towards the publication of this volume.

Printed in Great Britain at the Bath Press, Avon

CONTENTS

FOR VERONICA

PREFACE TO THE SECOND EDITION

THE first edition of this book was published in September, 1956. During the years which have elapsed, a great deal has happened in this field. Not only have researches vastly exceeded everything published prior to the date of the book's appearance; as a subject, Scottish silverware has attained independent status, and its history is no longer even putatively covered under the title of 'English Plate'. Much new silverware, newly-discovered silverware that is, has come to light. It is sad, certainly, that too many notable pieces have found their way into the market from the family homes where they have rested for generations, and for which in some cases they were made, and acknowledgements have to be changed; but at least some of these things have not been lost to the country, and the greater museums in Scotland have representative collections of Scottish silverware incomparably finer than used to be the case. That a small proportion of the silver which has gone should be ecclesiastical I do find regrettable, if inevitable. To purchase modern amenities by the sale of Communion silver for which past generations made great sacrifices is a form of betrayal if not a blasphemy.

For me, perhaps the most pleasing feature of this study over the years has been the sequel to the plea on the very last page of the book: the hope that growth of interest and vigilance in the smaller burghs where goldsmiths once flourished would result in such towns saving the products of their craftsmen and bringing together collections. This has come about to a degree I had not thought possible. As regards larger burghs, most can show some good examples and are eager to acquire more. Market prices of course have not made their task easier, but happily there are now funds they can draw upon in need, if and when they show their interest—funds which hardly existed all those years ago.

The need for a new edition, up-dated, corrected and improved, is therefore obvious. No alternative general history of the subject had appeared, as I had assumed it would. The relatively small printing of that first edition could not possibly meet present requirements. Surviving copies tend to fetch prohibitive prices.

Research and revision required for a new edition have proved an obstacle, so far as I was concerned, for a number of years. In the first place, for a long time I was too heavily committed to administrative work. When I retired in 1971 I had already moved to the field of Celtic art. It was therefore with the deepest pleasure that I welcomed Henry Steuart Fothringham's agreement to be Editor of the new edition. His devotion to the subject over many years and his scholarly work made him the ideal person to plan and oversee the volume; and his research into the provincial craftsmen in particular pointed to him for the authorship of a new chapter dealing with this subject. His re-casting of the lists of Scottish hall-marks for the new edition of Sir Charles Jackson's classical *English Goldsmiths and Their Marks* sets the seal upon his high qualifications.

I.F.

EDITOR'S NOTE

IT is with some diffidence that I have taken up Mr. Finlay's kind invitation to edit the second edition of *Scottish Gold and Silver Work*. Over the thirty-five years since it was written it has become a classic and is widely admired as a 'sacred text' by many enthusiasts of its subject matter. My task has been made much easier and more pleasurable than it would otherwise have been by having the kindly encouragement and help of Mr. Finlay who has smoothed my path at every turn and made many suggestions for which I am most grateful. The text of the first fourteen chapters has been altered as little as possible and I have merely added to the ends of the chapters anything that seemed needed to clarify or update them. I have also provided notes on the new illustrations which were not in the first edition. The number of plates has been increased from 96 to 120 allowing for seventy-four new illustrations to be included. Most of these are of items in the Royal Museum of Scotland to whose staff I am most grateful for the use of photographs and other facilities.

Chapter fifteen has been rewritten at Mr. Finlay's request and I have tried to cover as much ground as possible in the space available. I have also added a bibliography.

The last twenty years or so have witnessed many changes in who owns what, and not all of these changes have been mentioned where an item is in private hands. The John Noble collection, much referred to in the text, has now been dispersed, much of the best silver form Hopetoun House also, and the fine collections of Shaw of Tordarroch and Mr. Morris have come and gone in the same period. From these and other sources the national collection of Scottish silver has been vastly enriched to cover the whole field from mazers to teaspoons, and the provincial museums now possess fine representative collections of their locally-made silver.

One other change that needs to be noticed is the alteration of name of our two principal Scottish museums mentioned in the text, formerly known as the National Museum of Antiquities of Scotland and the Royal Scottish Museum. These two bodies have now merged to form a new entity called the Royal Museum of Scotland, which in turn is the principal component of a yet larger organisation called the National Museums of Scotland.

H.S.F.
Grantully 28th April, 1991

ACKNOWLEDGEMENTS

I wish to acknowledge my debt of gratitude firstly to Mr. Finlay himself for all his help and encouragement; to Mr. Stuart Maxwell, formerly Deputy Keeper of the National Museum of Antiquities of Scotland; to Mr. Jim Harper, the present assay master of the Edinburgh Assay Office, who have all been most helpful and longsuffering; to Mr. Tatton, present Deacon of the Edinburgh Goldsmiths Incorporation; to George Dalgleish and all his staff at the Royal Museum of Scotland (Queen St.) for giving up much time to my enquiries and facilitating the use of many photographs; to the staffs of the City Museums of Edinburgh, Glasgow, Aberdeen, Dundee, Perth and Inverness; to the private owners of items newly illustrated or mentioned in the text; to Mr. Kirkpatrick Dobie for kindly allowing me to make use of his original research into the goldsmiths of Dumfries; to the staff of the National Library of Scotland, the Edinburgh City Library and the Library of the Society of Antiquities of Scotland; to other interested parties who wish to remain anonymous; to Mrs. Davidson who kindly typed chapter fifteen; and to my wife who typed the bibliography.

H.S.F.

The Galloway Mazer: Canongate, c.1569.
Maker: James Gray (p.67)

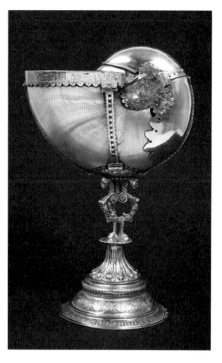

The Heriot Cup: Edinburgh, 1611–13.
Maker: Robert Denneistoune (pp.93-94)

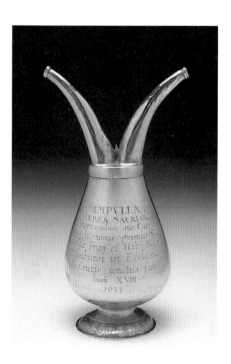

Gold Ampulla made for the Scottish Coronation of
Charles I in 1633: unmarked (pp.98-99)

The Feithie Salver: Dundee, c.1665.
Maker: Thomas Lindsay

Gold Tea Pot: Edinburgh, 1736.
Maker: James Ker (p.135)

The White Rod of Scotland lying in its fitted
case in two pieces: Edinburgh, 1758–59.
Maker: John Clark

The Royal Crown of Scotland: Edinburgh, 1540.
Maker: John Mosman (pp.54–57)

Obverse view of the Medallion appended to the
Gold Chain of the Usher of the White Rod of
Scotland: Edinburgh, 1758–59.
Maker: John Clark (p.167)

Chapter One

THE EARLIEST CELTIC GOLD AND SILVER WORK

THE blaze of glory which illumines the early pages of the history of the goldsmiths' art in Ireland casts only a fitful light on to the Scottish side of St. Patricks' Channel. Edinburgh's collection of Bronze Age treasures cannot match the national collection in Dublin. In the National Museum of Antiquities of Scotland there are some rich finds of early gold-work; but all too few of those relics can be credited with assurance to craftsmen of the region which is now Scotland, for archaeologists, on grounds of style or distribution, have linked one after another of them with southern Britain or with Ireland herself. There remains, however, a certain degree of tantalising uncertainty. Ireland and Scotland were closely linked in early times. Tradition hints at it: did not Cuchulinn go to Alba to learn chivalry of Dumnull and Scathach? The 'complete cultural identity' of the two countries in later, Christian times—I borrow Dr. Adolf Mahr's phrase—was not altogether a new thing. Scotland, therefore, may perhaps some day be shown to have enjoyed something more than crumbs from the rich table of Ireland's first golden age—that age when, if even a little of the *Yellow Book of Leacan* is based on truth, gold and silver adorned almost everything that men and women wore or wielded.

We know, of course, that men north of the Firth of Forth were skilled workers in metals long before the Christian era. There is ample evidence of this, and the superb bronze armlets peculiar to this part of the country hint at a craft of long standing. The constant coming and going between western Scotland and Ireland makes it likely that Irish skill as well as the products of it crossed the narrow sea. In most cases the gold ornaments found in Scotland are of types far commoner in Ireland, and because of this it is natural that they have generally been attributed to Irish origin; but it has been stated[1] that in the early Bronze

[1] Childe: *The Prehistory of Scotland*, p. 105

I

Pl. 1. i

Age native Scottish gold was being used to make dagger-mounts and ear-rings. The same authority quotes J. H. Craw's interesting theory that the beautiful golden *lunulæ*, so comparatively common in Ireland, have a Scottish derivation. It seems clear they are copies in gold of the crescentic jet necklaces of northern Britain, for the chevron-patterns engraved on them appear to represent the spacer-beads of the necklaces. Craw bases his argument on the fact that three out of the five *lunulæ* found in Scotland bear this chevron-pattern, whereas only nine of the fifty-two Irish examples are so decorated. It seems just possible that some at least of the Scottish *lunulæ* are of Scottish workmanship, and that the richer deposits of gold in Ireland are the reason for the much larger number of Irish pieces; but this view would find small support among archaeologists and the *lunula* must be abandoned as a starting-point for a history of Scottish goldsmithing.

Mention of native Scottish gold raises an important topic. Scotland did not share Ireland's fame as a source of the precious metal. She had no deposits comparable with the Wicklow Mountains, the wealth of which Mahr associates with the high pitch of perfection in Irish craftsmanship, yet there is reason to think the Leadhills and Crawford-Muir mines, perhaps also those of Sutherland and elsewhere in Scotland, were much richer many centuries ago than they have been in recent times.[1] Gold in these places was obtained mainly by washing the surface-soil—a simple matter compared with the complicated processes of mining and metallurgy necessary to procure silver—and it is probable the ground was quite systematically 'combed' long before James V established there the large-scale mining industry which will be described in its proper place. It is tempting to speculate whether some pointer to the native origins or otherwise of Bronze Age Scottish gold-work cannot be secured by assay. This, however, does not seem to hold out much promise. It is true that Scottish gold contains a rather high proportion of silver, that from Wanlockhead showing 12.39 per cent[2]; but a comparison of the analyses of Scottish and Irish gold[3] does not show such a disparity that the test would seem to serve a useful purpose. Dr. Callander inclined to the theory that prehistoric gold ornaments were of native metal,[4] disagreeing with the assertion that Irish gold was used; but since his belief was based on the factor of distribution it is doubtful if it

---

[1] D. Wilson: *Prehistoric Annals of Scotland*, Vol. I, pp. 323–4
[2] *P.S.A.S.*, Vol. XXIV, p. 91
[3] *P.S.A.S.*, Vol. LXIII, p. 188   [4] *P.S.A.S.*, Vol. LVII, p. 157

could be applied to objects found in western and northern districts, which could have got their metal as easily, if not more easily, from Ireland. On the other hand, it is reasonable to infer that the material of some at least of the Bronze Age gold-work is of native origin, for the observant eyes of that period cannot have overlooked the grains and occasional small nuggets brought to light by erosion along the courses of streams and in gulleys on the hillsides. Bronze and stone implements which may be pre-Roman have actually been found in the Leadhills and Wanlockhead surface workings.[1] They may, or again they may not, have been used by early lead-miners.

We must, however, return for a moment to the *lunulæ*. Whatever their origin, they are the most effective and perhaps the most interesting of the Bronze Age gold articles in the Scottish group. They alone show any serious attempt to carry out a pattern of surface decoration, although the tools used are only hammer and graver, and the pattern is a mere combination of engraved marks grouped in chevrons. This pattern, as Romilly Allen pointed out, founded as it is on the chevron, corresponds with the decoration of sepulchral pottery, which might be advanced as an argument against Craw's theory, quoted above, that the gold *lunula* was a Scottish invention. Other gold objects of the early period include torc bracelets, penannular rings and armlets, rings of plaited wire and at least four 'lock-rings', two with remarkably fine concentric circle decoration. Some of these things are of considerable beauty. The moving play of light on the torc bracelets renders them as desirable adornments as many a more sophisticated contrivance. Nor can they be dismissed as mere primitive gewgaws of drawn and twisted metal, for they call for a good deal of craft skill and, as a previous commentator remarks, are 'worked in a very careful and skilful manner'.[2] Yet similar things have been found over a wide area of Europe, and there is no modification here or scrap of decoration in which one might detect a local accent. There is in fact nothing of what Wilson calls 'defined ornamentation', and no more than the *lunulæ* do they give us a firm starting-point.

Pl.2.i

For this starting-point it seems we must look in the Christian era, although at a time when Scotland was still pagan. There is no doubt that by the Iron Age Scotland, north of the Forth at least, possessed metalworkers of the highest skill who were also men of excellent taste. Evidence of this is to be found in

---

[1] Wilson & Flett: *Memoirs of the Geol. Survey, Scotland*, Vol. XVII
[2] *P.S.A.S.*, Vol. XVIII, p. 234

the massive bronze armlets which are almost exclusive to this region, only two having been found outside it. They are of cast metal, some spiral, some ribbed, with flamboyant late La Tène decoration suggesting the *repoussé* work of the time. There is tremendous vitality in their design and execution, hinting at a vigorous community and culture. Their authors had not only a mastery of metal, but also some skill in the difficult art of enamelling followed by the Celtic peoples, for a number of the armlets retain traces of this. Where such technical skill and taste existed, there must have been essays in the precious metals and it is remarkable that few or none of them have been discovered. The one piece which might represent such essays is the gold torc terminal found at Shaw Hill, near Cairnmuir. It is a small relic, but a masterpiece of its kind, and illustrates well the Celt's unerring touch in contrasting decorated surfaces with plain, and massive designs with intricate. Authoritative opinion now appears to regard it as an import, probably from East Anglia, although its style at once suggests the spiral armlets, which are about a century later.[1] It is disappointing that this era, with its skill and taste and obvious vitality, should not have left us other treasures; but gold articles would naturally be the first objects to be seized by thieves and raiders and more often than not would go to the melting-pot.

The first few centuries of our era are a blank period indeed. It is, certainly, the period to which the Traprain treasure belongs. This, however, merely accentuates the blank in native craftsmanship, as the hoard is composed of late Roman provincial silver vessels possibly looted from colonies in Gaul and subsequently buried where they were found, on Traprain Law in East Lothian. Many of the vessels are of great beauty. But it would be out of place to describe the hoard even briefly in a history of Scottish work, and it is sufficient to make reference to *The Treasure of Traprain*, by Dr. A. O. Curle, the discoverer. This Roman hoard underlines also that extraordinary absence of objects made of silver which persisted generally up to the Iron Age, not in Scotland only, or even in Britain, but throughout northern Europe, as Dr. Wilson remarked.[2] It is not until about the late seventh century that the making of silver articles on any scale seems to have been carried on in Scotland. Wilson has already indicated the explanation. Silver-mining demands a knowledge of metallurgy and a use of tools which only the gradual mastery of iron brought about. It has been suggested that native smiths made use of such hoards as the Traprain one

Pl.1.ii

[1] See *Prehistory of Scotland*, p. 257   [2] *Prehist. Annals of Scotland*, Vol. II, p. 131

4

PLATE 1

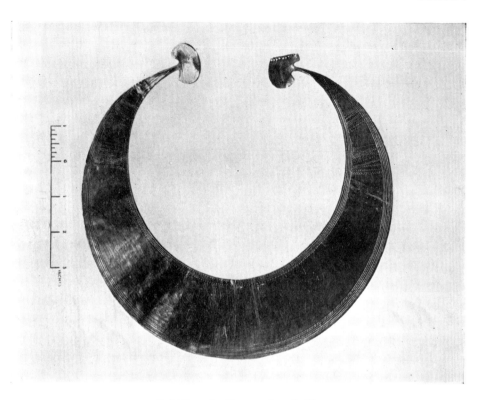

Gold Lunula: Bronze Age *(p.2)*

Gold Torc-Terminal found at Shaw Hill:
possibly 2nd century B.C. (2¼″) *(p.4)*

PLATE 2

Gold Armlet and Ear-Ornament (5½″): Bronze Age *(p.3)*

Silver Chain from Whitecleugh, Aberdeenshire: probably 8th century (20″ long)
(p.5)

PLATE 3

The Monymusk Reliquary: 7th to 8th Centuries *(p.11-12)*

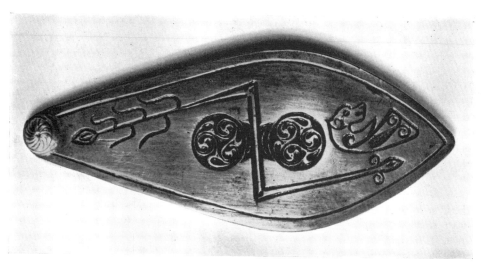

Leaf-shaped Silver Ornament, from hoard found at Norrie's Law, Fife: probably 8th century (3½″) *(p.6)*

PLATE 4

Fragment of a Brooch from Dunbeath: 8th to 9th centuries (2¾″) *(pp.14 & 16)*

as raw material for their own productions. This may be the case; but the only evidence available points to native sources of metal, for an analysis[1] made in 1880 of the silver chain found at Hordwell in the Lammermoors yielded these figures:

Silver	76·505
Gold	4·237
Copper	19·183
	———
	99·925

As the analyst stated at the time, this suggests that the silver was procured from ore by a rough metallurgic process, as otherwise no percentage of gold would have found its way into the alloy. He mentioned the possibility of the vein at Alva in Stirlingshire being the source, as argentiferous grey copper ore often occurs there.

This silver chain from the Lammermoors is one of a group of such chains which appear to date from about the eighth century. There are half-a-dozen of them in the National Museum of Antiquities, and there is a record of another found near Greenlaw which has long since disappeared. The first of the chains to be discovered turned up in a ridge of gravel forming part of a hill-fort when the Caledonian Canal was being excavated in 1809.[2] It is also the most massive: 18 inches in length, with a weight of 92 ozs. 2 dwts. The rings of all chains are in pairs, and the silver in each case has been hammered into a rod and bent to form a circular link with flattened ends brought together without soldering. How massive these are may be judged by the fact that in one instance the finder tried to use the chain for lifting sacks, with the aid of a pulley; while in the Greenlaw case the blacksmith, under the impression that the metal was iron, attempted to employ the chain to repair the 'rig-body' which passes over a horse's back to support the cart-shafts! The most interesting feature of the chains, however, is the stout penannular ring which, in two cases, forms a terminal. In the example from Parkhill in Aberdeenshire this ring is incised with a pattern comprising a thickened S-curve, two triangles and some triple dots, evidently filled with red enamel originally, a pattern clearly allied to some of those on the early sculptured stones of the region. The terminal ring of the Whitecleugh example is even more conclusively allied. It carries the 'spectacles and zigzag' and other devices from the symbol stones. These seem to establish the chains as Pictish. One may even venture with some confidence

Pl.2.ii

[1] *P.S.A.S.*, Vol. XV, p. 69
[2] Finlay: *Columba*, p. 129

to guess at the purpose of the chains. Dr. Wilson's contention that they were formed of ring-money[1] will not bear much scrutiny. It was based on the fact that the links are open, but he founded his opinion on the Inverness-shire chain, which has no large terminal ring. Full-length chains such as the Parkhill one—and in their original state all seem to have been about the same length— surround the neck comfortably, the open terminal ring serving as a clasp, and it appears to be a reasonable supposition that they were badges of office, ecclesiastical or civil. Dr. J. A. Smith gave convincing proof of this in a paper[2] read to the Society of Antiquaries of Scotland, describing in detail the use of neck-chains of gold by kings, chieftains and leaders among the Irish and the Welsh. These, indeed, not crowns, seem to have been insignia of the highest rank. Silver chains may well have signified dignitaries of lesser rank. Whatever their significance, the chains are evidence of high technical ability among the Pictish people.

Pl.3.i   Light is also thrown on this period by some of the remarkable silver articles found in the hoard at Norrie's Law, near Largo, in Fife, in 1819. The hoard, as discovered in or near a stone coffin, weighed 400 ozs. It comprises three pins with ornamental heads, two penannular brooches, two leaf-shaped plates, and a number of fragments. The leaf-shaped plates are specially interesting. They are alike, about $3\frac{1}{2}$ inches long, and engraved upon them is the 'spectacles and zigzag' device found on the terminal ring of the Whitecleugh chain, as on the symbol-stones. Here again the sunk spaces seem to have contained red enamel. I must resist the temptation to be lured aside by problems which belong to the field of archaeology, but this device clearly preoccupied the Pictish silversmith so that it is difficult not to speculate on his relations with rulers or priesthood. Like all Pictish devices, this one has remained without any convincing interpretation. The generical similarity of examples which occur on silver articles, as on the sculptured stones, is inescapable, although they come from widely separated sites; and as the silver articles are ornaments of importance and obvious significance its association with personages of dignity seems probable. It bears a certain resemblance to the stylised thunderbolt of classical art and in some vague way also recalls certain motives in archaic Chinese art. Pictish culture seems to have remained fundamentally pagan, whether or no the symbols were adapted for Christian purposes, and it is conceivable that the 'spectacles

---

[1] *Prehist. Ann. of Scotland*, Vol. II, p. 134
[2] *P.S.A.S.*, Vol. X, pp. 335 et seq

and zigzag' may have been connected with some princely or priestly powers over thunder and lightning, rain and the release of fecundity in the earth. One of the three pins from the Norrie's Law hoard, however, carries on its central 'finger' a cross, undoubtedly the Christian symbol. Its date is about 700, rather after than before.

This seems to be the natural point at which to end the first chapter of this survey. We have reached the end of the seventh century. The Picts, whose vigorously independent outlook is reflected in the originality of their art, are much subject to outside influences. St. Ninian had converted the northern Picts, who were probably at least nominally Christian in the seventh century; but lapses appear to have been frequent among them, and behind their barriers of mountain and bog the pagan element must have fought a long, stubborn rearguard action. As described already, the symbol-bearing silver chains and plaques themselves hint at a cult not obviously Christian. These objects, however, do not appear to have been made after the early eighth century. It may be significant that it was in the year 710 that Naitan, King of the Picts, sent to Abbot Ceolfrid at Wearmouth for architects to build him a church after the Roman manner, an event which must gradually have brought to an end the more easy-going ways of the Irish form of worship, although it is interesting to note that Bede records Naitan's request for enlightenment of him and his people as qualified by the words 'as far as their remoteness from the Roman language and nation would allow'. This remoteness insulated Scotland from direct Mediterranean cultural influences for many centuries. The beautiful metal-work of the period now beginning reflects Irish tradition and also the Scandinavian styles carried by the Northmen in their ceaseless forays to the west.

NOTES TO CHAPTER I

MAJOR ADDITIONS TO THE NATIONAL COLLECTION SINCE 1956 (p.1)

The first edition of this book referes to "some rich finds of early gold work" in the National Museum of Antiquities, now the Royal Museum of Scotland. Since its publication a number of important items have been added to the collection and much new scholarship and thinking has appeared in print. I will confine myself here to expanding a little on two of the items discussed in the text.

THE SHAW HILL TORC-TERMINAL (p.4)

This Torc-terminal should be compared with the torc from Snettisham, Norfolk, in the British Museum. As Mr. Finlay pointed out, it may not be Scottish at all. The technology involved in making this torc-terminal is discussed by Morna MacGregor in *Early Celtic Art in North Britain*, no.191, where she draws attention to the fact that one can still make out the hammer-marks inside the cast body of the ring, and see the ragged fluting where the multi-strand hoop was fitted to it with solder. Shaw Hill is close to the house of New Cairnmuir, in Netherurd parish, Peeblesshire. With the torc-terminal were also discovered two complete gold torcs of much lighter construction; one was a loop-terminal torc, 3½" diam., comprising two thick wires of circular section, twisted widdershins, formed into a hoop and terminating in a loop at each end; the other was of square-section, twisted clockwise, the ends turned out and flattened into lobes. Sadly, both these objects have disappeared, probably melted down, but they are cited by D. Wilson in *Prehistoric Annals of Scotland* (1851), *Archaeologia Scotica* vol.IV (1857) and by R. W. de F. Feachem in *The Cairnmuir Hoard from Netherurd, Peeblesshire* in 1957 (P.S.A.S. XCI, pp.112-16).

THE NORRIE'S LAW TREASURE (p.6, pl.3,1)

Probably deposited a century earlier than once thought, the famous pair of leaf-shaped ornaments are now ascribed to the mid-Seventh Century.

Besides those mentioned in the text, some other significant pieces from

8

the Norrie's Law Hoard have survived. One of these is a shaped oval plaque in beaten silver, some 5″ across, with a central more-or-less rectangular hole, and decorated with three raised coils. There were presumably four originally, but that section which would have included the fourth one is now missing. Two of the coils are relatively complex, having additional ground detail in the shape of curved trumpet stems, while the remaining simple coils is an unadorned keeled curve in equally high relief. It is not impossible that this plaque is all that remains of an annular brooch of an otherwise unknown type; this might explain the nicks in the inner and outer edges, just opposite each other, where the pin would have pivoted. The symbolism of the decoration is, like all things Pictish, obscure. The date of the hoard's deposition is now thought to have been in the late Seventh Century, but this plaque is probably anything up to a century earlier.

NOTES TO ILLUSTRATIONS

There are no new illustrations to this chapter. Note that the Monymusk Reliquary really belongs to the next chapter, but since it is coupled with the Ornament from Norrie's Law it has been left in its original position.

Chapter Two

THE CHRISTIAN CELTIC PERIOD

THE eighth century began a momentous era for the Scoto-Irish culturel. If, basically, it remained unchanged, the forms in which it showed itself underwent a revolution. The religious crisis was, of course, the factor responsible for this. For two centuries the little Christian world of Ireland and western Scotland had been isolated by a veritable iron curtain of pagan Saxondom, and what is perhaps too readily called its 'insularity' persisted for quite half a century after the defeat of the Celtic Church at the Synod of Whitby, for the monks of Iona did not accept the Roman form of worship until 716. It is sometimes argued on behalf of this absorption of the less by the greater that if isolation had persisted much longer the genius of this remote Celtic pocket would have spent itself in mere pattern-making, and that the latent craft skill of the metalworkers would never have flowered as it did. No such spirit of decadence had shown itself, however. In store of courage and initiative the Irish were rich. Irish missionaries had reached out southwards through pagan Europe long before orthodox Christianity penetrated into the north. While the Synod of Whitby hastened the downfall of the barriers between Rome and the nonconformist north, Hiberno-Saxon culture had already possessed Britain and left its mark in the shadow of the Alps.

This reunion of north and south did not destroy Irish Celtic art as it eventually destroyed the Celtic Church. From the earliest times the Celtic artist had hungered after union with the south, perhaps because his wayward, intuitive genius always needed the tectonic faculty and the powers of rationalisation of the Mediterranean mind to realise itself in full. Intercourse with Rome, and through Rome with the East, was precisely what the Irish monks and craftsmen required to stimulate their unrivalled capacity for decorative art. The result of this intercourse, in the words of Mlle. Françoise Henry, who has probably done more than anyone to place the contribution of the northern Celts in its true perspective, was 'an art of extraordinary strength, indulging in bold designs, rejoicing in the contrast of a plain surface with a broad pattern, and retaining much of the wild freedom of primitive times'.[1] The second golden age of Irish culture had arrived. This time there could be no question that the glory shed itself upon Scotland too and kindled there traditions which gleamed and glimmered fitfully for many centuries. To quote Mlle. Henry again: 'It is to be expected that the monastery of Adamnan'—Iona—'was a leading artistic centre and that it played a more important part in the elaboration of the new style than can now be proved'.[2] It must always be remembered that Iona was a stopping-place not only on the route out of Ireland but also on the route into Ireland by way of Lindisfarne and the east and south; and that on this small island the Irish genius may often have encountered for the first time many a strange and exciting new idea or *motif*, Norse, Saxon, classical and even oriental.

Metalwork was a ready medium, as always in Celtic art, and here this renaissance manifested itself brilliantly. Decoration, revitalised, in the seventh century spreads itself over the surfaces of metal objects in a variety of techniques which reveal not only the mastery of the craftsmen but also the confident, questing spirit in which they worked. From late in the century 'characteristic interlacing motives supersede pure La Tenè derivatives',[3] as can be seen also in another field, manuscript illumination, notably in the oldest of the Irish codices, the Book of Durrow. There is a combination of complicated design with delicacy of execution, although it is 'some emotional quality which constitutes its innermost essence'. Invention and originality enliven all the best examples of the *opus hibernicum*, no matter what the medium. And the zoomorph, as Dr. Mahr has stated, is a vital component of the new style: a supreme example of the foreign element—in this instance Teutonic—adapted superbly by the Celt for his own purposes.

Among the finest pieces of Scoto-Irish metalwork of this time are the little shrines or reliquaries of 'hip-roof' type. Scotland is the fortunate possessor of one which is probably the most outstanding of them all, the Monymusk Reliquary, otherwise known as the Brecbennoch of St. Columba. Its precise region Pl.3.ii of origin is, of course, unknown. Mlle. Henry describes it[4] as 'either of Irish workmanship, or a product of one of the Irish establishments in Scotland'. The beauty and interest of this reliquary have recently been enhanced by careful cleaning, and the sombre appearance which it wore when illustrated in colour in an earlier book, my *Scottish Crafts*, is now banished. It is in a sense the most

---

[1] Henry: *Irish Art*, p. 46   [2] Ibid., p. 52
[3] Adolf Mahr: *Ancient Irish Handicraft*, p. 13   [4] *Irish Art*, p. 70

notable of all Scotland's national relics. Traditionally, it held the Psalter,[1] chief relic of St. Columba, in the territory of his clan, the Cinel Conall Gulban.[2] It was styled the Cathach, or Battler, and carried suspended against the breast; and, it is recorded in Adamnan's *Life of St. Columba*, 'if it be sent thrice right-ways (i.e. sunways) around the army of the Cinel Conall when they are going to battle, they will return safe with victory, and it is on the breast of a coarb or cleric who is, to the best of his power, free from mortal sin, that the Cathach should be when brought round the army'. The relics of Columba are said to have been conveyed back and forward between Iona and Dunkeld, on the one hand, and Ireland on the other during the early part of the ninth century. It may be the reliquary took part in those journeys. Its history seems to enter the field of certainty when, shortly before the year 1211, it was deposited in the Abbey of Arbroath, with a gift of the lands of Forglen. In 1314 the Abbot of Arbroath apparently carried it with the Scots army at the Battle of Bannock-burn, when it momentously justified its reputation. One hundred and one years later it came to the family of Monymusk, in Aberdeenshire; and after a century in the possession of the Irvines of Drum it returned to Monymusk. In 1923, with the aid of a grant from the National Art-Collections Fund, it was purchased for the National Museum of Antiquities from the Grants of Monymusk.

The Monymusk Reliquary is a box 4¼ inches long, 3⅛ inches high and 2 inches wide. It is constructed out of two pieces of wood, one forming the box itself, the other the lid, each hollowed from the solid. On three of the sides the wood is covered by bronze plates fixed with small rivets, but the frontal plates are of silver, the corners and edges secured with rounded mountings riveted in position. An overall zoomorphic pattern decorates the two silver plates, a pattern recalling the Book of Durrow. This pattern is too delicate for effective reproduction, for it shows up only because it has been left in reserve on a ground of minute stippling. On the plates are imposed small circular and rect-angular panels contrived with gilt metal and red enamel. Yellow and red enamels are also employed for the hinged fitting attached to one end of the casket, a fitting which, with its companion, probably secured a leather strap for suspension round the neck of the priest. The decoration of this relic is of a very high standard, and Dr. Joseph Anderson's claim that it is the finest of its

[1] I understand this book is preserved in Ireland, but is too large for the Reliquary
[2] *P.S.A.S.*, Vol. XLIV, p. 259, and Finlay: *Columba*, p.17 et seq

type was well founded. The others include one from the Shannon, also in the National Museum of Antiquities, two in Ireland, one in Copenhagen and one in Trondheim. The Copenhagen example bears a scratched Runic inscription and the Trondheim one was discovered in a Viking grave-mound, so it is clear that both Scandinavian reliquaries were borne away from their proper sphere by Norse invaders or colonists. Dr. Anderson's contention that 'the architecturally shaped shrines of the Celtic Church . . . were fashioned in imitation of the form which the Celtic artist who illuminated the *Book of Kells* evolved from his imagination as a representation of the Temple at Jerusalem'[1] must be abandoned. However late in the seventh century these reliquaries may be placed, they appear to have been in existence two or three generations before the monks of Iona began work on the *Book of Kells*.[2] Resemblance between the form of the reliquary and the picture of the temple is, however, striking. If, as I suggested earlier, the reliquary in its travels found its way to Iona, it is not unreasonable to think the monkish illuminator may have borrowed from it the idea for his temple, instead of the other way about. But there is here, in any case, a typically Celtic architectural form which can be matched in early Irish churches and oratories, a parallel which Dr. Anderson himself drew.[3] It is probably a natural form for either shrine or temple image to take, and a similar form is of course followed by the familiar shrines of the middle ages, notably those embellished by the enamellers of Limoges, although there a normal gable-end replaces the hip-roof.

The technical skill, the level of sophistication and even, in some measure, the prosperity signified by the objects wrought in precious metal at this time must always cause surprise when they are regarded against a background of apparent primitive simplicity. 'There seems,' writes Mlle. Henry,[4] 'to be no proportion between the sumptuousness of the jewellery and the simplicity of the industrial objects'; and she pursues the contrast by citing dumps of bones, shells, remains of past meals in underground chambers and in crannogs. She points the parallel of similar contrasts in the tents of Arab chieftains. But it may be we assume too readily this picture of primitive domestic standards. No doubt we may discount as products of poetic licence bardic versions of the glories of Tara's Halls; but an absence of important building sites does not mean that important structures did not exist. Josef Strzgowski has long established the vital part

[1] *P.S.A.S.*, Vol. XLIV, p. 259   [2] *Irish Art*, p. 149
[3] *Scotland in Early Christian Times*, p. 248   [4] *Irish Art*, p. 88

played by timber in the ecclesiastical architecture of northern Europe, while Bede and other of the early writers recorded that timber was the Celt's natural building medium, as stone was the Roman's. I am convinced that the magnificent metalwork of the eighth and following centuries arose against a more stable and elaborate background than ascertained facts permit us to imagine, and it may be that the hip-roofed reliquaries hint at this, for their basic design suggests a house of timber rather than of stone construction.

Pl.4

The group of Scottish brooches is less important than the Irish group, but it is hardly less interesting and in itself forms a superb heritage from the early Christian period. It contains nothing quite so rich or intricate as the so-called 'Tara' brooch in Dublin; yet an unhappy accident robbed Scotland of one piece which, in delicacy of craftsmanship at least, might have compared with the Irish masterpiece. This tantalising object was brought up on the point of his pick by a man digging a drain at Dunbeath, in Caithness, in 1860. The pick-stroke shattered what seems to have been a complete brooch, and the finder, ignorant and careless, mislaid all fragments but one small one, which at the time of discovery he handed to an onlooker. Fortunately the fragment eventually found its way into the National Museum of Antiquities. It is of silver, inlaid with gold, and Dr. Joseph Anderson justifiably described it[1] as the most beautifully-executed specimen of Celtic goldsmith's work that he had ever seen in Scotland. Zoomorphic monsters comparable to those on the Tara brooch form the principal ornament, but the infilling of the bodies is composed of minute granules of gold. Ornament here is less riotous than on the Tara brooch, but the technique is almost as exquisitely fine.

Pl.5

The same may be said of the finest of the complete, or nearly complete, Scottish brooches, found at Hunterston in Ayrshire in 1826. This is a large brooch, $4\frac{3}{4}$ inches at its widest diameter. Full appreciation of it as a technical achievement can only be arrived at by examining the details under a mangifying-glass. It demonstrates exceptionally well the Celtic artist's infallible taste and his shrewd eye for contrasting textures—bold masses against intricate detail, plain surfaces against enriched ones, silver against gold, glinting gold against softly glowing amber settings. Even the narrow edges of the brooch have received the craftsman's careful attention, and they are engraved with panels of interlaced work so faultless that they lead us to wonder what sort of tools the man possessed. The Hunterston brooch is typical of the beginning of the finest

[1] *Scotland in Early Christian Times*, 2nd Series, p. 16, and Finlay: *Celtic Art*, p.122

period of Scoto-Irish jewellery, a period covering the eighth and ninth centuries: the period also of the great illuminated manuscripts, which in detail so closely resemble the brooches. Professor Mahr inclined to think the Hunterston brooch slightly later than similar Irish pieces, but he gave no reasons for this.[1] He dated the Tara brooch shortly before 750. It is a matter of considerable interest that the Tara brooch, like so many of the Irish brooches, is basically of bronze, whereas silver is characteristic of the Scottish brooches. This seems finally to dispose of the theory that the latter were importations from Ireland, and there would seem to be much substance in Mlle. Henry's suggestion[2] that silver came to the Irish jewellers from Scotland.

In these massive brooches the ring is completely closed, leaving no slot for the pin, while the pin itself has a great head shaped like a wedge or the keystone of an arch. Another type of brooch common to Ireland and Scotland is represented in the latter mainly by the Rogart group, a notable Irish example of the type being the Kilmainham brooch. The Rogart brooches were disclosed by a blasting operation during the building of a railway in Sutherland in 1868. As so frequently happens, the finder's first aim was profit, and he disappeared with what must have been a hoard of brooches. Three, however, were shed on the man's journey south. The two finest came into the possession of Macleod of Cadboll and are now in the National Museum of Antiquities. They, too, are of silver. Both are penannular. The larger is $4\frac{1}{2}$ inches in diameter and is plated with gold. Its two extremities are of quatrefoil shape, with an amber setting in the centre of each and four shallow compartments plated with gold and tooled with delicate interlaced work; but the peculiarity of this particular piece is the raised ornament of four bird's heads with bills dipping forward towards the amber setting, a motif employed, though less boldly, on the edge of the Hunterston brooch, and also in the manuscripts. The other Cadboll brooch is smaller, with trefoil extremities and without the bird motif. It possesses rich areas of ornament: interlacing on sunk panels of gold which by contrast is enhanced by the plain, rounded ring of silver. Less delicate in execution, though equally effective, is a brooch of the same sort found with another in the neighbourhood of Perth. The birds' heads of the larger Cadboll brooch are in this case represented by trios of animal heads. Here again the material is silver enriched by the application of thin gold plates decorated with interlacing and zoomorphic patterns.

Pl. 6

[1] *Anc. Irish Handicrafts*, p. 15   [2] *Irish Art*, footnote to p. 122

Another important brooch of silver and gold was found at Croy in Inverness-shire in 1875. It also is penannular, with terminals expanded into discs, the central setting on each of which is surrounded by double rope-twist moulding. Diametrically opposite, there is an oblong panel with interlaced ornament. This slight feature apart, the brooch is not markedly Celtic in feeling. Discovered with it were two coins, one of which is a silver penny of Coenwulf, King of Mercia (795–818), the other of Aethwulf (829–858). From its greater simplicity, Mlle. Henry suggests that it comes near to Saxon work.[1] It appears to me to belong with the Rogart brooch type, although it is later, for it resembles the smaller Cadboll brooch in spirit almost as closely as it does in size, the terminals developing in much the same way although without achieving the more elaborate trefoil design. Rope-twist ornament occurs on the beautiful fragment from Dunbeath, and this feature is no evidence of a non-Celtic origin.

Pl.4

A brooch from Dunipace in Stirlingshire Anderson describes as decadent and late,[2] yet the habit of identifying crudity of finish with lateness of execution is not in all circumstances reliable, for obvious reasons. To me, the features which indicate that this brooch is probably later than the finer ones are the contraction of the ring to take the pin-hinge and the lenticular settings of amber, both of which show a certain rough-and-ready idea of design foreign to the Scoto-Irish school in the period under review.

It is not unreasonable to believe these few brooches, together with other objects of the period such as the reliquaries, are the mere vestige of a great wealth of similar things once preserved in the monasteries and in secular houses.

Pl.5

On the back of the Hunterston brooch are scratched two Runic inscriptions which Anderson dates about the tenth century.[3] They read: *Maelbritha owns this brooch* and *Olfriti owns this brooch*. These names are characteristic of the Gallgael, Celto-Norse inhabitants of the Hebrides, and they commemorate the great and terrible pagan invasions which from the end of the eighth century began to penetrate and disintegrate the Scoto-Irish civilisation and culture—the descent of the 'Gentiles', as the Irish Annals call the invaders, or of the Northmen, as they are more commonly termed in our histories. These invaders established a plunder-route from the shores of the Irish Sea round the north of Scotland to the fjords of Norway, and it is impossible to calculate what quantities of booty were carried off from monastic establishments and dwellings in Ire-

---

[1] *Irish Art.*, p. 117   [2] *Scot. in Early Christ. Times*, 2nd Series, p. 24   [3] *Ibid.*, p. 6

land and Scotland. Impressed though their own craftsmen were, Viking warriors showed small respect for the artistic achievements of their victims and broke up their loveliest works into scrap-metal as heedlessly as they desecrated their altars from Iona to Armagh.

Many items of their plunder have of course come to light in Scandinavia, and they include Scoto-Irish reliquaries and brooches. Such plunder has also been discovered in Scotland itself, or the islands pertaining to it. The two most important finds are the Skaill and the Burray hoards, both of them now in the National Museum of Antiquities. The hoard from Skaill, in Orkney, is a particularly rich one. It may be said to have been unearthed by rabbits, since a boy found the first fragments of it at the mouth of a burrow in 1858. It consists of ring-brooches, neck-rings of twisted silver wire, penannular bracelets, ingots and odd fragments, and the total weight of silver is 16 lbs. avoirdupois. Dr. Anderson described the objects minutely some years after their discovery.[1] One or two of the ring-brooches are of the large, bulbous variety of the penannular form which came into fashion as late as the tenth century. The largest of the Skaill brooches has a pin 15 inches long, and the bulbs or knobs are incised deeply with a pattern of lacertine knotwork. High skill and excellent taste are reflected in this and other brooches in the hoard. Anderson tended to ascribe them to an oriental origin, partly because Cufic coins of the Abbaside series, one of them struck at Baghdad in 945, were found with the hoard. Certainly the bulbous brooches do not appear to be of Scottish origin, as no others have been found in Scotland; but the type is scattered along the Viking plunder-route and large brooches, no doubt of this sort, seem to have been a common enough article of adornment in the Scoto-Irish region, for in the Brecon laws there are regulations to limit the length of the pins, which must not project beyond the wearer's shoulder, as they were so long at times that they were capable of injuring neighbours in a crowd. Such regulations recall the limitations set upon the length of rapiers worn in Elizabethan England.

The decoration of the big Skaill brooch noted above links up with the Viking 'Jellinge' style, a squirming confusion of queer monsters. This, however, does not necessarily indicate an importation from Denmark. Forms of the Jellinge style became established wherever the Northmen settled,[2] from the Danelaw round to Ireland, and the ornament in question as well as other jewellery in

Pl.7

---

[1] *P.S.A.S.*, Vol. X, p. 574 et seq.
[2] Kendrick: *Late Saxon and Viking Art*, p. 89. Henry: *Irish Art*, p. 161

this hoard are characteristic of the large Irish thistle-brooches of the tenth century. Most of the evidence is consistent with the view that the traffic in valuables was from west to east rather than the reverse, although the coins must of course have found their way north by the trade route across Russia. For the neck-rings and armlets in this hoard Anderson again suggested an oriental origin, but the source is clearly much nearer to the place where the articles were found. Penannular silver armlets, either plain or decorated with small triangles containing pellets, have been found in various spots in Orkney, Shetland, Skye and Caithness. They may well have been intended as a form of currency, for there is a sharp interior ridge which would chafe against an arm. They were probably formed from melted Anglo-Saxon coins. Their distribution is all along the plunder-route, and almost as far as could be from native sources of silver. Similar penannular rings occur in the Burray hoard,[1] in the National Museum of Antiquities. Indeed this hoard consists mainly of such rings, although it includes a fine silver torc, of simpler construction than some found in the Skaill hoard.[2] Three coins found with it are Anglo-Saxon, dated between 901 and 1016. It is of considerably less consequence than the Skaill hoard; but, like the hoard found with Anglo-Saxon and oriental coins near the Storr Rock, Skye, in 1891, it is further evidence of that regular traffic in silver ornaments and bullion which passed through Scottish coastal waters during the centuries of Viking activity.

Metalwork of this Viking period, although it has so much in common with earlier times, is at once distinguishable from purely Scoto-Irish material. Mlle. Henry has contrasted the two styles perhaps more neatly than any other writer.[3] Interlacing is common to both, but she points out that Scandinavian interlacing is essentially inorganic, and she refers to the 'nightmarish' quality of eighth-century Norwegian decoration with its shapeless loops, disconnected tentacles, darting heads and fragments of legs. This nightmarish quality is totally absent from decoration of the Irish school, however fantastic that may be. The rhythms of the latter are easy and happy, never contorted; it maintains a delightful flow of lyrical invention, by contrast with the Teutonic 'crawling of reptiles seen by a dim light'; it is in fact the ornament of a civilised, even a sophisticated people, isolated by a world of darkness and violence from the older civilisations of the south; and whether we can or cannot claim that Scot-

[1] Cf. *P.S.A.S.*, Vol. XXIII, p. 318
[2] *P.S.A.S.*, Vol. XXVI, p. 225   [3] *Irish Art*, pp. 160–165

land had much share in making brooches, reliquaries and their like, we can at least claim that she had a share in forming the civilisation which gave them birth.

The peculiar character of Scoto-Irish culture was, however, altered for ever by the invaders. It continued for many centuries to be different from the main European stream, but outside influences poured into it. The Irish, or Scoto-Irish, church must have varied much in practice and ritual from the Roman church even as late as the eleventh and twelfth centuries, for the *cumdachs* or book-shrines, the bell-shrines and the crosiers make this abundantly clear. In these occurs a late flowering of the metalworkers' craft, and old forms are seen profoundly modified by new feeling under the impact of the outside world.

It is the crosiers which concern us here. The oaken staffs of the early saints were held in high regard, for oaths sworn upon them were especially binding and an exchange of staffs between two holy men was an act of deep significance. Naturally such staffs attracted the attention of craftsmen. To give them permanence and make their importance obvious, the heads of the staffs were encased in metal and much ornament lavished on them. The typical Celtic crosier had a special form which is clearly seen in certain stone-carvings such as the pillar at Killadeas, near Enniskillen, or more crudely on the slate slab found at Culbinsgarth, Bressay, in the Shetlands. The ordinary pastoral crook terminates in a short straight member, nearly vertical, and some notable crosier-cases possess an elaborate comb or crest. Among the finest Irish examples are those of Lismore and Clonmacnoise. The crook of the Clonmacnoise crosier shows marked Scandinavian influence, and the same is true of the comb, knop and ferrule of the Lismore crosier.

Scotland possesses one of the most celebrated of thcsc crosier-cases in the Quigrich of St. Fillan, preserved in the National Museum of Antiquities: a fine object of silver gilt enclosing an earlier crosier-head of bronze. It has an interesting history. It is conceivable that, like its companion piece, the Monymusk Reliquary, it may have been at the battle of Bannockburn, since Boece relates that Bruce prayed to St. Fillan on the eve of battle and that one of the saint's relics had a part in a miraculous happening on the field.[1] Boece wrote two centuries after the event, but the king undoubtedly had a special regard for St. Fillan,[2] while crosiers and reliquaries were of course borne in battle regularly. The first indisputable reference to the Quigrich appears to be an instrument

Pl. 8

---

[1] *Scotichronicon*: Lib. XII, Cap. XII   [2] *P.S.A.S.*, Vol. XII, p. 141

recording an inquest on the relic of St. Fillan commonly called the 'Coygerach', held at Kandrochit on 22nd April, 1428, when it was said that the office of custodian of the relic had been conferred *in perpetuo* by the saint on an ancestor of one Finlay Jore, bearer at that date. A letter of 6th July, 1487, from King James III proclaims that a certain Malise Doire (=Jore) of Strathfillan and his progenitors were custodians of the Quigrich since the time of Robert the Bruce and earlier. The name of Jore or Doire appears to come from the Erse word for 'exile' or 'pilgrim'; and since it seems to be widely connected with the office of custodian—for example, of bells—one may assume that the name of Dewar, which derives from it, has the same significance. The Quigrich continued in the possession of a line of Dewars for another three centuries and Pennant found it with one of them, a day-labourer, in 1782. An emigrant descendant of the family took it with him to Canada, and it was eventually secured for the National Museum in 1876.

In style, the Quigrich differs considerably from Irish crosiers already mentioned. Its general form is similar, but details are not so. For example, where the crook of the Clonmacnoise crosier is covered with Celto-Scandinavian interlacing, that of the St. Fillan's crosier is decorated with a design which has little or no Celtic element in it at all. The silver-gilt outer case, however, reproduces some of the main features of an older crook formerly contained in it, but now exhibited separately. This inner piece is of bronze with a raised design of lattice-work which once formed the basis of more elaborate ornament. Similar lattice-work appears on certain of the Irish crosiers, notably those of St. Blathmac and St. Tola (crosier of the Dysert O'Dea monastery). On St. Blathmac's the lattice-work is in silver, but St. Tola's crosier is of bronze with traces of gilding, and the lozenge-shaped spaces formed by the lattice once contained decorative panels. The bronze crook of St. Fillan also contained such panels and there are small rivet-holes in the angles of the lattice-work, so that in all likelihood it was an Irish type of crosier, attributable to the eleventh century. The silver-gilt outer case reproduces the lattice-work plan of the inner relic faithfully; and it is believed that the silver infillings of this have been transferred to the outer case, as in some instances they overlap the lattice framing slightly. These little plaques, lozenge-shaped and triangular according to the spaces they have to fill, are embellished with filigree work in the form of scrolls which, as Dr. Anderson long ago demonstrated,[1] are of two varieties or quali-

[1] *Scot. in Early Christian Times*, p. 220

ties. Some are executed with precision and elegance, and it may be assumed that these were transferred from the original crook; others, wrought with twisted wire, are weakly executed and have evidently been introduced when the new case was made. This filigree work is not Celtic in design. Dr. Anderson compared it with similar work on the cover of the prayer-book of Charles the Bald, in the Louvre, belonging to the first half of the ninth century. If this is a correct pointer, the bronze crook is older than any of the Irish crosiers. However this may be, Anderson clearly was right in looking southwards for the inspiration. As to the outer case, with the possible though doubtful exception of the triquetra ornament on the boss it is executed in what might be called an 'un-Celtic' style. Beautiful though it is, its beauty is of a rigid, repetitive sort foreign to the Scoto-Irish region, foreign indeed to the north. Dr. Stuart recognised this;[1] and, as the word 'quigrich' means 'stranger', he inclined to think the object was of foreign origin. This theory is difficult to reconcile with the close correspondence between the silver-gilt case and the older crook contained in it, for it is unthinkable that a relic so revered and cherished as the staff of St. Fillan would have been sent out of the country in order to be re-cased. The oval crystal set on the pendent part of the crook, the little bust—no doubt of the saint—above this, the Crucifixion on the terminal plate: all these are clearly medieval work, and Dr. Anderson has connected the convoluted ornament under the bust with the privy seal of David II, successor to Robert Bruce.[2] The outer case of the Quigrich can, therefore, with some confidence be assigned to the latter part of the fourteenth century; and as this was a period when many foreign craftsmen were working in Scotland in the service of the church, it may be this unique piece should be attributed to one of these.

Another important piece, also possibly attributable to the fourteenth century, is the Dunvegan Cup, but despite its long association with the Macleods this is certainly of Irish workmanship. Its nucleus is a wooden vessel of the mether type, square at the lip and rounded towards the base. There is now a deep silver rim, and the body is elaborately mounted in silver, much of it wrought in filigree, and enhanced by gilding and *niello*. There are a number of empty sockets which once contained stones or glass. The cup is supported on four legs, with feet modelled as shoes. Everywhere except on the rim the silver used is very thin sheet metal, and the cup has thus suffered a good deal of

---

[1] *P.S.A.S.*, Vol. XII, p. 166   [2] *Scot. in Early Christ. Times*, p. 222

damage. There is an inscription on the outside of the rim in Latin which has been much abbreviated, but may be rendered:

Katharina nigen uy Neill uxor Johannis Meguigir Principis de Firmanac me fieri fecit Anno Domini 1493. Oculi omnium in te sperant Domine et tu das escam illorum in tempore opportuno.

Meguigir is Macguire. John Macguire is referred to several times in the *Annals of the Four Masters*, and it is known that he became a chief of his clan in 1484, and that he died in 1503. Macleod tradition has it that the rim was affixed in 1493. The other mounts seem rather older than this, and I should be inclined to place them late in the final period of Irish art which followed the Anglo-Norman invasion. The six-pointed stars in circles are not unlike those on the top of the outer case of the Domnach Airgid, in the National Museum of Ireland.

The Celtic genius lost its force more abruptly in Scotland than it did in Ireland, and the reason is probably not far to seek. Attempts to bring the Celtic Church completely under the sway of Rome were periodic from the Synod of Whitby onwards, but the organisation of the Church of Rome would seem to have been fundamentally antipathetic to the nature of the Celt, as the elusiveness of the latter was no doubt aggravating to the Roman churchman. In art, regimentation had always been foreign to the Celt. 'The most permanent danger threatening Celtic decoration', declares Mlle. Henry,[1] 'was the assimilation into regular spirals of the curves derived from vegetal patterns.' That puts a great historical problem in an aesthetic nutshell. Some profound instinct prompted in the Celt, as in the Chinese, the knowledge that mathematical rigidity, no matter how beautifully precise, holds peril for the human spirit, and so in his masterpieces a vital restiveness and an untiring power of invention are the deeper qualities which delight and satisfy us.

In Scotland, so far as metalwork is concerned, those qualities seem to have disappeared by the eleventh and twelfth centuries. There is a record of a silver-gilt cross. described as *opus ibernicorum*, still preserved in the treasury of Aberdeen Cathedral in 1549.[2] This may very well have been decorated in the Celto-Scandinavian style of the Irish crosiers. There is also a fragment of a bronze crosier carried out in similar style in the National Museum of Antiquities. Certain zoomorphic features and scrolled engraving on the flat surfaces of the

[1] *Irish Art*, p. 191 [2] *P.S.A.S.*, Vol. XII, p. 162

PLATE 5

The Hunterston Brooch: 8th to 9th centuries (4¾″ diameter) *(pp.14 & 16)*

PLATE 6

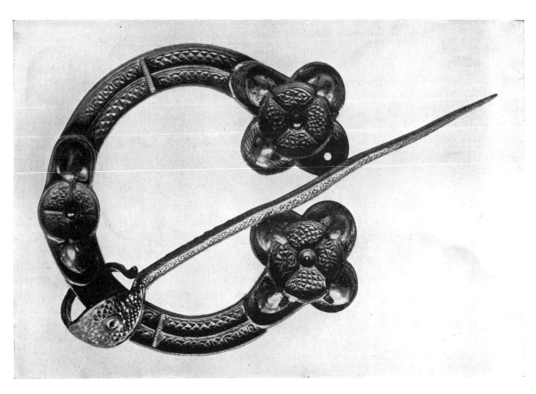

The larger Rogart or Cadboll Brooch: 8th to 9th centuries (4½″ diameter) *(p.15)*

The smaller Rogart or Cadboll Brooch: 8th to 9th centuries (3″ diameter) *(p.15)*

PLATE 7

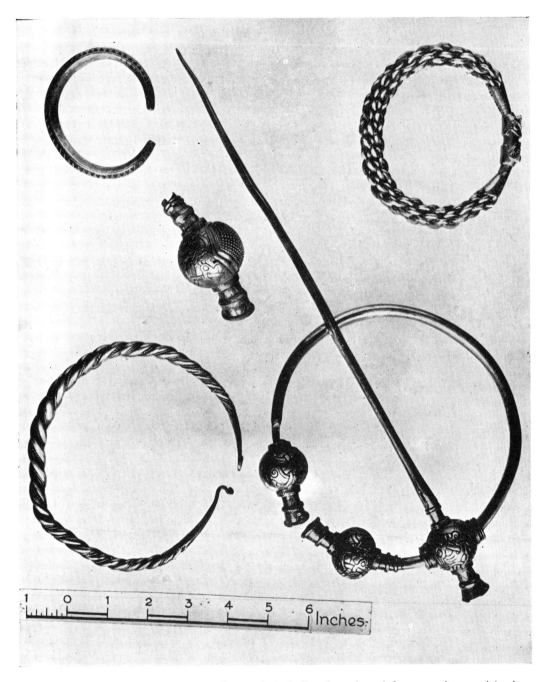

Group of Ornaments from the Skaill Hoard, including brooch and fragment decorated in the Jellinge Style: probably 10th century *(p.17)*

PLATE 8

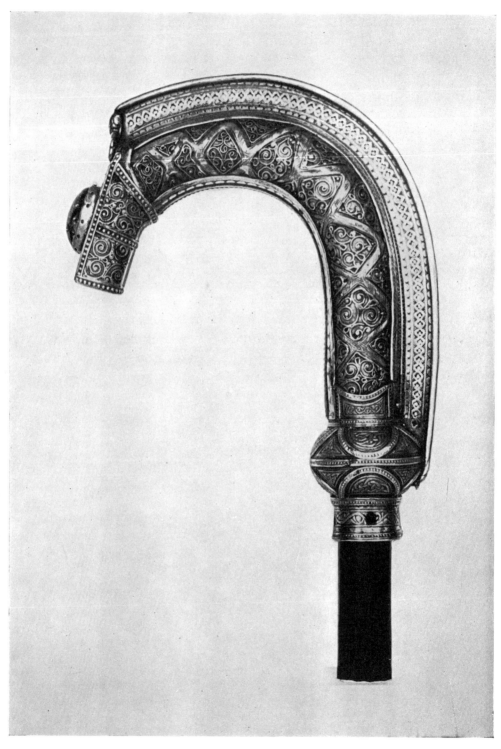

Silver-gilt Case of the Quigrich or Crozier of St. Fillan: second half 14th century *(pp.19-21)*

Kilmichael Glassary bell-shrine no doubt represent the afterglow of a golden age, but the Crucifixion and the Divine Hand above it, clearly twelfth century, are emphatically un-Celtic in every way.

It was at this time that the Celtic Church in Scotland made its final and complete surrender to the Roman faith. The sect of the Culdees had in some way maintained the Celtic tradition since the eighth century, when these monks of a lost cause came from Ireland to Iona; but David I, like his brother Alexander I and his mother Margaret, was hostile to the ancient tradition and vigorously sought to bring the Culdees within the orthodox fold, which he did with some skill, it would seem, by gently but firmly incorporating them as canons regular. The last strongholds of the Culdees were in the east and north-east of the country. Two of those strongholds were Brechin and Abernethy, the only places where the old Scoto-Irish round-tower has been preserved intact in Scotland, doubtless a fact of significance. Monymusk was also a stronghold of the sect, but the famous reliquary appears to have no connexion with this. Yet the Culdees may have had in their possession other examples of metalwork of earlier times which have disappeared for the very reason that they were associated with a body which the orthodox church was determined to extirpate.

NOTES TO CHAPTER II

THE MONYMUSK RELIQUARY (pp.12-13 & pl.3,ii)

This is illustrated in Chapter I. For an in-depth discussion of its symbolism,. see Finlay, Ian: *Columba*, p.17 *et seq.*

THE DUNBEATH BROOCH (p.14 & pl.4)

For more on this brooch-fragment see Finlay, Ian: *Celtic Art*, p.122.

ADDITION TO TEXT:
THE ST. NINIAN'S ISLE TREASURE (Not illustrated)

This amazing hoard of twenty-eight pieces of Celtic silverwork was discovered by the late Andrew C. O'Dell on St. Ninian's Isle, Shetland, on 4th July, 1958 in the ruined nave of the tiny church there. It was probably deposited, in its larch-wood box, around the year 800, although some of the items, not all of which are of Scottish origin, are a good deal older. The silver and silver-gilt pieces consist of eight shallow bowls, twelve penannular brooches, a spoon, a claw-like instrument, four mounts or pommels and two chapes. The chapes, probably intended for a scabbard, appear to be Scottish and of the very finest workmanship. One of them has been left in an unfinished state, suggesting that it was made locally. Controversy has raged in the past as to whether the hoard consists of secular or ecclesiastical items, but the weight of modern opinion favours the former view, despite Mgr. David McRoberts exposition of the other case (see bibliography). (See also Finlay, Ian: *Celtic Art*, pp.126-7.) The Treasure is now in the Royal Museum of Scotland.

Chapter Three

THE MIDDLE AGES

DURING the earlier middle ages the old culture so long established in Scotland by the Celtic peoples receded. There is a temptation to say it retreated into the fastnesses of the north and west, for it is in the north and west that it persisted in recognisable forms for many centuries and, indeed, persists to-day; but it must not be forgotten that it formed a substratum throughout the rest of Scotland and, broadly speaking, it is probably true to say it became recessive, not merely in the geographical area now called Scotland, but also in the nature of the individual Scot. The eastern or southern Scot became a microcosm of Scotland. Gradually his native cultural interests were driven under the surface by the pressure of an imported, an imposed culture. Malcolm Canmore's queen established not only the form of Christianity she had learned at the Saxon Court, but also its social and cultural accompaniments. The people of Scotland continued to live their lives as before. There can have been little interference with their folk traditions and crafts. But Court and Church, which were the only possible patrons for sumptuary arts such as the goldsmiths', were completely Normanised in their tastes by the beginning of the twelfth century; and the great church-building policy of David I, like his secular policy of granting lands to men of Norman extraction in order to safeguard his power, sent Romanesque feelers as far west as Iona and as far north as Orkney.

So little concrete evidence has survived from that time that any historian of the arts is forced to fill an embarrassing blank with a good deal of rather unprofitable speculation. One gains an impression of a country culturally divided against itself. The great churches of Scotland, even the earliest of them, are in an international style, yet a style so modified that the churches are unmistakably Scottish; on the other hand they are in their situations, many of them, alien and isolated in a way less often occurring in England or on the Continent, where the great cathedrals are usually the heart and expression of the communities in their shadow. The silver and gold vessels used by ecclesiastics and nobles were no doubt even more alien. There were no modifying factors. It is doubtful, indeed, if native craftsmen were concerned in the making of any of the finer work, for we have no evidence whatever that Scotland in the twelfth century possessed goldsmiths skilled enough to satisfy the taste of priests familiar with the rich services of plate of the great Continental churches and abbeys. Probably in early times the priests imported some of their craftsmen, as they imported their masons, but the more usual practice must have been to import the finished wares.

Although the complete disappearance of early vessels of the precious metals is surprising, reasons for a dearth of them are not far to seek. One of the principal reasons is, of course, the Reformation. This does not mean that the Reformation in Scotland was more destructive of works of art than iconoclastic movements elsewhere. The subject is one which I have discussed at some length in another place[1] and I do not propose to re-state my views here, except to emphasise the historical fact that violence towards the artistic achievements of past generations was formerly the rule rather than the exception, and that the violence of the Reformers was on a modest scale compared with some of the orgies of destruction which swept away treasures on the Continent. For the practice of impious vandalism one need look no further than the first of the Plantagenets, whose looting of sacred places in Scotland included the removal of plate from abbeys in order to enrich the coffers of his family, as will be seen when we come to discuss the records of gold and silver vessels in religious houses. The Reformation, however, by bringing the older form of ritual completely to an end, scattered the vessels and treasures in use by the Church and substituted vessels of quite different form. Such vessels of the Church as survived the mob and the melting-pot—ultimate destination of the bulk of secular plate in all ages before the present historically-minded one—were no longer protected by sanctity from the grasping or the careless hand.

That the Church in medieval Scotland possessed a considerable store of sacred plate is something that can almost be taken for granted. Regarded in all its length and breadth, Scotland was then a poor country, but considerable tracts of it compared quite favourably with other countries, and an examination of the state of agriculture in early times shows that the monks enjoyed substantial wealth, especially in such fertile districts as the Laigh of Moray and the Carse of Gowrie and in wool-producing regions such as the Border coun-

[1] *Art in Scotland*, Ch. IV

try. The researches of Mr. T. Bedford Franklin into Scottish monastic farming
have thrown much new light on this. In 1275, he writes, 'when Boiamund de
Vicci came to Scotland to collect the Tenths of ecclesiastical Benefices for the
relief of the Holy Land, some of the richer abbeys already had incomes of over
£2,000 Scots—equivalent to £30,000 sterling in 1950'.[1] Their prosperity seems
to have remained constant up to the time of the Reformation. It was derived
from rent and sale of corn and wool, and from rents in kind. Mr. Franklin
makes some useful comparisons between English and Scottish abbeys. He
shows that big Cistercian houses such as Melrose, Holm-Cuntram and New
Minster got a yield and price of wool rather less than those of the best English
houses, but the figures are not very much lower. It is inconceivable that prosperity drawn from fat lands skilfully managed should not have been reflected
in fine church furniture, although, as Mr. Charles Oman points out to me,
Scottish abbeys were mainly of 'reformed' orders, which sometimes, as in one
case of the Cistercians, made a merit of not having too much plate. Yet it is an
easy matter to find references to silver and silver-gilt plate in the inventories
and chartularies of the abbeys, and in other documents. Even in the earlier
middle ages seemly equipment of the altar must have formed an objective of
some importance, for in those times the Church was still fighting hard to make
an impression on the people who, in the northern half of the country at least,
were still deeply conscious of an older tradition. It was laid down, for example,
in the Constitution of the Bishop of St. Andrews (1242) that every church
should have a silver chalice, and that 'flagons or cruets for keeping the wine
and the water for the eucharist of the Lord should be of silver or pewter'.[2] A
similar order is recorded in the Aberdeen Statutes, also of the thirteenth century. At Dundemor, a chapel under the jurisdiction of Lindores Abbey, in
1248, monks were to pay to Sir Henry de Dundemor twenty-five shillings for
the maintenance of a chaplain and to provide in the first instance a chalice and
the necessary books and vestments. This order appears to have been duly
carried out, as the *ornamenta* of the chapel were a silver chalice, a full vestment
and a missal.[3] In the early documents there is a certain amount of support for
my assumption, above, that the priests imported sacred vessels even after the
middle ages and at a time when Scotland certainly possessed good goldsmiths.

[1] *A History of Scottish Farming*, p. 84
[2] *Statutes of the Scottish Church* (Scot. History Socy.), p. 58
[3] *Chartulary of Lindores* (Scot. Hist. Socy.), p. lxx

It is recorded that in 1520 the Abbot of Kinloss sent Sir Thomas Cumein to Flanders to buy richly-wrought vestments, consisting of copes, chasubles, dalmatics, stoles and albs, and he also procured a mitre ornamented with gems and pearls.[1] Such a supply of vestments implies a similar lavish standard in vessels for the altar, and there is an actual reference to silver vessels brought from France and Flanders. The most lavish of recorded services of plate is listed in the Inventory of Jewels found in Cupar Abbey by Edward I in 1296.[2] It includes silver dishes, salt cellars, cups of silver-gilt, some with foot and cover, and many spoons. These were 'delivered to Adam the King's goldsmith at Westminster . . . to be broken up by order of the King to make thereof new vessels (dishes) for the Lady Elizabeth the King's daughter'.

Although no pre-Reformation metal chalice has survived, the form is not in doubt. It is depicted several times on the medieval sculptured stones of the western Highlands and the islands. Among these are the Priest's Stone at Balquhidder, the headstone of St. Oran's Chapel, Iona, two other carved stones on that island, a tombstone at St. Duthac's, Tain, and a slab at St. Magnus' Cathedral, Kirkwall. Two of the Iona stones are quite elaborately carved, but in all cases the chalice is shown in much the same, simple form: a bowl and spreading foot which balance each other, divided by a substantial knop. Two such chalices have actually come down to us, although neither is of precious metal. They are in the National Museum of Antiquities. One of them, of wax, was found with a paten in the tomb of Bishop Thomas Tulloch in St. Magnus'.[3] Tulloch was bishop from 1418 to 1461. The other chalice and paten are of pewter and were found at Bervie in Kincardineshire. The two chalices are uniform in size. Uniformity was, of course, strictly adhered to in the pre-Reformation Church, shape being determined by modifications of ritual such as the fourteenth-century practice of laying the chalice on its side to drain at ablutions.

Of surviving pieces of medieval silver in Scotland, the earliest are the Iona spoons, preserved in the National Museum of Antiquities. They were discovered in 1922, in the ruins of the Nunnery on Iona, and were probably for ceremonial use. Three of the spoons are in more or less damaged condition, but the fourth is complete and in good condition. It is parcel-gilt. Its shallow, fig- or leaf-shaped bowl with gilt border and engraved floral design passes into

[1] *Records of the Monastery of Kinloss*, p. xlvi
[2] *Register of Cupar Abbey*, p. 364 (quoting Wardrobe Account of Edw. I in British Museum)
[3] Cf. *Rights of Durham* (Surtees Society), Vol. 107, pp. 52, 53, 57

a long neck of panel form decorated with a series of arches linked by inverse curves, and this narrows to a slim stem ending in a knop resembling a mulberry in a calyx, which the late Commander G. E. P. How believed to be of the type referred to in wills and inventories as 'de fretelett' or 'cum fretlettez',[1] terms evidently signifying 'fruitlet'. The Iona spoons belong to that exclusive little group of early examples which includes the Coronation spoon as well as the Taunton and Pevensey spoons, the Coronation spoon differing from the others in having a step-junction between stem and bowl.

Dr. A. O. Curle has dated the Iona spoons to the twelfth or thirteenth century.[2] They belong to a well-recognised European type. Their use may have been to ladle the water into the chalice. Dr. Curle found the closest analogy to the ornament in an enamelled plaque from the tomb of Geoffrey Plantagenet, Count of Maine, made in 1151 and now in the museum at Le Mans. With the same plaque of Limoges enamel he compared a gold fillet found with the spoons, a narrow strip of metal ornamented in *repoussé* with a running design of foliaceous scroll-work, bordered by pellets. How, broadly speaking, accepts this dating of the spoons, recording it as about 1150–1250. Their arrival on the island is easily explained. In 1203, Reginald, Lord of the Isles, founded a convent of Benedictine nuns with his sister Beatrice as the first abbess, and a group of Benedictine monks was introduced at the same time. Connections with a parent house in England or on the Continent would account for the presence of the spoons and the fillet, which may have formed part of the treasure of the Nunnery. One thing at least is certain: we cannot make the Iona spoons the starting-point for an account of native Scottish medieval plate. Two other spoons in the National Museum of Antiquities have perhaps slightly better claims. The Brechin spoon, ascribed by How to the thirteenth or early fourteenth century,[3] was found in a grave at Brechin with coins of Alexander III, Edward I and Edward II. It has a long, thin stem, a small finial and a roundish bowl, slightly pointed. How allocates this to the Scottish group, although he draws attention to its resemblance to the Rouen diamond-point type. Then there is the spoon found at Windymains Water, Haddington. It is a simple type of acorn-knop, belonging to the late thirteenth or early fourteenth century. I feel strong doubt that either of these spoons originated in Scotland, for they have every appearance of being strays.

[1] *English and Scottish Silver Spoons*, Vol. I   [2] *P.S.A.S.*, Vol. LVIII, p. 108
[3] *English and Scottish Silver Spoons*, Vol. I, p. 40

Pl. 9

The earliest important piece of silverwork repeatedly and authoritatively claimed as of Scottish provenance is the print, or boss, of the Bannatyne or Bute mazer. This fascinating relic is generally admitted to be older than the mazer-bowl itself of which it forms a part, although how much older has been a matter for argument. The print is of silver, heavily gilded. It is a disc 5 inches across containing a 'platform', hexafoil in outline, on which lies a lion *couchant* a little less than 2 inches in length. In each bay of the hexafoil is set a heater-shaped shield with coat-of-arms in *champlevé* enamel. Around the lion and the shields twines a tendril of what has been described as a strawberry plant; while in the angles between the bays are set a cinquefoil and an animal apparently derived from the bestiaries. This remarkable print, like the mazer itself, has been an object of study for what might now be called a 'working-party' of authorities.[1] The heraldic shields have been interpreted as representing the High Steward, Sir James Douglas, Sir John Menteith, a Crawford, Walter Fitzgilbert, and an unknown cadet of the Fitzgilbert family, all duly surrounding or supporting the lion of the King himself. J. H. Stevenson, at the time Marchmont Herald, has in an ingenious and scholarly paper surmised that the unknown cadet was John (?) Fitzgerald, Keeper of Rothesay Castle, and that the mazer, or at any rate the print, was made for him. A combination of known circumstances brought together by Stevenson certainly seems to fix the date of the print in its present form as between 1314 and 1318, and he hazards the guess that the Bruce himself may well have drunk from the vessel at the High Steward's table. The style of ornament of the print is quite consistent with a fourteenth-century date.

Invaluable as it is, the paper of Stevenson and his associates remains inconclusive. Two contributors who were acknowledged authorities on old silver, Lionel H. Crichton and William Brook, differ over the provenance of the print. The first sees no reason why it should not have been made in Scotland and declares that the design has strong Celtic influence. The second suggests the print originated in the East and was adapted by a Scottish silversmith to fit into the bottom of the mazer. Now, to me, only one feature of the decoration possesses anything resembling Celtic feeling, and that is the three monsters; but not for a moment would any student of Celtic art accept the print as belonging to this field. An Eastern origin is even more improbable. The lion may have some faint air of the Byzantine, as Brook asserted, but no

[1] *P.S.A.S.*, Vol. LXV, p. 217 *et seq.*

oriental artist could possibly have executed the tendrils, the cinquefoils or the monsters. On the other hand, Brook has established beyond reasonable doubt that the heraldic shields were let into the print by a craftsman of less skill than the maker of the original piece. The problem remains: who made the shields themselves? Clearly they were made to the order of a Scot—John Fitzgilbert, for the sake of argument. Were Scottish silversmiths of the period of Bannockburn skilled enough in the making of *champlevé* enamels to produce these technically excellent little shields? The alternative theory is that the enamels must have been executed by a foreign craftsman, probably French, and perhaps fitted by some local metalworker into a piece of silverware which in all likelihood was not intended to serve as the print of a mazer at all. It is far larger than any other known print. My feeling is that the high relief of the lion and the presence of the enamelled shields indicate that the piece was intended to decorate a place of eminence rather than a depression where such choice things would be submerged under 'the bluid-red wine' when the mazer was put into use as a grace-cup.

Stevenson in his paper[1] tends to assume that, if the print be attributed to the years 1314-1318, the mazer as a whole belongs to approximately the same time, although presumably exemptions were made of the silver mazer-band, foot and straps. It seems certain that mazers were in fact much used and prized in Scotland by the late fourteenth century. Two or three are mentioned among Edward I's spoil from Edinburgh Castle in 1296,[2] while an inventory of the 'Jowellis' found in the Castle in 1488 has an even more significant entry: 'Foure Masaris callit King Robert the Brocis with a cover . . . Item the hede of silver of ane of the coveris of the masar.' This reference to a cover is tantalising, for a cover is not a normal adjunct of a mazer, and yet it happens that the Bute mazer possesses a cover of carved whalebone which is unique. Mr. Stevenson constantly connects the print of the mazer with Bruce. There is, for example, the significance of the lion. The monsters he interprets as wyverns and connects them with two such creatures on the seals of Robert Bruce, Earl of Carrick, father of the King[3]; but wyverns as usually defined are equipped with wings, and these are wingless. On the whole, I see no good reason to make the mazer's bowl antedate its silver mounts. These last clearly belong to the sixteenth century, and a description of them will be given in the appropriate place.

[1] *P.S.A.S.*, Vol. LXV, p. 251   [2] Burns: *Scottish Communion Plate*, footnote to p. 191
[3] *P.S.A.S.*, Vol. LXV, Footnote to p. 232

PLATE 9

Print or Boss of the Bute Mazer: early 14th century *(pp.30-31)*

PLATE 10

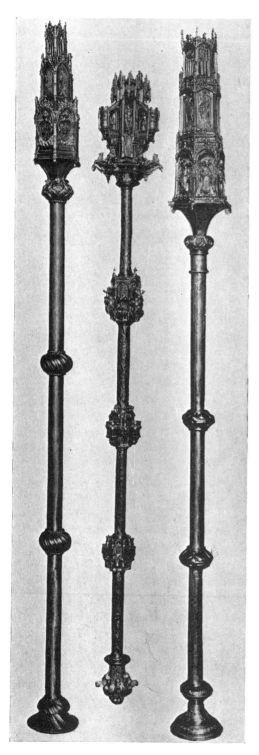

Maces of the University of St. Andrews:
(1) Faculty of Canon Law: French;
(2) St. Salvator's College: French (Paris), 1461;
(3) Faculty of Arts: Scottish, see editor's note p.36 *(pp.32-34)*

Head of the Faculty of Arts Mace,
St. Andrews University
(pp.32-34)

PLATE 11

Medieval Brooches of octagonal type (largest brooch 2¼″) *(p.41)*

Gold Ring Brooch found in the Ardoch Burn, Doune: 15th century *(p.43)*

Silver Brooch found at Canonbie: 14th century (3½″ diameter) *(p.41)*

PLATE 12

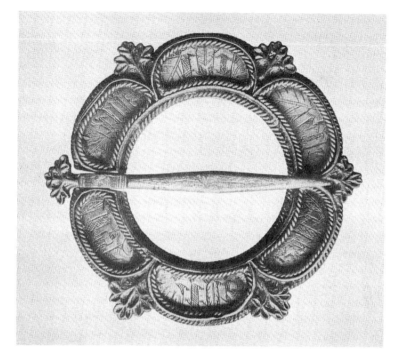

The Kindrochit Brooch: first half 16th century
(3½" diameter) (p.43)

The Brooch of Lorne (p.46)

Medieval secular plate, like sacred plate, must have existed in considerable quantities in Scotland. The completeness of its disappearance remains a puzzle. We know that a great dispersal of royal treasures occurred after the downfall of Queen Mary.[1] The queen's jewels fell into the hands of the Confederated Lords. It may be that they sold them, for 1300 ounces of her silver were turned into coinage. After her surrender at Carberry, the Palace of Holyroodhouse was broken into by the mob, not for the last time. Among the treasures which were turned into money during those years was the gold font of 333 ounces presented by Queen Elizabeth I of England for the baptism of the prince who became James VI and I.

The first piece of medieval silverwork for the native Scots authorship of which a good case has been made out is the mace, or verge, at St. Andrews University which the late A. J. S. Brook identified as once belonging to the old Faculty of Canon Law.[2] It is partly gilt and has a wooden core to the shaft. The head is of gothic tabernacle form, in three stages, each recessed a little so that they diminish towards the top. The shaft is plain but is divided into three sections by belchered bands, with a terminal knop of later date than the rest of the mace. Interest centres principally on the head. It is a remarkable piece of architectural design. The lowest and deepest stage is divided at the corners by buttresses connected at the top by crocketed arches, each bay so formed containing the winged figure of an angel with expansive halo. It appears certain, as Brook records, that each angel once held an armorial shield such as occurs on the companion mace of the Faculty of Arts, for the fixture-holes are there. In the second stage again each bay contains a figure, this time in flat chasing only, and the six figures represent the Trinity, the Virgin Mary, St. Mungo, St. John the Baptist, St. Andrew and St. Peter. In the third stage each bay contains a window carried out with pierced tracery, no two windows being of the same design. No maker's mark of any kind appears on the mace. No record contains any information pointing to its origin. The first mention of it is in a Register of Vestments of St. Salvator's College which is believed to have been made soon after 1461. Brook, however, admitted of little doubt in assessing period and provenance.[3] He judged the first to be early fifteenth century, basing his view on the architectural design; and he considered the workmanship 'manifestly Scottish', holding that the mace came out of the workshop of one of the early burgh craftsmen, the earliest surviving piece of its kind.

Pl. 10

[1] *Scottish History and Life*, p. 243 (James Paton, editor)   [2] *P.S.A.S.*, Vol. XXVI, p. 451 *et seq.* But see Editor's Notes, pp. 37-38   [3] Ibid., p. 454

There is no good and substantial reason for contradicting Brook's verdict. The case must be considered again, however, against the background of the three other gothic tabernacle maces or verges which survive in Scotland: those of the Faculty of Arts at St. Andrews, St. Salvator's College in the same university, and the University of Glasgow. Together, the four are the oldest ceremonial maces in Britain, and are quite unlike any other maces in the country. The gothic form is appropriate in a symbol carried before a rector who, as Brook remarked, in pre-Reformation times was always a churchman; and pyxes, ciboria and other ecclesiastical vessels on the Continent in this period were commonly made in the same architectural mode. It is because of the tabernacle form of the head that I have suggested 'verge' as an alternative to mace. The mace in fifteenth-century England still bore some resemblance to a weapon, and it is Mr. Oman who has pointed out to me that these Scottish university beadle's wands are really connected with ecclesiastical verges—the inscription on the Glasgow University piece (see p. 101) uses the word *virga*. Canopied gothic verges are still to be found in Spain.

The only one of these four maces which carries a definite indication of its origin is St. Salvator's. Above the fleuron is the inscription: *John Maiel govldsmche and verlete off chamer til ye Lord ye Dalfyne has made yis masse in ye toune of Paris ye zer of our Lorde MCCCCLXI.* John Mayelle was a warden of the Paris Incorporation of Goldsmiths in 1460. Brook makes out a convincing case for the Faculty of Arts mace also having been made in France. A Faculty meeting on 9th August, 1418, decided that someone should go the goldsmith commissioned to persuade him to come to St. Andrews to complete the mace there or to send it with the messenger, and it is argued that the place of manufacture must have been at a considerable distance. The quality of the enamelled shields, which on this mace are still retained by the angels, makes France seem the likely place of origin. The quality of the enamel work on the Glasgow mace likewise points towards France, although the only definite evidence of the mace having been in that country is the inscription recording that it was carried to Paris for safety in the year of the Reformation and restored to Glasgow in 1590. Presumably, however, the missing shields of the Canon-Law mace were of this same high quality. Inevitably the query passes through one's mind: would the scholarly author of the paper have felt so confident of the Scottish workmanship of the Canon-Law mace had the shields been in position? Alternatively, enamel-work apart, might he not then have considered a possible Scottish origin also for the Faculty of Arts and Glasgow maces? Those three—the Arts, Canon-Law and Glasgow maces—so resemble one another and so differ from the mace of St. Salvator's that there is a reasonable case for grouping them together, and Brook's distinction between the workmanship of the Canon-Law mace and that of the others is not so finally convincing that the subject should be considered closed. It is not at all clear why he should so confidently attribute it to one of the 'burgh craftsmen', if by this he means a craftsman of one of the burghs outside the capital, for it is hard to believe that any town except Edinburgh could at that time have produced such a work; and this somewhat loose remark tends to draw the question of the origin of all three maces back into the current of speculation. But, if we allow that the workmanship of the Canon-Law mace shows less technical efficiency than that of the other two, this is not conclusive evidence that its provenance is different. It is proof only that it comes from the hand of a different craftsman. Quite as significant as any difference in quality of craftsmanship is the general similarity of the trio. Of their kind they are, together, unique. Whether the origin of any or all of them is a Scottish workshop, they must be classified as the type of the medieval Scottish mace, and there is ample documentary evidence that two of them were commissioned in Scotland, although we do not know whether there were detailed instructions as to the form they should take. As Brook pointed out,[1] the founders and early professors of the Scottish universities had received their training abroad and would be familiar with the ceremonial equipment of the great universities of the Continent, and they must have drawn their ideas of the proper form of their maces from examples they remembered. This explains the tabernacle ornament, whatever the provenance of the maces.

It is in the fifteenth century that the Scottish goldsmiths first make their appearance in the records as an organised craft. An act of James II, of date March 6th, 1457, is devised to control the practice of adulterating gold and silver brought by the customer to the goldsmith to be wrought.

'As anent the reformacione of golde and siluer wro[t] be goldsmythis ande to eschewe the desaving done to the Kingis liegis thair salbe ordanyt in ilke burghe quhair goldsmythis wirkis ane understandande and cunnande man of gude conscience quhilk sall be dene of the craft. And quhen the werk is bro[t] to the goldsmy[t] and it be golde quhar golde that ever it beis bro[t] till him he sall give it fur[t] agane in werk ne we[r] than xx. granys. And

---

[1] Ibid., p. 484

of siluer quhat ever be brot him he sall gif it furt agane na wer ne xj. granys. And the said goldsmyt sall tak his werk or he gif it furthe and pass to the dene of the craft and ger examyn that it be sa fyne as is befor wrettyn. And the said dene of the craft sall set his merk and takyn thairto togidder wt the saide goldsmytis. And gif faute be fundyne thairin afterwartis the dene forsaide and goldesmytis gudis salbe in eschet to the King and their liffis at the Kingis will. And the saide dene sall haid to his fee of ilk vnce wrot jd. And quhair ther is na goldsmyt bot ane in a towne he sall schawe that werk takinit wt his awne merk to the hede officiaris of the town quhilkis sall haif a merk in like manner ordanyt thairfor and salbe set to the saide werk. And quhat goldsmyt that giffis furth his werk vtherwayis thane is befor wrettyn his gudis salbe confyskyt to the Kyng and his life at the Kingis will.'

This act discloses a number of things more interesting than the moral weakness of certain craftsmen. It is clear not only that practising craftsmen existed in considerable numbers, but also that they were distributed among several of the burghs. It would seem to suggest that before this date there was nothing in the nature of a craft or guild organisation such as existed on the Continent, or such as London had known since 1180. Alternatively, if organisation there were then it came under no strict discipline and was not responsible to the community, nor can it have been presided over by a dean or similar official performing the function which the dean subsequently performed. Whether the unelaborated reference to 'merk and takyn' implies that certain goldsmiths had been in the habit of using such a device cannot be determined. In London the Master Goldsmith had been required to set his mark on approved pieces since the year 1363, so the practice must have been known well enough to craftsmen north of the Border. The enactment, however, is concerned purely with honest dealing in the matter of the metal's purity: in every 24 grains or carats of wrought gold not less than 20 of fine gold, and in every 12 grains or ounces of wrought silver not less than 11 of fine silver; so that the idea of the guild as a guardian or guarantor of excellence in workmanship was not yet born in Scotland.

A second enactment, of February 24th, 1483, is little more than a repetition of that of the previous reign, already quoted. Yet it is apparent that by 1483 the guild principle of good measure and good work in return for protection and privilege had become established, for in that year the goldsmith members of the Edinburgh Hammermen Incorporation petitioned the Town Council against certain practices prejudicial to the 'auld guid rule and statutes of their craft'; and two years later it was required that 'al goldsmytis werk be markit wt his avn mark, the dekynis mark, and the mark of the tovne, of the finace of xjd fine'.

It may be contended, therefore, that by the end of the middle ages the gold-smiths of Edinburgh, at least, had emerged as an organised body and had laid the foundation on which were built the splendid achievements of the next three centuries.

The picture for the rest of the country is less clear. The guild principle, how-ever, was long established in a general way. It is first encountered in Scotland in 1249, in the Statute of the Guild for regulating the Guild of Merchants at Berwick. It animates David II's charter of 28th March, 1364, in favour of the whole Burgesses of Scotland, which requires that merchants 'effectualie pro-duce and offer the saidis merchandrice withoute fraude or gylle'. It is crystal-lised into the typical Scots craft organisation by an Act of James I of 1424. This rules: 'The Craft suld have ane Deaken. That in ilk Toune of the Realme of ilk sundrie Craft used therein be chosen a wise man of that Craft, and be consent of the Officier of the Toune; the quhilk sall be halden Deakon or Maister-man over the laife for the time, to governe and assay all warkes, that beis maid before the Craftismen of that Craft; swa that the Kingis Lieges be not de-frauded and skaithed in time to cum, as they have beine in time by-gane, threw untrew men of Crafts.' The goldsmiths were not numerous enough to form a craft of their own in those times. They belonged to the craft of the hammer-men, which embraced pewterers, armourers, locksmiths, cutlers, blacksmiths and all other workers in metals.

NOTES TO CHAPTER III

THE ST. ANDREWS MACES (pp.32-34, pl.10)

There has long been a considerable confusion as to the correct identities of the maces of the Faculty of Arts and the Faculty of Canon Law, and modern opinion has reversed their traditional identification. Mr. Finlay followed the view taken by A. J. S. Brook (see p.32), but it now seems much more likely that the French mace is that of Canon Law, while the Scottish one pertains to the Faculty of Arts, as per the captions to Plate 10. The identification depends on how one interprets the available evidence, which is incomplete. The writer of the catalogue *French Connections: Scotland & The Arts of France*, which accompanied an important exhibition of that name at the Royal Scottish Museum in 1985, argues the case for the latter view (catalogue, pp.23-4), the opposite of Mr. Brook's. He does so very convincingly and I have to say that, having examined the evidence for myself some years ago, I had already arrived at the same conclusion. While I have altered the captions of Plate 10 accordingly, it was found too difficult to change the text to match, and so it remains as Mr. Finlay wrote it, setting out the other point of view. The arguments and evidence are much too long to enter into here. To sum them up, the cruder of the two maces, now identified as that of the Faculty of Arts, is deemed to be Scottish, and is clearly based upon the slightly earlier and more proficient Canon Law mace, which, together with the maces of St. Salvator's College and Glasgow University, was made in France.

THE EDINBURGH GOLDSMITHS INCORPORATION
(p.36, first paragraph)

The Goldsmiths of Edinburgh had indeed gained a corporate identity, separate from that of the Hammermen. In 1492 a goldsmith named Patrick Forrester sat with the town council, along with the other deacons of the incorporated trades; it is clear from this that they were independent of the Hammermen by that date. This is confirmed by an early reference to corporate entertainment in the Hammermen's accounts for May 1495, where the two incorporations are clearly separate:

"*Item*: Expensis given for ij pynts of wyne at ye feasting between us & ye goldsmyths, xvjd."

Much more has recently been learned about the early history of the Incorporation of Goldsmiths and the manner in which they did or did not observe the requirements of the various Acts of Parliament which concerned them. The subject is a long and complex one that cannot easily be reduced to a few paragraphs. One point ought to be made, however. The first sixteen names in the list of Edinburgh goldsmiths which appeared in the first and second editions of Jackson's *English Goldsmiths and their Marks*, have fictitious dates of admission set against them. All sixteen men were already freemen of the Incorporation by 1525, some of them for as long as twenty years or so. The latest edition of Jackson, edited by Mr. Ian Pickford, corrects this to some extent, but more revisions of the early Edinburgh list are on the way.

Chapter Four

BROOCHES, MEDIEVAL AND LATER

At the beginning of the last chapter reference was made to the retreat of native culture before the advance of foreign modes promoted by Church and Court. Almost the only surviving evidence of the art of the goldsmith or silversmith in anything like wide distribution in medieval Scotland is of such a humble sort that neither Church nor Court could have had any use for it. It takes the form of a number of small ornaments, principally brooches, a few of them of gold but the majority of silver. They were first given serious study by Dr. J. Graham Callander, a former director of the National Museum of Antiquities, and they were classified in a paper which must form the basis of this survey.[1]

Dr. Callander began his examination with a description of a small mass of silver coins discovered in a purse in the wall of an old house in Dumfries. When cleaned and carefully separated, the coins were found to be associated with a little cross, a brooch and portions of other brooches, as well as other ornaments, all of silver; and the coins, mainly of the reigns of Alexander III, John Balliol and Edward I of England, established approximately the date of the jewellery as early fourteenth century. In general terms, brooch and cross were very similar to the humble ornaments mentioned in the previous paragraph, so that it is reasonable to date all in or about the fourteenth century.

The cross, about 1¼ inches in span, is equal-armed. Each arm tapers a little towards its extremity, and three of the arms terminate in a flattened knob, while the fourth ends in a collar and suspension-loop. The junction of the cross is flattened into a disc, on which are engraved the letters AGLA, latinised initial-letters of a Hebrew phrase translated as : 'Thou art mighty for ever, O Lord!' On the arms of the cross are ridges or transverse cuts filled with *niello*, the use of which in conjunction with silver is typical of medieval Scottish jewellery, and of some of the brooches subsequently made in the Highlands. *Niello* is a composition formed of silver, copper, lead and sulphur pounded down and

[1] *P.S.A.S.*, Vol. LVIII, p. 160 *et seq.*

applied like enamel, although it does not require the same degree of heat. It may be that its use here is an attempt to perpetuate an art in which the ancient Celtic metalworkers were notably proficient, and it is not perhaps unreasonable to suggest that the native tradition in enamel-working was, in some obscure way, handed down among the people while David I and other sovereigns were normanising the outlook of the ruling castes. The cross has been compared with a cross of jet of similar design which, by means of the lettering on it and the pottery found with it, has been dated to the early thirteenth century. A talismanic purpose has been attributed to the crosses, and it is thought that many of the medieval brooches were made with the same end in view.

With the cross were some fragments of brooches and a complete brooch. This last is of ring type, with transverse pin, measuring $1\frac{1}{4}$ inches in diameter. Like the fragments it is notched or indented, and there are traces of *niello* in the hollows. This is the type of the Scottish medieval brooch in its simplest form. Callander divided the brooches into several distinct categories.

The first type is, broadly, of the sort just described, with the addition of an inscription. The front is flat, the reverse either flat or convex in section. Where the back is convex it is plain, but where it is flat there is either an inscription or some form of ornamentation. The most common inscription is IESVS NAZARENVS REX IUDEORVM, while the names of the Three Wise Men occur, no doubt for their talismanic properties. The brooches vary from about $\frac{1}{2}$ inch up to about 2 inches in diameter, and the metal may be silver, gold or common brass. One of the finest and most important examples is the gold 'Annunciation' brooch exhibited to the Society of Antiquaries of Scotland in 1936[1] by Theodora, Lady Forbes of Neme, and subsequently described by Dr. W. Douglas Simpson. It was found during excavations at the Doune of Invernochty, in Strathdon. It is flat in front and the reverse is convex, while the loop-hinge of the pin has a collar decorated with granulation. Marginal lines run along the inner and outer edges of the face of the ring, and between them is inscribed the phrase AVE · MARIA · GRACIA · PLENA. As Dr. Simpson remarked, there is no evidence of illiteracy here. Further, the gothic letters are formed with the greatest care and nicety, and the brooch evidently is not the work of a travelling tinker. The diameter is only $\frac{13}{16}$ of an inch. Naturally, the gold brooches tend to be on a smaller scale than the silver. Traces of *niello* sometimes appear in the inscriptions of the silver brooches, and it seems probable that this method of emphasis-

[1] *P.S.A.S.*, Vol. LXX, p. 179

ing the formula was widely used. Distribution throws no clear light on possible localities of manufacture, and it is likely that the brooches were in use from the English Border to the western islands.

The second category comprises only octagonal brooches. In section, the metal is triangular; but the eight sides are so arranged that every alternate one exhibits a flat face, while the others are ridged. Inscriptions occur as a rule on the flat faces. These take the form of variations of IESVS NAZARENVS REX IUDE-ORVM. The phrase is much contorted and mis-abbreviated, and often is scarcely recognisable. This type of brooch has been found mainly south of the Highland Line. It is of pleasing design, but the meagre attempts at decoration of the surface are crude. In all cases the brooches are of silver. Pl.11.i

A third category is devised as a circle of thick silver wire with a swinging pin attached. Around the circle are mounted rosette-like ornaments alternating with small punched knops. A fine example found at Canonbie possesses six rosettes, which are firmly and neatly modelled and more tastefully conceived than other ornaments of the kind. Dr. Callander's fourth category is so closely allied to his third that I should be inclined to describe it as a mere crude attempt to achieve the rosette brooches. Here the rosettes are replaced by lozenge-shaped plates punched with radiating lines or scored with a criss-cross mesh, originally emphasised by the use of *niello*. Traces of gilding represent another method of enhancement. The tools used must have been few and primitive. One of the favourite instruments seems to have been a small ring punch, the marks of which appear on examples of all categories, but most clearly in the third, where they occur on the knops between the rosettes. Pl.11.ii

The subject of tools raises the question of the identity of the makers of the medieval brooches, and the primitive nature of the tools together with the standard of craftsmanship and the confusion of so many of the inscriptions point to men of no great accomplishment. Certainly the brooches are not the work of professional silversmiths, even if we interpret the term liberally. Some ability to work with metals goes without saying; but it is the ability of a general handyman rather than the skill of a man with a craft. A curious feature of the brooches is that the earlier ones reveal a greater familiarity with Latin than do the later, and with the sixteenth century the 'Latin' tends to become quite unintelligible and indeed little more than a decorative pattern with the general appearance of black-letter script. Does this indicate that the earlier talismanic brooches were executed under the influence of the monastic establishments,

PLATE 13

Group of silver-mounted Charm Stones: 16th century (enlarged one-eighth) *(pp.44-45)*

PLATE 14

The Ugadale or Lossit Brooch; The Lochbuie Brooch; The Glenlyon Brooch: all 16th century (scale approximately two-fifths) *(pp.46 & 43-44)*

The Brooch of Ballochyle: 16th century (5⅖″ diameter) *(pp.46-47)*

and that those earlier brooches were later imitated by handymen in the remoter parts? A. J. S. Brook discussed the problem at length nearly seventy years ago.[1] He came to the conclusion that this brooch-making was the work of men in whom it was one of many accomplishments, rather than their trade. He based his arguments mainly on the fact that the constructive ability revealed is small by comparison with the taste in decoration, although it should be added that this taste develops rather in the later examples, from the fifteenth century onwards, with which we have yet to deal. Brook gives examples of brooches, both of silver and of brass, in which the technique betrays avoidance of difficulties, particularly hard-soldering, so comparatively simple to a trained craftsman but so baffling to the inexperienced. The brooch-makers invariably riveted where they might have soldered. Dexterity in the use of tools was a widespread accomplishment in the middle ages, and this dexterity was evidently handed down in the remoter parts of Scotland together with so much else of the medieval tradition. Indeed, there would be little to wonder at in the production of such brooches were it not that the average man of to-day has largely lost his manual faculties through the excess of mass-production and, even more, through the disastrous influence of a system which everywhere exalts paper qualifications above creative skills.

The brooches so far examined belong to a period probably not later than the fourteenth century. The ring-brooch continued to develop and, if its authors were the *ceardan* or travelling tinkers, as they are reputed to have been, then we cannot deny them a considerable amount of technical skill allied to much natural taste and ability. Towards the end of the fifteenth century a new type of annular brooch evolved from the old ring of wire. It is flat and, on its external edge, octagonal, clearly derived from the talismanic brooch; but the simple octagon has been given elegant curves, so that the brooch has a star-like outline accentuated at the points by means of small finials. In the beautiful example described by Brook,[2] both sides of the brooch are divided into eight panels, filled alternately with black-letter inscriptions and animal and other ornament. This decoration is engraved and inlaid with *niello*. The inscription on the obverse, divided by the panels, reads IHS MAR IA-DEO GRATIA, and that on the reverse OMATE R-DEI MEM ENTOI, the 'memento mei' having been telescoped for want of space. The animals represented include a wolf, a human-headed creature, and another beast which has been thought to resemble a bull. On the reverse,

---

[1] *P.S.A.S.*, Vol. XXIII, p. 196   [2] Ibid., p. 192

the animals are even more difficult to identify, but they are accommodated to the panels perhaps with even more sense of the decorative. More sophisticated although it may appear, the workmanship of the brooch is still fairly crude and, as Brook remarks, it is simply cut from a piece of silver which has been cast in a skellet and hammered to the required thickness. This type of brooch is rare, but not unique. In the National Museum of Antiquities there is a similar piece, inscribed IHCN, and there is also a bronze version of the type.

The medieval ring brooch is, by the fifteenth century, beginning to disappear, although it seems to have lingered in Scotland longer than it did in England.[1] A most important and attractive Scottish example of this period is a small gold one discovered by some boys 'guddling' for trout in the Ardoch Burn, near Doune Castle, in Perthshire.[2] The ring is twisted or fluted spirally, rather in the prehistoric manner, as noted by the writer of the first paper describing it. This fluting is emphasised by neat borders of finely-twisted wire, and in the spiral channel there is a black-letter inscription in old French: *Avez de moy mercie et pite moun coer en vous repoce. Niello* appears to have been used to emphasise the inscription, which is precisely inscribed considering the small scale of the brooch, which measures only $1\frac{1}{2}$ inches in diameter. It is of a gold which is almost pure and weighs 19.5 dwts. There is no reason to think the piece has any direct connexion with France, for its design is quite consistent with a Scottish origin. The most notable of these ring brooches, however, is the Kindrochit. It might be described as a medieval brooch carried out in the spirit of the Renaissance, which had found an echo in Scotland by the first half of the sixteenth century, the period to which it can be ascribed. The ring portion is broad and is divided into six kidney-shaped compartments, outlined with filigree work of twisted wire. The black-letter inscription so characteristic of medieval pieces of this sort is introduced within the six compartments, but the cast leaf-shaped ornaments inserted wedge-like between the compartments is a new element which helps to give grace and elegance to the brooch. The pin, a strong member reinforced functionally in the centre by thickening, terminates at the swivel end in a leaf ornament uniform with the rest. This brooch is of silver gilt, and has an air of much greater sophistication than others of its kind.

A variation of the ring type is to be found in the Glenlyon brooch, now in the British Museum. It is very large, 3 inches in diameter, and the ring is channelled transversely and embellished with six gold turrets on top of each of

Pl. 11.iii

Pl. 12.1

Pl. 14.i

---

[1] Joan Evans: *English Jewellery*, p. 44   [2] *P.S.A.S.*, Vol. VIII, p. 332

which a pearl is set. Alternating with the pearl turrets are amethysts set within a beaded edge, while other turrets are mounted with crystals. An unusual feature is a thick bar set across the diameter of the brooch. On this bar are two groups of sockets or *cloisons*, from which the stones have been lost. At the back is a black-letter inscription with the names of the Three Kings and the word *consumatum*—'It is finished'— that last saying of Christ reputed in the middle ages to have great talismanic powers. There is a curious arrangement of two pins, hinged on the inner circumference of the ring and resting their points on the edge of the cross-bar. Formerly in the possession of the Campbells of Glenlyon, this brooch would appear to be of a transitional type, retaining much of the medieval tradition and mystical purpose and combining these with the more elaborate style evolved under the impact of the Renaissance. It may have been made somewhere in the second half of the fifteenth century, or early in the next.

Pl.14.i   The occurrence of crystals on prominent settings on the Glenlyon brooch is one of the features which suggest its transitionary character, for the combination of brooches and crystals is a practice which seems to have been common among Scottish brooch-makers during the sixteenth century, in the Highland area at least. Crystals are, of course, thought by peoples in all parts of the world to be endowed with magical powers; but in such a region as the Highlands, where veins of quartz occur fairly frequently in the rocks on the high hills, superstitions of this kind are particularly widespread and tenacious. Such stones were supposed to possess curative properties, both for human ills and for maladies among cattle—'adder-stones' were worn by children as a protection against whooping-cough—and they were also closely linked with the rites of witchcraft. Usually, it seems, the stones were dipped in water, which then acquired special properties from the stones. It is related that at the trial of Hector Monro in 1598 one Marion Macingarath gave 'thrie drinks of watter furth of thrie stanes' to Hector Monro of Foulis, stones later deposited with the Justice-Clerk.

Pl.13   Those charm-stones in certain instances gained repute over wide areas for their potency, and as the legends grew about them nothing was more natural than that their owners should pay them the tribute of special settings. The Glenorchy charm-stone has been dated to about 1440.[1] It is a polished pyramidal piece of rock-crystal mounted in a roughly octagonal frame of silver ornamented with eight small pearls. Master William Bowie, pedagogue to the

[1] *Scottish National Memorials*, p. 337 (James Paton, editor)

44

Campbells of Glenorchy about the end of the sixteenth century, described it in the *Black Book of Taymouth* as 'ane stone of the quantitye of half a hen's eg set in silver, being flatt at the ane end and round at the uther end lyke a peir, whilk Sir Coline Campbell, first Laird of Glenurchy, woir when he fought in battell at the Rhodes agaynst the Turks, he being one of the Knychtis of the Rhodes'. The Maclean Leug in the National Museum of Antiquities is a similar relic; and among others in the museum is one associated with the Stewarts of Ardsheal, a polished crystal ball mounted in silver straps. Probably the most celebrated of all crystal balls so mounted is the Clach-Dearg of Ardvorlich. This is about $1\frac{1}{2}$ inches in diameter, secured by two intercrossing hoops of silver, lightly engraved and fitted with clasp and chain for suspension. It belongs to the Stewarts of Ardvorlich and is reputed to have been used for curing cattle as lately as 1830. The story has it that the charm was brought from the East by the Crusaders. The precise reason for the chain attached to these charms is explained in a description of the Keppoch charm-stone given in 1890 by the Rev. Dr. Alexander Stewart of Ballachulish. It was for suspending the stone when dipping it in water, in this case Tobar-Bhride—Bridget's Well—near Keppoch. The Keppoch stone, which is believed to have been carried to Australia about a century ago, was 'about the size of a small egg', mounted in a silver setting shaped like the claw of a bird. Dr. Stewart related that the following incantation was repeated when the stone was dipped in the well, the lines being his translation from the Gaelic:

> *Let me dip thee in the water,*
> *Thou yellow, beautiful gem of Power!*
> *In water of purest wave,*
> *Which (Saint) Bridget didn't permit to be contaminated.*
> *In the name of the Apostles twelve,*
> *In the name of Mary, Virgin of virtues,*
> *And in the name of the High Trinity,*
> *And all the shining angels,*
> *A blessing on the gem,*
> *A blessing on the water, and*
> *A healing of bodily ailments to each suffering creature.*

Sometimes the patient drank the water or had it sprinkled over him; at other times the stone was applied directly to the painful part.

45

In the sixteenth century a very few of these charm-stones were mounted in brooches, which also appear to have formed reliquaries. All the brooches are outstanding. The three 'turreted' brooches—the Lorne, the Ugadale or Lossit, and the Lochbuie—may safely be placed in the first half of the century. The Lorne brooch consists of a silver disc $4\frac{1}{2}$ inches across, on which is a massive socket or reliquary compartment capped by a big crystal fixed within a crenellated border, while standing around this central feature are eight *chatons* or turrets $1\frac{1}{4}$ inches high, slightly inclined inwards and each surmounted by a large pearl. A profusion of filigree work in the form of stellate *appliqué* ornaments and cabled borders provide detailed contrast to the generous proportions of the piece as a whole. It has been in the possession of the Macdougalls of Dunollie for more than a century, so far as its recent history is concerned. Before that it is said to have belonged to the Bragleen Campbells since the sacking of Gylen Castle on Kerrera, opposite Oban, by the troops of General Leslie in 1647. Tradition maintains stoutly that the brooch was carried by Robert the Bruce, and that at the battle of Dal-Righ he left it with his plaid in the possession of his foes, the Lords of Lorne. The stone itself most probably acquired fame long before the silver setting was formed round it, and it may be the stone and not the brooch to which the tradition properly attaches.

The Lochbuie brooch is generally similar. Its diameter is $4\frac{3}{4}$ inches. The central crystal may be lifted out, disclosing the reliquary cavity. Small bosses and cabled wire filigree form the detail, and in this case there are ten turrets, each 1 inch high and set with a river pearl. There is a story that the brooch was made by a local *ceard* or tinker from silver found on the Lochbuie estate on Mull. It is impossible to substantiate this in any degree from the evidence of local deposits. It is true there is a tradition that argentiferous galena occurred at Croggan, on the Lochbuie estate, but there are no records of actual finds of silver, or even of lead, on Mull. Pennant saw the brooch during his tour. It subsequently found its way into the Bernal collection and at the Bernal sale in 1855 was acquired by the British Museum.

The Ugadale or Lossit brooch differs from the others in certain minor respects. The central crystal is oval, its setting is an oval capsule, while the eight turrets are crowned by red corals and pearls alternately. On the broad outer rim there is strapwork decoration which is rather Elizabethan in character. The brooch is of silver gilt.

The last of these large silver brooches is the brooch of Ballochyle, quite un-

Pl.12.ii

Pl.14.i

Pl.14.i

Pl.14.ii

like the others. It is in the form of an eight-pointed star, with a small trefoil loop of open-work at the tip of each ray. In the centre is a large rock-crystal, seen *en cabochon*, in a setting with vandyked edge surrounded by the inscription: DE SERVE AND HALF THE HEVIN BABAIF. In compartments formed by the rays of the star are cut the initials MC, for McIver-Campbell of Ballochyle. With them are the leopard's head of McInnes and the gyronny of the Campbells. Like the other talisman brooches, it was used as a charm against witchcraft and disease, but the setting is perhaps rather more sophisticated in general appearance, if crudely-enough cut on close examination. It is a very fine and striking piece of jewellery, and belongs to the second half of the sixteenth century.

These great brooches, associated though they are with Highland families, stem from the medieval tradition of the smaller brooches discussed earlier in this chapter, and are in no sense a link between the art of the Celto-Norse group and the Highland brooches of the seventeenth and eighteenth centuries.

THE KAMES BROOCH (Not illustrated)

One of the most remarkable pieces of Scottish medieval goldwork is the Kames Brooch, a beautiful cast zoomorphic example, only just over 1½″ across. It is probably unique in several respects, having no known really close parallel. Dated by Mr. R. B. K. Stevenson to c.1300, it consists of a chain of six miniature wyverns, each one gripping the beast in front of it with its left fore-paw and teeth while coiling its tail around the neck of the one behind. The back is inscribed with a talismanic inscription in sunk Lombardic lettering which may originally have been enamelled or filled with niello. (The museum has another gold brooch, from Islay, with a very similar inscription.) The Kames Brooch shares its history with the Bute Mazer (p.n), both objects having descended through the MacGregors of MacGregor, by virtue of a marriage in the late eighteenth century with the heiress of MacLeod of Bernera, from the Bannatynes of Kames, Isle of Bute. (See Stevenson, R. B. K.: *The Kames Brooch* in *P.S.A.S.* Vol. XCV, pp.308-9.) The brooch was purchased, with help from the Pilgrim Trust and a Special Treasury Grant, by the National Museum of Antiquities of Scotland in 1961, where it is displayed under a large magnifying glass, a necessary provision because of its small size and the delicacy of its workmanship.

Chapter Five

THE REIGN OF JAMES V

AT his marriage to Mary of Guise, James V set before each guest a covered cup filled with 'bonnetpieces' of Crawford gold, telling the assembly that this unusual dessert consisted of 'the finest fruits' of a barren moor. In the history of Scottish gold and silver work, this picturesque incident is significant. Little has survived to tell factually the tale of this golden age; but the records of gold and silver mining in the sixteenth century, together with what we know of the expanding craft of the goldsmiths, provide ample circumstantial evidence of the temper and prosperity of the time.

Whether or not it was worked in earlier times, the existence of gold on Crawford Muir is said to have come to light in the reign of the fifth James. Small particles were doubtless gleaned regularly before then. The river gravels of the Leadhills were found to be auriferous as early as the reign of James IV, although it is interesting to learn that at that time lead was actually imported to the district to help in refining the gold. Stephen Atkinson in 1619 states that 'The vulgar sort of Scotsmen usually sought for it uppon these moores, after a great raine, and after the splitts of raine had run his course'.[1] Outside Scotland, for a time there appears to have been a rooted scepticism about the possibility of such precious metal occurring in such a cold country. 'Some say', Atkinson asserts, 'that gold and silver cannot engender with any other stones or meneralls, without the helpe of the sonn by day, and the moone and starres by night. Neither is it to be found in any place under the influence of the heavens but in hot countries.'[2] The author himself, however, did not share this notion, and it was exploded by sixteenth-century adventurers, especially the Elizabethans, such men as—in the phrase of Atkinson—'one Captain Furbisher, a famous gent', who took with them on their quests men of all arts and sciences.

[1] *The Discoverie and Historie of the Gold Mynes in Scotland* (Bannatyne Club, 1825), p. 14. Original MS. in the Nat. Library of Scotland
[2] Ibid., p. 16

At various times during this century concessions and monopolies were granted in Scotland to prospectors from England and other countries. The cupidity of Queen Elizabeth herself was aroused by rumours of rich veins of gold in the north, and among her emissaries was a certain George Bowes. 'It is so, and most trew', relates Atkinson,[1] 'that Mr. Bowes discovered a small vaine of gold, which had much small gold in it, uppon Winlocke-head. But he swore all his workmen to keepe it secrett, and never to disclose the same unto the King of Scotland, nor his Counsell: for so he had promised to do, at his departure from the Queene of England, if he found it.' Bowes worked under a warrant from 'the Lords of Scotland, by vertue whereof he was suffered quietly to digg and delve, where he would'. For a time he prospered in his duplicity. He filled up the shaft and again swore the workmen to secrecy, while he carried his samples of gold—'a long purse full thereof'—to Elizabeth, his mistress, who 'liked well thereof, and kept it secrett from all others'. But the secret remained an eternal one, for shortly after Bowes lost his life in a copper mine in Cumberland.

Another enterprise, perhaps on a larger scale, started in 1567, when a company under Cornelius de Vois—Devosse is Atkinson's version of the name—partner to Nicholas Hilliard, 'principall drawer of small pictures' to Queen Elizabeth, got a licence from the Regent Morton to work all the Scots mines. Both De Vois and Hilliard seem to have taken part. Hilliard was, of course, by training a goldsmith, and De Vois must have been an experienced mineralogist. With them was an Arthur van Brounckhurst. Here again, as with Bowes, the aim seems to have been to convey as much as possible of the gold into England, but Morton was well aware of this and Brounckhurst had to leave his gold at the Mint in Edinburgh. Eventually Brounckhurst was forced to become one of the King's servants-in-ordinary in Scotland, 'to draw all the small and great pictures for His Majesty', while Hilliard and De Vois lost all they had invested.[2]

Native sources of silver naturally attracted much less attention. It was, as remarked in an earlier chapter, much less easy to extract than gold, but its close association with lead caused jealous attention to be paid to the lead-mines. A lead-mine worked on the confines of the parish of Glenorchy in Argyllshire in 1424, for example, was declared a Royal Mine under the Scots Parliament's grant to the King of all lead-mines which yielded more than three-ha'pence' worth of silver to the pound of lead. Until the sixteenth century many of the

[1] Ibid., p. 33 *et seq.*   [2] Erna Averbach: *Nicholas Hilliard* (1961) pp.17-18

mines appear to have been worked principally for silver, the lead being lost during the process of cupellation. Before the end of this century the extraction of silver had become unprofitable, and the mines were worked for lead alone.

Profits were for a long time substantial in the Crawford-Muir gold mines. Three hundred people are believed to have found employment in washing gold on the moor, and for eighty years the value of the output is reputed to have been £100,000 Scots (about £30,000 sterling).[1] In an MS. in the Cottonian collection there are references to Germans employed to refine the gold here in 1526. From 1538 to 1542 the working is for the first time associated with the name of an actual Scottish goldsmith, John Mossman, who used 113 ounces of the metal for making crowns for James V and his Queen, for enlarging the King's chain, and for making a belt for the Queen.[2] Porteous maintains[3] that the miners under the direction of Mossman were French, imported from the Duchy of Guise. He quotes entries of payments in the Royal Treasurer's books for 'interpretours to pass with the French mynours till they learn the language', and also a grant of 'ane Scottish boy that speaks French, to serve them till they get the Scottish language'. The output during this time must have included some considerable nuggets, for one worker, John Gibson of Crawford, found them as large as birds' eggs, the largest of them 'uppon Glengaber Water, within the Forest of Attrick' (Ettrick). He sold it to the Regent Morton for 6s. 8d. sterling the ounce. Another incomer of the time was Abraham Grey or Greybeard, a Dutchman.[4] He got 'a good quantity of naturall gold' in the valleys around Wanlockhead, enough to make 'a very faire deepe bason', large enough to contain an English gallon. This basin was filled to the brim with gold coins called unicornes, and basin and coins were presented to the King of France by the Regent Morton, who declared to him: 'My Lord, behold this bason and all that therein is: it is naturall gold, gotten within this kingdom of Scotland, by a Dutchman, named Abraham Grey.' Here again we have a link with a Scottish craftsman of the time, although he is nameless, for the basin was made 'att Edenborough, in Cannegate Streete; it was made by a Scottsman'.

This is an interesting pointer to the activities of goldsmiths in the Canongate, at that time not merely an Edinburgh thoroughfare but a burgh in its own right, embracing within its boundaries the royal palace of Holyroodhouse.

---

[1] J. Moir Porteous: *God's Treasure House in Scotland*, p. 35
[2] Heddle: *The Mineralogy of Scotland*, Vol. I, p. 8
[3] Ibid., p. 37   [4] Atkinson, p. 21

The earliest recorded name of a goldsmith within the burgh is that of Ogier Coquele, a German.[1] It is recorded that he appears in a protocol of November 10th, 1552, as obtaining possession of a house in the High Street. Two years later the Edinburgh Town Council brought from him a goblet as a present for Marie de Lorraine, the Queen's mother, and it is thought he came over in her train from Lille. A certain Ferdinand Coquele, or Cokquall, is mentioned in a Canongate charter of 1589. From the middle of the sixteenth century a number of goldsmiths were always located in the Canongate, but the high quality of their work is something which belongs properly to the next chapter. The majority of those men were native Scots, and the gold basin proves that the craft did not come into the burgh with Ogier. It is all the more surprising, as Commander How has remarked, that in the Canongate there appears to have been no official 'tryar' or assay officer; for the rival craftsmen of Edinburgh, with whom there was constant dispute over trespasses against the rights and privileges of one group or the other, were, long before the Reformation, organised fully on the lines of the medieval guild.

The goldsmiths of Edinburgh, as we have seen, were included within the Incorporation of Hammermen, together with the blacksmiths, pewterers, lorimers, saddlers, cutlers, buckle-makers and armourers. The Incorporation was granted its charter, or Seill of Cause, in 1483. Like all such guilds, it had close links with the Church. An altar to St. Eloi, patron saint of goldsmiths, was founded in the High Kirk of St. Giles before 1483, and by 1494 the control of this altar and its chaplaincy had passed to the Hammermen, who exercised it until 1558.[2] Ceremonial associated with the craft does not reflect any very great wealth, but it indicates that the Hammermen played a distinctive part in the life of the city. All members were entitled to the use of the crafts' 'mort-cloth', evidently an elaborate pall, embroidered by one Gerard de Haustin, and costing £30 15s. 11d. The Incorporation staged various processions and sacred plays, as for example the drama of 'King Herod' on Corpus Christi Day. Such processions have an intriguing sound. They were headed by musicians, most of them French but among them a certain native element which performed on such cruder instruments as the swash or drum—violently belaboured, if we may judge by the cost of hides for re-covering it!—and the buzoon or bovum, apparently the bagpipe. The Incorporation was associated with the Magdalen

[1] Comm. How in *Burlington Magazine*, Vol. LXXIV, p. 287
[2] J. Smith: *The Hammermen of Edinburgh*, Ch. VIII

Chapel, in the Cowgate. This is first mentioned in 1544, and was conveyed to the Hammermen craft three years later by Janet Rynd, widow of Michael Macquhan. In secular affairs, the craft fought a long battle for the interests of the craftsmen as against those of the merchants of the town, for example in such matters of dispute as the import of manufactured articles from abroad. When in 1543 the Deacon of Crafts appeared before the Provost and Council to demand redress for grievances, four out of the eleven craftsmen who accompanied him were members of the Hammermen Incorporation. The delegation added point to its arguments by drawing its swords in the faces of the city fathers, an incident which ended with the delegates being thrown into prison.

There is little enough material by which to judge the skill of the Scottish goldsmiths of the earlier part of the sixteenth century. The print or boss of the Bute mazer, belonging to the early fourteenth century, has already been examined; but the silver mounts of the bowl have been claimed as work of the Pl.15.i third decade of the sixteenth century in the scholarly paper by J. H. Stevenson already quoted.[1] The inscription on the exterior of the lip-band, engraved in characters transitional as between the Lombardic and Gothic of the middle ages and the revived Roman of the new age, reads: NINIAN BANNACHTYN LARD OF THE CAMISSOUN TO UMQHIL ROBERT BANNACHTIN OF THE CAMIS. There was only one Ninian Bannatyne of Kames whose father's name was Robert, and he evidently succeeded his father in 1522. Stevenson considered that, as Ninian is described merely as the son of his father, he was a young man when the inscription was done. This seems likely enough.

The lip-band is generally characteristic of that feature in English mazers of the late fifteenth and early sixteenth centuries. It can be compared with, for example, the mazer at Oriel College, Oxford, while Stevenson drew a parallel between the lettering and that on the Rochester mazer in the British Museum. The notched or scalloped lower edge of the band may be matched, more or less, on a number of English mazers. Altogether it is clear that if the lip were made in Scotland, which there is no good reason to doubt, the pattern was an English one, probably of a period slightly earlier. The execution of the lettering is rather less sure than it is in the case of the Rochester mazer, but is no less decorative. Introduced among it are various punctuation marks such as the mullet, bearing of the Bannatynes, and the cinquefoil of the Fitzgilberts, a version of the sacred Monogram, and an 'I' which for some reason Stevenson

[1] *P.S.A.S.*, Vol. LXV, p. 223

treats as a blunder of the engraver but which is clearly intended to separate the beginning and end of the circular inscription. Inscription and punctuation both go to confirm the case for native workmanship. Lip and foot are connected by means of six silver straps, ½ inch in width and with scalloped edges which to some extent repeat the lower edge of the lip-band. Each strap has a spine which is, in heraldic terminology, counter-embattled, and is connected to lip and foot by a hinge. This is the only Scottish mazer to possess straps, and only a very few English mazers do so, although of course straps were to be used commonly on coconut-cups of both countries.

Pl.15.ii At one time the cover of the mazer also has been mounted in silver: that is, there has been a narrow rim to it in addition to the small, central silver knob which survives. The cover has been carved from a piece of whalebone which Professor Ritchie has identified as a slice from the ramus of the lower jaw of a sperm whale.[1] As bone-carving, it would not directly concern us here were it not that it perhaps goes a little way to help confirm again the suggested date of the mazer as it stands. The very beautiful overall pattern has no parallel in Scotland, for in spite of a certain amount of interlacing this cannot be grouped with Celtic work. There seems no reason to doubt it is Scottish. Clearly it has been made to fit the mazer, for there is no sign of adaptation. It is not unusual for sperm whales to be stranded on the Scottish coasts, and the shrinkage of the lid shows that the carving was done before the process was complete. The carving is more sure and sophisticated than that on the Fife and Eglinton caskets, of the fifteenth century, and it seems to point to a date rather later than theirs. Altogether, in conjunction with the other features already discussed, the cover adds weight to the surmise of the date at which the mazer was assembled in its present form. The cinquefoil plates securing the silver knob above and below are possibly a repetition of the bearing of the Fitzgilberts.

Pl.16 The principal surviving piece of evidence of the attainments of Scottish goldsmiths in the first half of the sixteenth century is the Royal Crown of Scotland, constructed or reconstructed by John Mosman for James V, so that it is the oldest of the crowns in the British Regalia. Evidently James was much concerned with the insignia of royalty and felt the need to make a braver show, for he constantly commissioned modifications and additions. The Crown has occasioned a great deal of controversy since 'the Honours of Scotland' were rediscovered in 1818, for Sir Walter Scott maintained that the refashioning of

[1] *P.S.A.S.*, Vol. LXV, p. 233

the Crown in 1540 merely amounted to the addition of arches to an open crown dating back to the time of Robert the Bruce. That something like the reverse is true was proved by Alexander J. S. Brook's investigations in 1890.[1]

There is no authentic record of the form of the older crown. Principal sources of information about it are four: an inventory of the Royal Wardrobe taken in 1539, a representation in a panel of the altar-piece removed from the old Trinity College Chapel in Edinburgh, representations on the coinage of the times, and certain features of the existing Crown. Brook has set out the evidence in much detail, and his paper remains the one full and authoritative work on the subject; but one may summarise by saying that the open crown of the Trinity College painting cannot be accepted as an authentic or at least complete picture, for coinage ascribed to James III and James IV depicts a closed crown, while Brook showed conclusively that the existing arches pre-date the refashioning of 1540. The gold of the arches is of 20 carats $3\frac{7}{8}$ grains fineness, as against the 21 carats $\frac{1}{2}$ grain of the fillet. Additional jewels were added to the fillet at the reconstruction, and it is clear that a phrase used by Lord Fountain-hall in his manuscript diary, 'that the Crown of Scotland is not the ancient one, but was casten of new by James V', applies to the fillet, which is in part literally cast, and not to the arches.

If we accept Brook's view, which there is every reason to do, since he supports it minutely and abundantly with first-rate evidence, it may be taken that the existing Royal Crown of Scotland consists of (1) a fillet, refashioned— 'casten of new'— in 1540, but incorporating most of the jewels of the older crown; (2) the arches of the older crown and, surmounting them; (3) a mound and cross *pattée* added by James V, demonstrable by the cipher IR 5 enamelled on the foot of the cross. We know that John Mosman was entrusted with the work of refashioning. The probability that native gold was used amounts almost to a certainty, for the high percentage of silver in the gold supports the documentary evidence regarding '113 ounces of the metal for making crowns for James V and his Queen', while sentiment increases the likelihood of native metal being employed for the sovereign's emblem.

Briefly to describe the Crown's form: the fillet, $1\frac{9}{16}$ inches deep, has a moulded edge above and below, and is surmounted by ten crosses fleury alternating with ten fleurs-de-lys. From the crosses fleury and fleurs-de-lys rise four radial arches $\frac{7}{16}$ inch wide, ornamented with oak leaves in gold and red

[1] *P.S.A.S.*, Vol. XXIV, p. 49 *et seq.*

enamel. At the intersection of the arches is fixed the mound or celestial globe of gold, $\frac{5}{32}$ inches in diameter, enamelled blue and powdered with stars, and surmounting this is the cross *pattée* of the same height as the mound's diameter, enamelled in black with decoration reserved in gold. The fillet is ornamented with nine carbuncles, four jacinths, four amethysts, two white topazes and two rock-crystals backed with green foil to represent emeralds, and one white topaz foiled with yellow. Some of the stones are cut *en cabochon*, others are rose or table cut, and yet others irregular. Between the stones are pearls, thirteen of them oriental and seven Scottish. There are pearls also on the crosses fleury. Beneath the crosses fleury and the fleurs-de-lys are settings filled alternately with diamonds and blue enamel. In the centre of the front of the cross *pattée* is a table-cut amethyst, and the angles and extremities of the cross are fitted with oriental pearls. The weight of the Crown is 56 ounces 5 dwts. This may be compared with the 71 ounces of the old English crown, minted down into coin in 1649, but the English crown was much more richly adorned with gems than is the Scottish.

The principal work done by John Mosman must have been the casting of the fillet with its crosses fleury and fleurs-de-lys, and the setting of the gems. In the accounts of the Lord High Treasurer there is an item of 15th January, 1540, of payment to John Mosman 'for making and Fassoun of the Kingis crowne', for 'gold of the mynde' and for 'xxiij stanes thereto'. The arches, belonging to the older crown, must also have had their older mound and cross *pattée*, for these appear on the coins; but the present mound and cross are of much finer execution than the rest of the Crown, and are probably French. French also are the oak-leaves on the arches. Brook, himself a goldsmith, had a devastatingly poor opinion of the old Scottish goldsmiths, declaring that their shrewdness as bankers was greater than their skill as craftsmen[1]; and there is no doubt that when we are faced with a close juxtaposition of Scottish and Continental work, as in the Crown, the ruder execution of the Scot is at once apparent. Even the finish is inferior: file marks are to be found on the fillet. Insecure settings, too, have resulted in the loss of a number of the gems. Mosman no doubt modelled his crown on the preceding one; but the question arises whether he merely took moulds from it, or from the details of it, or whether he drew up his design anew, copying the main features of the older piece. It is probable that he did the latter, for he was set the problem of incorporating many stones

[1] *P.S.A.S.*, Vol. XXIV, p. 70

which were not in the original crown, and we have seen that he added a quantity of new gold. We may conclude, therefore, that the leading Scottish goldsmiths of the time were reasonably skilled in the crafts of casting and engraving, but that the finer points were beyond their powers.

The Crown is quite the most interesting item in the Regalia, but not the only one in which native craftsmen were concerned. It will be remembered that Mosman was also commissioned to make a crown for the Queen of James V, for which he used 35 ounces of gold. It is now lost or destroyed, but the weight suggests the probability that it was an open crown or diadem, set with jewels, such as Queen Margaret of Denmark is shown wearing in the Trinity College altar-piece; while in 1503 James IV had commanded one John Currour, an Edinburgh goldsmith, to make a crown for his queen, the Princess Margaret of England. So the Edinburgh craftsmen by 1540 had at least two generations of experience in attempting pieces of the more sumptuous kind. The surviving Sceptre, a gift from Pope Alexander VI in 1494, might be passed by as Italian work; but it, too, has been 'casten of new' by an Edinburgh goldsmith, Adam Leys, in 1536. It is not of gold, but of silver gilt, and in its present form it weighs 25 ounces 12 dwts as against the 15 ounces of the piece originally given by the Pope. James V appears to have had a marked obsession for rendering the symbols of his kingship more massive, if not more decorative, but whether this is a sidelight on his lusty temperament, or whether it is simply a question of the 'Gaberlunzie King's' patronage in his close relations with his people, cannot be judged. Not all of the Sceptre has been remodelled, and the shape of the older emblem has been perpetuated by casting. Brook records that no attempt has been made to finish the castings except in so far as the three figures have been smoothed with a steel scraper. In the original, much of the decoration must have been carried out in beautiful *repoussé*, as on the hilt and scabbard of the Sword of State presented by Pope Julius II. The mounts of the rock-crystal sphere and the finial above are part of the original Italian sceptre.

Pl.17.i

Of rather more significance in the story of Scottish goldsmiths is the Lord High Treasurer's Mace, not properly part of the Regalia but discovered with it in the oak chest in 1818. It is of silver gilt and is 3 feet long, not including the oval, faceted globe of rock-crystal surmounted by a cross *patteé*, which measure $2\frac{3}{4}$ inches. The mace may be taken apart in three sections, and there is a wooden core. Sir Walter Scott first connected it with the Lord High Treasurer, although there is no real evidence to support his contention. It cannot, on the other hand, be the missing Queen's Sceptre made by John Mosman in 1540, as the weights do not correspond, and it appears more likely to have been a rod of office than a sceptre. Its special interest, however, lies in the maker's mark, F.G, punched on two of the sections. Brook first suggests that it belongs to an early period, since only the maker's mark is present, and then in the following paragraph concedes that Scottish plate was often irregularly marked.[1] He proceeds to state that no freeman in the minute-books of the Edinburgh Incorporation of Goldsmiths, which date from 1525, bears the initials F.G., and that the mace may therefore date before 1525. The only goldsmith in Scotland whom he could find with the correct initials was one Findlay-Goldsmyth of Perth, mentioned in the minutes of the Perth Hammermen for 1519. The mark does not suggest an early Scottish provincial type, and indeed Brook did not press the attribution. Nor does it appear to be an English mark, for London goldsmiths of the early sixteenth century used symbols rather than initials, as a rule, and it does not seem to have been the practice of English craftsmen to use their personal punches unaccompanied by any other, although it was common in Scotland. It is assuredly not a Continental mark. In style it is quite in keeping with other Edinburgh marks, and it is reasonable to refer the Mace to that town.

Pl.17.ii There is one other piece of about this period which must be described: the Methuen Cup. It was sold at Christie's in 1920, for £3,200, and is probably in the United States. I have not had an opportunity of examining it, but it has been fully described in a paper read to the Society of Antiquaries of Scotland.[2] The cup is shallow, with a shaped cover surmounted by a crystal ball with a ring of serpent form. The stem is of rock-crystal, octagonal in section, and there is a spreading foot. Four S-shaped brackets link base with stem, and the stem is fitted with a collar. The total height is 7 inches and the bowl is $4\frac{1}{2}$ inches in diameter. There are five incised inscriptions, the lettering being Roman with an occasional Lombardic intrusion. These inscriptions are as follows: (1) GIF · YAT · YOV · HES · AFRIND · OF LANG · SVPPOS · HE · SUMTIM · DOV · YE · VRANG · OPPRES · HIM · NOT · BOT · AY · OF · MEIN (on cover); (2) THE · KANDES · YAT · AFOR · HAS · BEIN · MAL (top of cover); (3) AT · YI · BURD · QVAN · ART · SET · THINK ON YE · PVIR · STANDIS · AT · YI · ZET · LOVE · GOD · DO · LAV · KEIP · CHERATI · SVA · SAL · AL · GRACE · ABOVNDAND · BE (around bowl); (4) EX · DONO · G · D · B · M · (on ring around stem); (5) QVCQVID · AGAS · SAPIENTER · AGAS · ET · RESSPICE · FINEM (around foot). The contributor of the paper, Francis C. Eeles,

[1] P.S.A.S., Vol. XXIV, p. 117   [2] P.S.A.S., Vol. LV, p. 285

PLATE 15

The Bute or Bannatyne Mazer: first half 16th century *(pp.53-54)*

Carved whalebone Cover of above *(p.54)*

PLATE 16

The Royal Crown of Scotland: Edinburgh, about 1540. Maker: John Mosman (*pp.54-57*)

PLATE 17

The Methuen Cup: 16th century, possibly c.1530
by John Vaiche (*pp.58-59*)

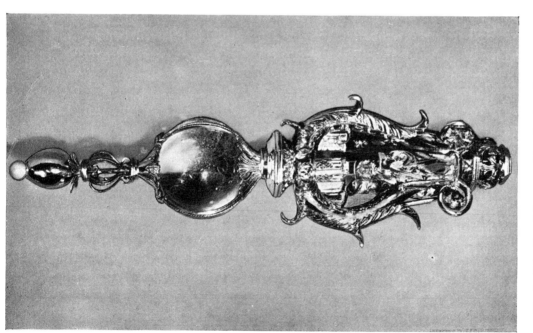

Head of the Royal Sceptre of Scotland: re-fashioned
in 1536 by Adam Leys, Edinburgh (*p.57*)

PLATE 18

The Watson Mazer: mid–16th century *(pp.61-64)*

Detail of rim of above, showing maker's punch
(pp.61-64)

suggests that the inscription on the ring may well be later in date than the others. Inside the bowl is an incised medallion containing the sacred monogram in black-letter enclosed within two concentric circles with leaves in wreath form. The maker's mark is vh, and there is no other mark. Eeles dated the cup as belonging to the second quarter of the century, but the maker has not been identified. The Methuen family is probably descended from John Methuen and his son Paul, who left Scotland in the sixteenth century, and it is possible the cup came originally from Methven, near Perth. The piece has every appearance of being of Scottish workmanship, but more than that cannot be said without a close examination.

NOTES TO CHAPTER V

NICHOLAS HILLIARD (p.50, second paragraph)
For more on Hilliard's envolvement in the goldmine adventure, see Auerbach, E: *Nicholas Hilliard*, 1961, pp.17-19, and Edmond, M: *Hilliard and Oliver, the lives and works of two great miniaturists*. London 1983, pp.54-58.

CANONGATE GOLDSMITHS (p.52, top)
Several goldsmiths worked in Canongate before Ogier Coquel in 1552. Two men called Matthew Auchinleck, father and son, Joachim Hochstetter, James Achesoun, elder, John Achesoun, elder and Patrick Gray are all found there earlier in the same century. Some of them were also concerned with the operation of the Royal mint, which was established at Holyrood by 1504. More is said about this in Chapter XV, page n.

"THE LORD HIGH TREASURER'S MACE" (pp.57-58)
The paragraph beginning at the foot of page 63 discusses a staff of office which was known at the time, due to a false assumption by Sir Walter Scott, as the Lord High Treasurer's Mace. It is still exhibited with the Honours of Scotland in the Crown Room in Edinburgh Castle, but it is a Sceptre, not a mace, and is unconnected with the Treasurer. It turns out to be the sceptre of the Duke of York (afterwards King James VII and II), used by him while

he was Lord High Commissioner for his brother, King Charles II. It was made in London by Francis Garthorn in the early 1680s and is marked with his maker's mark only, a fact that contributed to the confusion of its identity.

THE METHVEN CUP (pp.58-59)

The Methven Cup is now in the Los Angeles County Museum of Art, having been given to them by William Randolph Hearst. There is still a lingering doubt as to its date and the identity of its maker, but I would like to offer my own suggestion, which I believe to be a correct one. I feel that the cup could easily be as early as 1530 or even 1525. When trying to make sense of the maker's mark it should be remembered that it consists of a capital V and a lower case h; we are therefore not looking at a pair of initials, VH or WH, but at a contraction of a single name. I suggest that it is in all probability the monogram of John Vaich, an Edinburgh goldsmith who became a burgess in 1517. He is mentioned again in the Edinburgh City Archives on 23rd October 1520 when he valued a silver-gilt belt and a gold ring; and he comes sixth in order of seniority in the list of the sixteen Edinburgh Goldsmiths in 1525-6. There is nothing to prove that this mark pertains to Vaich, but it seems to me to be the most likely of all the possible explanations so far, and a very reasonable probability.

Chapter Six

THE STANDING MAZERS

THE second half of the sixteenth century is one of the most interesting periods in the history of Scottish silver work. There is no plenitude of pieces to reflect its achievement as the great salts and standing cups still in the possession of colleges and corporations reflect Elizabethan England; but the few things which have survived are of the greater significance for that.

Most noteworthy is the group of standing mazers. Standing mazers, that is, mazers raised on a stem or foot to a height of several inches, are not peculiar to Scotland. It is probable that they were not uncommon in England, although the only surviving English examples admitted by Jackson to be in their original state are three: those of All Souls College, Oxford, and Corpus Christi and Pembroke Colleges in Cambridge. Others, such as the Harbledon Hospital mazer and the triple-supported Scrope mazer at York, have had the foot added at a later date. The two Cambridge pieces have a trumpet-shaped foot, a feature shared by the three earliest Scottish standing mazers, the Watson, the St. Mary's and the Fergusson; but the English trumpets are elaborated in a style wholly different from the Scottish.

I will deal with the Watson mazer first, because it may represent a link be- Pl. 18
tween the much earlier Bute or Bannatyne mazer and the rest of the Scottish group, and I take leave to deal with it at some length because it has for a number of years been an object of controversy, and remains so. Its wooden bowl—I hesitate to pronounce upon the wood since Mr. Edward H. Pinto dismissed the customary attribution of bird's-eye maple to the bowls of mazers—is fitted with a deep silver-gilt lip-band, escalloped along its lower edge, with feathered piles. A pattern of foliaceous scrolls proceeding from a sort of cornucopia is engraved rather crudely on the outer side of the band. Occupying most of the well area of the bowl, which measures $7\frac{1}{2}$ inches in lip diameter, is a print with an engraved coat-of-arms surrounded by sixteen radiating lobes, stepped down to the well. The silver-gilt stem has a band of decoration about the waist, while

the foot is boldly ornamented with lobes in *repoussé* and inscribed with the legend: TYNE GEIR TYNE LITIL TYNE HONOVR TYNE MUCKIL TYNE HART TYNE AL. This Old Scots wording may be rendered as:

> *Lose wealth, lose little,*
> *Lose honour, lose much,*
> *Lose heart, lose all.*

The mazer is not in its original condition. Apart from any modification in design, it would seem to have received at some time an impact which has driven the stem up through the bowl, for modern silver plates have been inserted above and below the bowl, clamping the wood between them. They are secured by a bolt passing down through the stem. The rim is struck four times with a mark, a fleur-de-lys enclosed in a shield with invected margin. This mark occurs singly, and again in a group of three. Endeavours were made at one time to associate it with Aberdeen by comparing it with the Fintray Communion cup of 1663, the Drainie-by-Elgin beakers of 1750, and the Monymusk beaker of 1691. I have examined the first and last, but found no significant similarity between their marks and those on the mazer. There appears to be no ground for associating the fleur-de-lys with any Scots burgh. In estimating the date, therefore, we have to fall back on style. The mazer has many features typical of the late Gothic period. The rayed lower edge of the lip-band, with its notching and hatching, may be matched on a number of mazers of the years between 1470 and 1530. The treatment of this rim is altogether more suggestive of the Bute mazer than of the later Scottish group, and it might belong to the early part of James V's reign, but the engraving seems to reach forward towards the animals and scrolls of the much later Craigievar mazer, although the execution is much inferior.

The main burden of the case for the mazer's Scottish provenance is not stylistic. It rests on the inscription around the foot of the stem, and on the coat-of-arms engraved on the print. The inscription has been quoted. The arms on the print are those of Watson, *argent an oak tree proper and a fess, azure*, while the shield bearing the arms is flanked by the initials DV. The original records of the Lyon Office and all but a few scattered grants of arms in private hands were destroyed in the seventeenth century, and it is understood these arms are unrecorded in the *New Register* of Scottish arms. However, they have been attributed to the parent stock of the Watsons, of Saughton, now within the city boundary of Edinburgh. The initials may well represent David Watson, who was alive in the middle of the sixteenth century. The earliest Watsons of Saughton recorded in the Register of the Privy Council in Scotland were James and John, portioners of the lands of Saughton in 1572 and 1576–7. They may have been the sons of David.

Commander How[1] has questioned the case for the Scottish provenance of the mazer as re-stated by myself, and it is only right that his argument should be summarised here. I trust my brief summary is fair to him, but a full statement of his point of view is on record. The bowl and its mounts he considers genuine, although originally they might have formed a low mazer of English type. The decoration of the rim 'is typical of the period 1560–1590 and cannot with certainty be ascribed either to England or to Scotland'. The marks he likens to one which Jackson attributed to Lincoln,[2] an attribution with which he disagrees in the belief that the mark 'may eventually be shown to pertain to Chester'. He considers the print is built up and was not originally the print of a mazer at all, but perhaps the cover of a mounted jug such as the Erskine ewer. He maintains that the foot, although similar to the boss or print, is by another hand, that it may be English or Continental of the first half of the sixteenth century, and that it belonged to a 'totally different object'. The engraved band on the upper half of the foot—the waist, as I have described it—'might reasonably be ascribed to the second half of the seventeenth century'. As to the legend inscribed on the foot, it is his opinion 'that the addition of the proverb would present no difficulty to a competent craftsman, thereby connecting the foot and the print together and giving a specious air of homogeneity to two pieces which otherwise I consider show only superficial kinship'. He supports his view on the proverb by quoting the comment of the Edinburgh City Archivist, Dr. Marguerite Wood, that the words LITIL, MUCKIL and HART 'are not commonly used in that form in sixteenth-century Scots'. 'The use of one', Dr. Wood continues, 'might be possible, the use of four seems to show that the inscription was made not at that period, but by someone who was trying to reproduce the spelling of the period, but did not know quite enough about it.'

In brief, Commander How has come to the conclusion that the mazer is a made-up piece, and although he allows the arms of Watson to be perfectly genuine, he believes the Scots inscription to be a later addition to lend unity to the whole. The genuineness of the 'parts' of the mazer is not in question: the

[1] *Apollo*, Vol. XLIX, p. 16 [2] *English Goldsmiths and their Marks*, p. 443, l. 1

Wardens of the Goldsmiths' Company, to whom the piece was submitted, were agreed upon their antiquity. In the absence of any better guide, much seems to hang upon the inscription, and I took the precaution of referring it to that most eminent of authorities on Old Scots, Sir William Craigie. Sir William replied to my query that LITIL and HART are common forms in the sixteenth century, and that MUCKIL, though certainly rare, was in use. He ended: 'I shall have no hesitation in quoting it (the inscription) as sixteenth century if the other features of the mazer indicate that date.' The other features do indicate that date. Both print and foot, then, appear to have passed through the hands of Scots craftsmen of the period. The possibility of the later assembly of the parts remains, and I agree with Commander How's rejection of the Aberdeen-shire origin of the marks, although I feel that is as far as the matter can be carried in our present state of knowledge. The mazers which we are about to discuss prove that the mounts and decoration of the Watson mazer were well within the powers of Scottish goldsmiths of the time. On the strength of two proved Scottish features, therefore, I consider we are entitled to include the mazer in the Scottish group.

Pl.19.i The trumpet-shaped stem and foot of the Watson mazer is found again, in a simpler and more elegant form, in the St. Mary's and the Fergusson mazers. The first of those is simple to the point of severity, but is of unique interest as the oldest fully hall-marked piece of Edinburgh silver. Scarcely more than half an inch deep, its lip-band is without ornament except for its notched or van-dyked lower edge. Its stem is of silver, also undecorated, spreading into a reeded foot. The only engraving on the mazer is on the print, which is 4 inches across and inscribed with two texts from the Vulgate: LEX · PER · MOISEN · DATA · EST · GRTA · ET · VERITAS · PER · IESV · CHRM · FACTA · EST · IO · I and, on a shield in the centre, SIVE · MADVCATIS · SIVE · BIBITIS · VEL · ALIVD · QVID · FACITIS · OIA · IN · GLIAM · DEI · FACITE · I Corin · 10. On the shield also is the date 1567, and it is surrounded by another inscription: COLLEGIV · NOVVM · SCTE · ADREE. The mazer is a little older than the date inscribed. In addition to the triple-castle mark of Edinburgh, it carries the punches of the maker, Alexander Auchin-leck, and of Thomas Ewing, the deacon. Date-letters had not made their appearance on Scottish silverware at this time, and the dating of early pieces can be done only approximately, by comparing the maker's and deacon's marks and referring to the maker's recorded date of entry into the craft and to the deacon's period of office. Ewing occupied the deaconate from 1552 until

1554, in 1556–7, and again in 1561–2, so that the latter is the latest year in which the mazer could have been made. Commander How, whose papers on the mazers[1] admirably complete the work done on them by Brook, inclines to the belief that the latest period, 1561–2, is the most likely one. Burns notes that the mazer was used at the St. Mary's College table on high occasions, and handed round from guest to guest.[2]

The Fergusson mazer is a more elegant piece. The everted lip-band is much   Pl.19.ii
deeper than the band of the St. Mary's mazer. It is quite plain, but the lower edge is notched and engraved with a formalised leaf-like effect. The stem itself is also plain but spreads into a rolled and moulded foot the enrichment of which is in contrast to the severity of the stem. Around the print is inscribed QVID · HABES · QVOD · NON · ACCEPISTI · SI · ACCEPISTI · QVID · GLORIARIS · I CORIN 4, with the date 1576; while in the centre, rather rudely engraved in outline, are the arms of Fergusson impaling Durham with the initials DF and ID, for David Fergusson and Alice Durham, his wife. It is no longer in the possession of Fergussons, but the belief is that it was the gift of James VI, when a small boy, to his tutor, David Fergusson. David was a glover by trade in Dundee, although of Ayrshire extraction, but, like many Scots of later times, he was drawn to the church and, at the Reformation, received a charge at Dunfermline, where he became tutor to the King. The mazer found its way to Ayrshire, where it came to another branch of the family, the Fergussons of Kilkerran. For a long time its existence was forgotten, but someone discovered it in a hatbox about to be burned with a quantity of rubbish. Its date may well be as engraved. It is marked fully, on lip-band, stem and print. Adam Craige, admitted to the craft in 1562, is the maker, and the deacon is James Mosman.

To diversify for a moment the subject of mazers, once associated with the piece just described is the Fergusson spoon. Now in the collection of the Marquess of Bute, this spoon has a bowl which is nearly round, and a short, straight stem with a decorative collar round the neck, the whole completed by a version of the seal-top. On the back of the spoon is a short, stubby rat-tail, peculiar to Scotland. This is one of the very earliest of Scottish spoons. It is stamped with the pot of lilies, hall-mark of Dundee, and with the maker's mark, RG. This last appears to refer to a member of the family of Gairdyne. The earliest mention of a Dundee goldsmith with those initials is a reference to a Robert

---

[1] *P.S.A.S.*, Vol. LXVIII, p. 394 and *Connoisseur*, Vol. XCIII, p. 313
[2] *Scottish Communion Plate*, p. 193

Gairdyne in a statute of the Hammermen Craft dated 8th April, 1663. A maker's mark with the same initials occurs on a Brechin Communion cup of more than thirty years earlier. The oldest of surviving craft records in Dundee is the 'Lockit Buik' of the Hammermen, but it dates only to 1587. However, the spoon bears on its seal-top the initials DF and, on the back of the bowl, ID, confirming the link with the mazer. How cites another Scottish seal-top spoon.

Pl.33.ii
Inscribed with the date 1573, it is an Edinburgh piece by William Cok with the deacon's mark of Adam Craige. The Canongate spoon in the National Museum of Antiquities introduces a second type of Scottish spoon of this time. The stem ends in a form of trefid, and the spoon is dated 1589. Jackson estimated the age of it at half a century later, but How—whose researches on Scottish spoons have clarified the whole subject—identifies the maker's mark, GC, as belonging to George Cunningham, senior, whom the Canongate records prove to have been at work at least in 1593.[1] The Canongate mark, a stag lodged, is also present. A number of other spoons have survived from this time.

Antiquarian interest is at once superseded by aesthetic considerations when we come to examine the Tulloch, Craigievar and Galloway mazers, which may be claimed as the three finest standing mazers in existence. Their proportions are good and their workmanship and decoration of the highest order. Contemplating them, we realise how far the powers of the Scottish gold-

Pl.20.i
smiths have developed since the day of James V. The Tulloch mazer, like the Craigievar, is in the Marquess of Bute's collection and is perhaps the most beautiful of the three. The mounts are of silver gilt. Its height is precisely equal to the diameter of the bowl, a clearly deliberate device which lends the piece faultless balance and symmetry and marks the maker as an artist among his kind. The baluster stem is designed with similar subtlety. The lip-band is deep in proportion to the amount of wooden bowl left visible and is finely engraved with foliaceous scrollwork and figures on a hatched ground, while the lower edge is neatly cut as an even fringe of notched leaves. The stem is chased with finely designed acanthus-like ornament, inverted, while the foot is embossed with oval lobes recalling those on the Watson mazer but far more delicately conceived. On the print are the arms of Tulloch of Tannochy, and the mazer remained in the possession of the Tulloch family until a few years before the Second World War. This print, inscribed with the adjuration HONORA DEVM EX TOTA ANIMA TVA, was in its original condition apparently enamelled, and it

[1] *Connoisseur*, Vol. XCVIII

carries the date 1557. The Canongate stag lodged, cross between antlers, is stamped on the rim, and Commander How, working with the aid of Dr. Wood's invaluable researches, has identified the maker's mark as that of James Gray. Gray later became Master Coiner to the King, although the mazer, if we accept the inscribed date, belongs to the time of Mary of Lorraine's regency. This remarkable craftsman, who is also the author of the memorial to the Regent Murray in the High Kirk of St. Giles in Edinburgh, worked almost in the shadow of the Palace of Holyroodhouse. An achievement such as this—not the only surviving example of his mastery of silverwork, as will be seen presently—emphasises the heights to which the presence of the Court stimulated craftsmen to attain and encourages speculation about what might have happened if there had not been the exodus to the English capital a generation or two later.

The Galloway mazer is a little larger, both in height and in diameter. Also worked in silver gilt, it closely resembles the Tulloch and is also the work of Gray. In general design, the chief difference between the two pieces lies in the proportions, since the Galloway mazer is less tall in relation to its diameter, while on the lip-band three shields are substituted for the engraved figures. The shields contain the arms of Archibald Stewart and his wife Ellen Acheson, the Acheson crest of an eagle displayed, and the initials AS · EA. Archibald Stewart was Lord Provost of Edinburgh in 1579. It seems not unlikely that he saw and admired the Tulloch mazer and commissioned a similar one for himself. He had no descendants, but the daughter of a nephew married the brother of the first Earl of Galloway, and the mazer appears to have come into the possession of the Earls of Galloway about the middle of the eighteenth century, and remained so until sold in February, 1954. The initials AS · EA occur also on the print, with some leafy decoration. In an oval space reserved in the centre is the inscription: *Proverb · 22 · Ane · good · mane · is · to · be · chosen · above · great · riches · and · loving · favour · Is · above · silver · and · moste · fyne · golde · 1569.*

The third mazer of this type, the Craigievar, measures 9 inches across the bowl and is 8½ inches in height, so that it is the largest of the three. Its mounts are not gilt. No hatched ground offsets the engraving on the lip-band, but this enhances the effect of lightness. In the engraved pattern are various birds and animals alternating with flowers. The handling of the lower fringe of the band is perhaps less inventive. Acanthus again decorates the baluster stem. The oval lobes on the foot are here replaced by gadrooning emanating from the stem.

Pl. 20. ii

Pl. 21. i

PLATE 19

The St. Mary's Mazer: Edinburgh, mid-16th century. Maker: Alex. Auchinleck *(pp.64-65)*

The Fergusson Mazer: Edinburgh, about 1576. Maker: Adam Craige *(p.65)*

PLATE 20

The Galloway Mazer: Canongate, about 1569. Maker: James Gray (p.67)

The Tulloch Mazer: Canongate, about 1557. Maker: James Gray (pp.66-67)

PLATE 21

Coconut Cup with Sinclair arms, dated 1588 (pp. 94-95)

The Craigievar Mazer: Edinburgh, 1591. Maker: James Craufuird (pp. 67-68)

PLATE 22

The Macleod Cup: late 16th century. No hall-marks *(p. 80)*

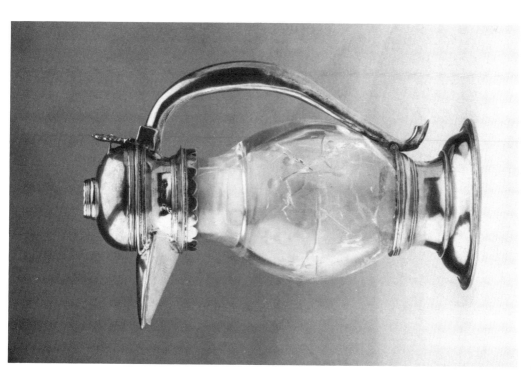

The Erskine Ewer: Edinburgh 1565-57. Maker: James Cok *(pp. 68-69)*

On the print are the arms of another provost, Robert Petrie, who presided over the affairs of Aberdeen; but this is a later addition, as he married in 1665 Anna, second daughter of Sir William Forbes of Craigievar, whose arms are impaled by Petrie's on the print. The mazer is reputed to have belonged to the Forbes-Sempill family. On the lip are struck the mark of James Craufuird, the Edinburgh hall-mark, and the deacon's punch of George Heriot, father of the celebrated 'Jinglin' Geordie'. As Heriot was deacon for the last time in 1591 and Craufuird was only admitted to the craft towards the end of that year, the mazer may be narrowed down to a matter of months, almost of weeks. It should be added that above the hall-mark is the wriggled assay-groove so characteristic of Scottish silver. This method of taking metal for assay is a Continental one, and was adopted in Scotland—perhaps the minutest of all of the many links between Scotland and the European countries.

These standing mazers are not undeserving of Commander How's praise of them as 'the most beautiful objects ever produced by the goldsmiths of this or any other country'.[1] They are elegant and impressive enough to satisfy the most sophisticated taste, and there is nothing in them of the extravagance or misplaced ingenuity which mar so much of the finest Continental work and even some English plate of Tudor times. They are also, in their way, peculiar to Scotland. I would hesitate to go so far as Commander How does when he says they show no sign of foreign influence, for the general form of bowl and lip-band follows the precedent of the English mazers and is obviously derived from it, while the decoration of the foot of the Tulloch, Galloway and Craigievar mazers has marked affinities with Elizabethan silverware and even furniture and is wholly Renaissance in spirit. The Scottish goldsmiths, however—and perhaps the credit should go primarily to James Gray—contrived from their knowledge of foreign styles something quite original and executed it with admirable taste. It should be remembered that Brook, when he summarily dismissed the technical ability of Scottish goldsmiths, had not set eyes on the Tulloch mazer.

Pl.22.i The deacon's mark of George Heriot is on another celebrated and unusual piece, the silver-mounted jug of rock crystal known as the Erskine ewer. Its body is formed from a very large lump of crystal, which has been given a baluster shape. Flaws running through it lend special character to the vessel and banish any first impression that the material is mere glass. As to the mounts,

[1] *P.S.A.S.*, Vol. LXVIII, p. 411

the neck-band is concave and its lower edge, which is scalloped, projects from the neck of the vessel itself, producing a somewhat ill-fitting appearance. A very large beak-like spout adds to the strange look. There is a domed cover, hinged to the neck-band and surmounted by a disc-like finial, while a thumb-piece is attached to the rear. A long, swelling, tubular handle connects the neck with the foot, which consists of a concave member spreading into an ogee base-moulding. The scalloped fringe of the neck-band apart, there is nothing which can be called ornament about the ewer, which stands $9\frac{1}{2}$ inches high. This vessel is said to have been presented by Queen Elizabeth to the Regent Mar on the baptism of one of his children. It came eventually to Sheriff Erskine Murray and, at Christie's in 1904, passed into Lord Swaythling's possession. It is now in Lord Bute's collection. Assay grooves and hall-marks are on several portions of the mounts, which are the work of James Cok; and his mark, read in conjunction with the deacon's, suggests a date of 1565–7.

Most of this chapter has been devoted to description of individual pieces, which, in a history, is in a sense a digression, but this may serve to establish the maturity to which the craft had come. Their quality tempts us to speculate upon the circumstances in which they were made. From 1560 onwards the times were, of course, disturbed. The immediate influence of the Reformation on the goldsmiths' craft is a subject for the following chapter, but it is clear that there was a certain amount of patronage and demand for expensive plate, and the quality could scarcely have been achieved had there not been a considerable output of humbler, domestic silver, although little other evidence of it has survived except a few spoons. Of direct royal patronage there is not much evidence. Mary had perhaps small leisure or peace of mind to interest herself for long at a time in the craftsmen about her doors, and she and her household probably looked to foreign sources for more sumptuous furnishings, although the only really notable foreign silver which has come down from that time is the so-called 'Queen Mary cup' and its companion belonging to St. John's Kirk in Perth. Her son, James VI, has left no reputation as a connoisseur. He had much curiosity but probably little taste, and his chief interest in the gold-smiths was for what he could get out of them. The story of his court gold-smith, George Heriot, has been told often enough, but in relation to his craft Heriot emerges as a baffling figure. We know that his father was a goldsmith and a deacon of the Incorporation. We know that the son was admitted to the craft in 1588, and that he was deacon ten years later and on two other occasions. We know he became goldsmith to the Queen in 1597 and later to the King and that he went south with his sovereign and prospered in London, and that he died leaving a large fortune, with part of which the present Heriot's Hospital was built in the seventeenth century. What we do not know is whether he ever practised his craft. No piece of silver has yet been discovered bearing his punch, either as maker or as deacon, and indeed his father's punch seems to occur only as a deacon's mark. It is of course quite reasonable to argue, on the other hand, that the minutes of the Incorporation contain the names of many goldsmiths none of whose work has survived. This must always be kept before us when contemplating the more extreme arguments against George Heriot as brought together by the late Professor D'Arcy Wentworth Thompson in a typically ebullient article published in 1935.[1] Thompson avers that Heriot was purely a banker, that he never made anything with his hands, and that the romantic idea of his labouring in his little 'buith' in the High Street to make the vast sums—£50,000 has been mentioned—to lend to the King is sheer nonsense. This hearty critic sweeps aside the theory that the Heriots were of East Lothian stock and boldly endeavours to connect them with a family of Jews from Augsburg who banked in the manner of the Fuggers themselves. It is all very tenuous speculation; but that the Heriots were principally financiers may well be the case, and certainly 'Jinglin' Geordie' must have had small opportunity of doing anything else after he moved with the Court to London.

King James's interest in the precious metals reflects his shrewdness, as we should expect. It was directed towards seeking for them rather than towards turning them into fine plate. On his succession to Elizabeth's throne, he lost no time in investigating the possibilities of the Scottish gold mines, and in his first year as sovereign of England he sent for his predecessor's Master of the Mint, Sir Bevis Bulmer, then plain Mr. Bulmer. The conversations as related by Atkinson[2] are diverting. ' "I doubt the silver Mines of England decayes, (quoth the King,) else are not to be found so plentifull, as in times past." "It is true," said Mr. Bulmer. "And therefore (quoth the King) as I desire to have a new onsett to find out whence this naturall gold doth descend, so I have meditated thereuppon; and have devised a Plott how the gold Mines may be sett open, and thereby become profitabler than heretofore." ' James swept aside Bulmer's doubts. ' "Lett Bulmer," he directed, "procure or move 24 gentlemen within England of sufficient lands and livings, or any other his freinds of Scotland,

[1] *Blackwood's Mag.* Sept., 1935.   [2] *The Gold Mynes in Scotland*, p. 44, etc.

70

that shall be willing to be Undertakers thereof, and to be adventurers towards the discoverie thereof; and see that all these gentlemen, be of such sufficencie in lands, goods or chattelis, as the worst be worth ten thousand pounds starling, else £500 per annum starling. And all such gentlemen to be moved to disburst £300, starling, each man in monies, or victuals, for maintenance of the gold mynes in Scotland; for which disbursement each man to have the honour of Knighthood bestowed uppon him, and so for ever to be called the Knight of the Golden Mynes, or the Golden Knight." ' This picturesque scheme produced only one knight. The mines, however, produced a certain amount of gold, if scarcely enough to induce twenty-four men to 'disburst' £300. Bulmer is said to have employed about three hundred miners around Leadhills and Wanlockhead for several years, during the summer months, and to have collected metal to the value of £10,000 sterling. The search became unprofitable when wages rose above 4d. per day. The heaps of gravel and sand cast up by the miners are still to be seen and are known as the Gold Scaurs. Silver, too, seems to have attracted a certain amount of attention. Atkinson[1] mentions the discovery in Linlithgowshire by a collier named Sandy Maund of 'a heavy peece of redd-mettle' containing silver. He found it 'at the Silver bourne, under the hill called Kern-Popple', and took it to Bulmer at Leadhills, who tested it again and again, 'and still it proved rich, and wonderous rich'. The mine was called God's Blessing. A similar piece of silver-bearing stone from the mine was sent by Atkinson to his uncle in London, where it was much praised by the goldsmiths. The Earl of Salisbury asked if he might show it to the King; 'but it was never more seene to Mr. Atkinson, neither had he ever content for it'.

[1] Ibid., p. 47

NOTES TO CHAPTER VI

THE FERGUSSON MAZER (p.65)

This mazer once formed part of the Hearst Collection but has now returned to this country and presently resides in the hands of a London dealer. A most interesting feature has emerged concerning its marks, which has led to a re-identification of its maker. In 1576, the year when it was made, the deacon was Michael Gilbert. He, for reasons unknown, refused to act as assayer to the Incorporation and was brought unwillingly before the Privy Council to explain himself. The outcome was that he continued to be obdurate and the Privy Council appointed Adam Craig to act as assayer in his place. Thus, Adam Craig's mark is struck on the mazer as that of the *deacon*, not the maker, even though it is not in the conventional place on the right of the Town Mark, while the mark of James Mosman, who was not deacon at the time, is struck as that of the *maker*, not the deacon. Why there should have been such an irregularity over the relative position of the maker's and deacon's marks is unclear, but it may have been nothing more than absent-mindedness on the part of Adam Craig.

THE GALLOWAY MAZER (p.67)

The Galloway Mazer was bought at Sotheby's on 25 February 1954 for £11,000 by Garrards on behalf of an American museum. The Reviewing Committee on the Export of Works of Art recommended that a licence to export it should be refused and it was thereafter acquired by the National Museum of Antiquities of Scotland.

THE CRAIGIEVAR MAZER (pp.67-68)

There is some doubt as to the date of this mazer and the identity of its maker. If the maker's mark is truly that of James Craufuird, then one has to accept the date as being 1591-2, as given by Jackson. (There is a serious misprint in the first impression of the 1989 edition of Jackson, p.541, in which the maker's mark of this mazer has been accidentally transposed with that of the Erskine Ewer on the line below, thus making nonsense of my footnote on that page.) The usually accepted date of 1591-2 seems to me to be a little too late on stylistic grounds although one may cite one or two parallels in the 1580s and '90s. Looking to see if there are any other possible makers in Edinburgh with the same initials in the 1560s and '70s, there seem only to be James Cok I, the maker of the Erskine Ewer, who's mark is very different and who, in any case, was hanged from the ramparts of Edinburgh Castle in 1573, James Cok II who was admitted a freeman in that same fateful year, and John Cunninghame, who was admitted in 1588. The deacon's mark is that of George Heriot II, father of the famous "Jingling Geordie". He was deacon in 1565-6-7, 1575-6, joint deacon in 1579-80-81 and 1583-4, and deacon again in 1584-5, 1586-7 and 1589-90-1 which latter period seems to me to be too late. My own view is that the mazer was possibly made by James Cok II in 1575-6 or possibly 1579-81, but no later. This is by no means certain and there remain other possibilities.

Chapter Seven

THE REFORMATION

THE impact of the Reformation on the goldsmiths' craft in Scotland must be examined from two angles. First, there are the consequences of the disturbed state of the country, and of reforming zeal, on existing plate, especially ecclesiastical, to be considered; and secondly there is the effect of the Reformers' attitude on the output of the goldsmiths.

Inventories of the time show that the store of plate in the Church's possession before the Reformation was considerable.[1] In 1493 Holyrood Abbey could boast a variety of crosses, including one of pure gold set with thirty precious stones, reliquaries, texts, candlesticks, vials, thuribles, twelve chalices, one of them of gold weighing, with its paten, 46 ounces, and a large silver Eucharist of 160 ounces. Glasgow Cathedral was also richly endowed. In Aberdeen Cathedral in 1549 there were eleven silver chalices with patens, one weighing as much as 41 ounces.[2] Burns lists important silver in the collegiate church of St. Mary, Haddington, the college kirk of Crail, Dunkeld Cathedral, Coldingham Priory and the church of St. Nicholas in Aberdeen. Indeed, as regards burgh churches, as Mr. Oman remarks to me, in Scotland there was usually only one per town, so they must have been well provided since the only competition came from the friaries.

The total amount of important ecclesiastical plate in Scotland must have amounted to many hundreds of pieces, but none appears to have survived unless we except the 'Queen Mary' and 'Nuremberg' cups of St. John's Kirk in Perth. A certain amount of this plate undoubtedly vanished with priests and members of the old Church. Some, it has been stated, including the vessels used in Glasgow Cathedral, went to the Scots College in Paris.[3] This assertion is supported by the evidence of the Glasgow University mace, which is inscribed: *Haec Virga empta fuit publicis Academiæ Glasguensis sumptibus A.D. 1465 in Galliam ablatam A.D. 1560 et Academiæ restituta A.D. 1590*; while the Inventur

---

[1] *Bannatyne Miscellany*, Vol. II, p. 22   [2] Burns: *Scot. Comm. Plate*, p. 129   [3] Ibid., p. 121

of the Gudis of the University relates the story of the abstraction of the 'Silver Warke and hail juels of the Hie Kirk'. At Aberdeen the plate and vestments were committed to various members of the chapter, among them the Dean, the Archdeacon and the Treasurer, while among the plate entrusted to the Earl of Huntly, Chancellor of Scotland, at Strathbogie Castle, were a chalice and paten of gold with three diamonds and 'two great rubies of Bp. Dunbar's gift', the whole weighing no less than 59 ounces. It is probable, however, that the greater part of the treasure of the old Church came into the hands of the Reformers. Iconoclastic zeal may have caused the destruction of much of this. The Aberdeen burgh records of 1559 urge the Provost and Council to protect the silverwork and vestments[1] since it was 'notowrly knawin that certane personis in to the soutt partis of Scotland hes interpryssit at thair awin hands . . . to destroy kirks . . . and the ornaments and polacie of the same'. Yet most of the destruction of plate was brought about by the need for money of both sides in the struggle for power between Mary and Knox, and there is no real evidence that the Catholic party was more reluctant to melt down its plate than was the Protestant. In 1556, to defray the cost of the war with England, Mary had sold the church plate and vestments she brought from France, with much secular plate including 'twa lytill small culppis of gold maid to quene Magdalene quhane scho was ane barne'. In 1567 she melted down the gold font given to her by Queen Elizabeth, and it produced a sum of 5,000 crowns. It cannot be emphasised too often that plate, however much its beauties were appreciated, was in past times regarded as so much capital to which recourse might be had in the day of need, and that the sentimental or scholarly viewpoints from which we now regard it had no more power to restrain the possessor of a fine chalice from melting it down than they would have in restraining us to-day from settling a bill with the coin of the realm in our purses. It must be admitted that, had the Reformation not intervened and caused the church treasuries to be thrown open, we might now be the heirs of some fine sacred plate, of gold and of silver. On the other hand, even had there been no Reformation, much of the old material would have been refashioned into monstrances and other such later requirements of the Roman Catholic Church. Mr. Oman tells me that in Sweden, where the Reformation was much less thorough, there are many part-medieval pieces, such as chalices with medieval stems or feet but seventeenth or eighteenth-century bowls.

[1] Ibid., p. 137

The general practice at the Reformation appears to have been to hand over the plate of the old Church to the secular authorities. In Aberdeen in 1561 the sacred vessels were to be 'sauld and disponit to thame that vill offer maist for the same', and the money obtained had to be handed over 'for the common weill and necessar adois of this guid toun'.[1] In Stirling chalices were sold up to mend the streets, while in Peebles 'all kirk geir' in the possession of the laity was to be recovered and applied 'to the commoun use of the tovne'.[2] It is needless here to repeat the results of the researches of the Rev. Thomas Burns into the disappearance of the old church plate; but in summary it may be said that the Reformed Church inherited none of the treasures of its predecessor.

The direct effect of the Reformation on the goldsmiths' craft is more difficult to gauge. We must assume that a high proportion of pre-Reformation church plate, at least for ordinary requirements, was made by Scottish craftsmen, for it is hardly credible that the Church should have ignored the existence of the men who built up the tradition which culminated in the mazers and other plate described in the last chapter. Factual knowledge of such patronage is meagre, but the Records of the Hammermen of Edinburgh for the year 1550 show an item of £27 paid for a silver chalice of $25\frac{1}{4}$ ounces and another twenty shillings paid 'to ye goldsmyt to ye burnissing of ye challece'. We have no parallel, however, to the Communion plate produced in Scotland for the Reformed Kirk. All we can say is that the latter's requirements were met almost wholly by native craftsmen.

The organisation of the craft does not seem to have been affected materially by the religious revolution. The Hammermen's devotional activities in Edinburgh underwent a certain gradual change, if we read between the lines of the first volume of their Records. Coming events cast their shadows before. Entries such as 'four quarter pund candell to ye saule mass and dirge' occur for the last time under the year 1557, and from 1558 items are mainly of a secular nature, noting moneys received from members of the craft. References to priests and ritual are replaced by such entries as that which relates that the Hammermen have 'chosin elecket and nominat William Barbour yair ministir'.[3] A certain pre-occupation with fiscal detail is reflected also in the proceedings of the Hammermen of the Canongate, who in 1560 for the first time appointed a 'boxmaster' or treasurer.[4] In Edinburgh, relations between the

---

[1] Ibid., p. 138   [2] Ibid., p. 140   [3] *The Hammermen of Edinburgh*, p. 172
[4] *Book of the Old Edinburgh Club*, Vol. XIX, p. 3

crafts and the merchants seem gradually to have improved and by the end of the century the position of the deacons was so far regularised that some of those officials gained seats on the Town Council.[1] St. Eloi ceased in 1560 to be worshipped as patron saint of the Hammermen except, as might be expected, in the consistently reactionary town of Aberdeen, which retained Episcopal sympathies. But, generally speaking, the development of the craft incorporations seems to have proceeded with little interruption throughout the sixteenth century and there is no doubt they were much stronger and more valuable elements of society by the time the century came to its close. Supervision of the craftsmen became more strict. In 1586 the 'deacon and masters' of the Edinburgh goldsmiths were granted by James VI a letter empowering them to search for 'all gold and silver wark wrocht and made in ony pairt within this realme', and to impound any plate found deficient in fineness.

The direct effect of the Reformation on plate produced by the goldsmiths was considerable. Before 1560, the Church was chief patron of workers in the precious metals. It was impossible for the Reformed Kirk to stand in the same relationship. The main obstacle to this was not a religious one, but the utter poverty of the new organisation, which took no material profit from the wealth of its predecessor. It appropriated the churches, but the shells of their structures only. Neither furniture nor fittings were utilised, and in the smaller buildings at least, floors of beaten earth were not unusual.[2] Burns has recorded that the pulpit and the stool of penitence were the only fixtures. Congregations sat on stools, which might be brought in by the worshipper or hired from the beadle, the fees affording that officer a part of his income. Another function of the beadle was to go around with a sharp stick 'to wauken sleepers, to drive out the dogs, and remove greetin bairns'. We learn that about the end of the sixteenth century a few amenities were introduced, such as the ordinance of the Glasgow Kirk Session of 1586 that the pulpit stones be removed and laid in ranks for the women to sit upon and, two years later, the cutting down of an ash-tree to supply forms. But it may be assumed that sacred services were for a very long time housed in the most rough-and-ready style, and it is surprising that any vessels of silver were made at all. Stipends were miserable. Most of the clergy led lives of extreme poverty, and some were even forced to sell ale to their parishioners to augment their tiny incomes.

In the Reformed Kirk, occasions for the use of sacred vessels were two in

[1] Ingleby Wood: *Scottish Pewter Ware*, p. 16   [2] *Scot. Communion Plate*, p. 13

PLATE 23

Communion Cup of Rosneath: Edinburgh, 1585.
Maker: John Mosman (*pp.80-81*)

Communion Cup of Forgue: Edinburgh, 1563.
Maker: Henry Thomsone (*pp.78-79*)

PLATE 24

Communion Cup of Currie: Edinburgh, 1596-1600. Maker: Hugh Lindsay (p.81)

The St. Leonard's Mazer: mid-16th century. No hall-marks (pp. 79-80)

number only: Communion and baptism. It was recommended in the *Booke of the Universall Kirk of Scotland* that Communion 'be ministrat four tymes in the yeir within burrowes, and twyse in the yeir to landwart'.[1] Several circumstances made compliance difficult. Clergymen were few, one sometimes serving several parishes. Poverty made the provision of worthy sacramental vessels a great burden. Quite as important is the third point, which Burns makes, that examinations in knowledge of religious truth in the early days were obligatory for all participating in the Lord's Supper, not merely on the first but on every occasion, and the ignorance and illiteracy of the great majority rendered the numbers of participants few. It was this circumstance of lay participation in the supreme ceremony of religious observance under Presbyterianism which stimulated that wide diffusion of scholastic learning for which Scotland was at one time justly famous, as no doubt it also stimulated that less admirable feature of Scottish life, the confusion of the idea of education with the capacity to pass examinations. At any rate, those three factors combined to limit the requirements of the Kirk for ceremonial plate, as the Kirk's loose-knit and democratic organisation made the provision of specially designed vessels unnecessary.

From the beginning there is a quality of experiment in the shapes of Communion pieces, in contrast to the centuries of uniformity which went before. The chalice and paten of Rome have remained fairly constant in their general design from the dark ages to the present day, and notably so in the fourteenth and fifteenth centuries. Before the sixteenth century had ended the Communion cup had appeared in forms ranging from the standing mazer to a secular wine-cup. Partly this is due to the confusion of the times, when secular vessels were often adopted for sacred purposes, in the eyes of the Kirk's adherents a practice no more objectionable than the habit of bringing one's seat to church. No uniform times were laid down for the observance of Communion, except that it should not coincide with the feast-days of the old Church; and in the same way the only stipulation about the vessels used was that they should not follow the pattern of those used on the altars which had been cast down. Probably the only consideration which influenced form was the fact that the cup was used not by the priest alone, but by the laity. This necessitated a greater capacity. The Communion cup, therefore, was made rather larger in the bowl than the chalice.

A case in point is the earliest Communion cup still in the possession of the

[1] *Bannatyne Club Misc.*, Vol. I, p. 30

Church of Scotland, a place of honour given by Burns to one of the pair at
Forgue, in Aberdeenshire. The bowl of this cup is the work of Henry Thom-   Pl.23.i
sone of Edinburgh and the deacon is James Cok, a combination which points
to the date 1563, just three years after the Reformation. This bowl, which is
less than a hemisphere, is quite plain, except for an inscribed date 1633, which
may indicate the time when the cup was adapted to its present form. Stem and
foot are characteristic of the early seventeenth century, and the inscription on
the bowl indicates that the cup, like its fellow, was given to Forgue by James
Crichton of Frendraught. Burns relates in full the story of how Frendraught
Castle was destroyed by fire in 1630, and of how Viscount Melgum and the
Laird of Rothiemay were burned to death. Frendraught was wrongfully
accused of being the author of a crime and offered to stand his trial, but an old
servant was eventually executed for the deed. In view of the dates it is reasonable to think Frendraught may have given the cups to his church as a thank-
offering for his escape, and that the gift involved the modifying of an existing
cup. Whether the original portion of date 1563 was made for Communion
purposes is impossible to say, for there is no other cup of the kind within a
generation of this date. I feel it was probably for secular use. Indeed there is no
evidence and small likelihood that the Reformed Kirk in its earliest days commissioned silverware of any sort. Burns quotes from *The Buke of the Four Scoir
Three Questions*, in which, in the year when the Forgue cup bowl was fashioned,
Ninian Winzet, Knox's bitterest opponent, denounces the 'Calvinian preche-
ouris' in Scotland for using basins and tavern cups for dispensing the Sacraments; and it is recorded that Knox himself inverted silver candlesticks to use
the hollow bases as cups. The form of vessel used was in no way regulated
until 1617. Cups which came into use about or after this year faithfully reflect
secular forms and make clear what had been happening in the intervening
period. There is no better example of this than the cups of the Town Church
in St. Andrews, which are standing mazers executed wholly in silver, and the
prototype of them is the St. Leonard's so-called mazer in the same town. The   Pl.24.i
style of the lip-band of the St. Leonard's 'mazer' suggests that the present silver
bowl has replaced a wooden one, as Burns maintained,[1] and the pins used for
fastening tend to support this view; but Commander How believed it to be
the original bowl.[2] The piece is quite unmarked, but Burns points to the possibility of its being the mazer referred to in the Inventory of the Chamber of

[1] *Scot. Comm. Plate*, p. 193   [2] *Connoisseur*, Vol. XCIII, p. 319

St. Leonard's college, of 1544. For a long time it was used for collecting the offerings in St. Leonard's Church, and doubtless it was put to sacred uses after the Reformation.

A number of interesting Communion cups belong to this period when secular cups were in such general use. Notable among them is the Macleod cup, which Burns included in his book although there is no evidence that it was ever used for sacramental purposes. It is a fine piece, but a baffling one. In outline similar to the Forgue cup, in detail it is very different. Some of the decoration on the bowl and all that round the moulded foot is in the Celtic manner, but the stem is ornamented in an Elizabethan style which forms a curious contrast to the rest. I have examined the cup closely and there are no marks. To guess its provenance is difficult. The Celtic ornament has an air of sophisticated adaptation which does not accord with the practice of Scottish silversmiths of the time; yet it is even more difficult to think a southern craftsman would have used the Celtic motifs in this way. Clearly the print inside the bowl is a piece of native work. The general resemblance of the stem to the stem of the Forgue cup may not be without significance and is a point in favour of Scottish authorship.

Of the secular cups used for Communion, many are not Scottish and therefore have no proper place here unless it is to indicate the catholic tastes of the Reformed Kirk in the first half-century of its existence. Not many of the surviving ones date from the sixteenth century, and the most celebrated example is the 'Queen Mary' cup of St. John's Kirk, Perth. Perth is exceptionally rich, for it possesses also the 'Nuremberg' cup and two very good London steeple-cups, all three of the early seventeenth century. The Canongate Church in Edinburgh has two rather odd-looking cups of London make, of date 1610. Duirinish-Bracadale owns a handsome pair of London cups of 1612, richly decorated in *repoussé* in typical Jacobean style, while Newtyle has cups of equally fine quality dating from 1606 and 1610. The date-letters of the English pieces make it evident that they were bought specially for Communion use.

Two Scottish-made vessels which may well have begun as secular wine-cups are now among the oldest Communion plate in the Church of Scotland. They belong to Rosneath, and their delicate bowls poised on long, slender stems are of a type in wide use a generation later. John Mosman's punch appears twice on each, as maker and as deacon, and as Mosman's deaconate covered only the period 1585–6 this fixes the date. It is probable that they were not given over

Pl.22.ii

Pl.23.ii

to sacred use until early in the seventeenth century, but neither date, initials nor the name of the church is engraved on them. A secular origin is perhaps less likely in the case of the older of the two Communion cups of Currie, in Mid- Pl.24.ii
lothian. This possesses the same wide, less-than-hemispherical bowl as the Forgue, although it measures 6½ as against 7¼ inches in diameter. There is a graceful baluster stem with engraved collar and knop, and the foot is engraved also in a style which appears to have become an accepted one for the purpose about this time and for many years after. The interior of the bowl is engraved rather sketchily with a circular device containing a shield with the initials MML; evidently done by a man much less skilled than the man who engraved the foot of the cup. The initials refer to Matthew Lichtone, minister of the parish from 1591 to 1631, and no doubt the cup was got in his time although, like its younger companion, it bears an inscription, FOR x THE x KIRK x OF x CVRRIE x 1657. The maker is Hugh Lindsay of Edinburgh, the deacon David Heriot, which places the time of origin at either 1596 or 1599–1600. This is a particularly beautiful cup, and its companion is a copy made in 1617–19 by a man whose punch is indistinct but slightly resembles Jon Scott's.

A smaller and more delicately formed type of cup of the pre-1617 period is represented in the parish of Fala and Soutra. The Fala cup is of what may be termed the 'champagne-glass' form: a small bowl, almost hemispherical, a long and slender baluster stem with one disc-knop above and three below and a trumpet-shaped foot stepped down to an edge embossed with a tongue design. In the interior is engraved a leafy circlet, and the foot is inscribed FOR YE KIRK OF FALA. George Craufurd, junr., is the maker, and David Palmer the deacon, so that the cup may be dated as between 1611 and 1613. A similar though rather larger cup at Straiton, by Gilbert Kirkwoode, could be as early, but as the deacon is James Denneistoune it might be as late as 1644.

Early baptismal vessels are rarer even than Communion cups. The font used for the purpose of baptism in pre-Reformation times became anathema in 1560, and many fine old stone fonts must have been destroyed. Yet strict regulations on the conduct of baptism prevailed. There was strong condemnation of private baptism—'Sacraments are not ordeined of God to be vsed in private corners as charmers or sorceries'—and the infant had to be brought to church on a day of 'common pryare and preaching'.[1] Burns points out that this reference to private corners in *The First Book of Discipline* is related to the position

[1] *Scot. Comm. Plate*, p. 470

of fonts near the doors of churches, for it was an important contention of the Reformers that all sacraments be administered in full sight of the congregation. It may be that basins of many sorts were adapted for this sacrament, as cups were for Communion, for all that is laid down in Knox's Liturgy is that the minister should take water in his hand, sprinkle it on the child's forehead and then give thanks. Whether the only surviving baptismal basin of the sixteenth century is of secular origin cannot be said. This is the magnificent basin belong-

Pl.25.i

ing to St. John's Kirk in Perth. The rim is inscribed FOR THE KIRK OF PERTHE 1649; but the maker is David Gilbert of Edinburgh and the deacon William Cok, so that the piece was made somewhere between 1591 and 1594, and it may well have been in use for many years before the inscription was added. Indeed, this is probably the case, for in 1617 the custom altered and basins with lavers or ewers were introduced. The Perth basin is simply a great platter, over 18 inches in diameter, and may never have possessed a laver, as there is a raised centre with a massive boss so decorative that it is plainly not intended to be hidden by a laver. The basin is parcel-gilt, the gilding showing no evidence of renewal. The rim has a moulded edge with an intricate vandyked pattern punched on its inner side, and it has at one time been repaired and is now in a rather fragile state. The only other baptismal vessels of a date approximating to the date of the Perth basin are the ewer and basin belonging to the Old Kirk, Edinburgh. They are elaborate and lovely pieces made in 1602, but their place of origin is London and they do not appear to have been adapted for sacred use at the Old Kirk until 1728.

Chapter Eight

EARLY COMMUNION PLATE

I N 1617 the Scottish Parliament passed an Act requiring that 'all the paroche kirkis within this Kingdome be prowydit off Basines and Lavoiris for the ministration of the Sacrament of Baptism, and of couppes, tablis and table clothes, for the ministratioun of the holie Communion'. This Act took immediate effect. There is ample evidence to indicate this in the numbers of Communion cups bearing hall-marks of the period 1617–19. It did not lay down or suggest any approved shapes for the vessels, and there are wide divergences both in form and in size. Burns points to a very likely reason for the contrasting sizes.[1] He refers to the fact that the small-bowled, 'champagne-glass' type of cup, with slender baluster stem, is usually associated with small country parishes with sparse populations and therefore smaller numbers of communicants, whereas the large-bowled types as a rule belong to town parishes. This compulsory expenditure must have been a severe drain on the smaller parishes and one assumes they would commission cups as light in weight as possible. It should also be noted, however, that cups with a very large bowl, such as Dalkeith's or St. Giles', Edinburgh, generally belong to the middle or latter part of the seventeenth century, and that most of the cups made about the time of the Act are of the light variety.

There can be no question that some of these cups, perhaps a majority of them, were made specially for the Sacrament and were not secular wine-cups adapted. The Cawdor cups provide us with a documented case. Burns quotes the following extract from the Spalding Club publication, *The Thanes of Cawdor*:

18 of March 1619 . . . Sir becaus the communion approches I have maid your tua cupis reddie weyand ilk cup ten unce weacht and ane half unce, and ilk unce at £4, and the workmanship of ilk unce 8s. The gilding of thame is £12, and the cass £3, summa of the haill £86 : 6 : 8d. They are baith weill and cheip done as ye may sie.

The passage is from a letter written by James Mowat, W.S., to Sir John

---

[1] *Scot. Comm. Plate*, p. 259

Campbell who, it is interesting to note, in 1636 was put to the horn for popery. An inscription round the rim of the bowl of each cup records that Campbell built the kirk of Cawdor before furnishing it with Communion vessels. These are Edinburgh pieces made by John Craufurd during the deaconate of John Lindsay (1617–19), and they are unique in having prints within the bowl, inscribed with an appropriate text from Corinthians. They have the hemispherical bowl and a baluster stem with some engraving on the moulding of the foot. A variation of this shape is found, with a blunt, conical bowl, good examples of which are at Middlebie and Carstairs.

It is significant that all those early cups are the work of Edinburgh silversmiths, and the craftsmen of the capital must have experienced a profitable time following the Act of 1617. The man whose output exceeds by far that of all the others is Gilbert Kirkwoode, responsible for the cups of Balmaghie, Carstairs, Fyvie, Blantyre, Cambuslang, Tynron, Inchture and Glencairn, among others. All those belong to the period immediately following the Act, so that Kirkwoode's workshop must have been exceptionally busy. He was as talented as he was industrious, for his cups are all marked by delicate balance and peculiarly fine lines, and the pose of his conical bowls is such that one can almost recognise his hand at a glance. The Fyvie cup, although more heavily proportioned, exhibits a subtle relationship between the angles of the sides of the bowl and the straight-sided baluster-stem, and the angles again are offset by the splay of the foot. It is most instructive to compare it with the Blantyre cup, which is basically similar but has the straight lines translated into the softest of curves. Kirkwoode was evidently a man who took delight in contriving subtle variations within the narrow limits set by regulation, economy or fashion in the years immediately after the Act, and his apparent popularity is a tribute not only to his craftsmanship but to the discrimination of his patrons, a quality we have sometimes been driven to wonder if they possessed. It is true, of course, that such patrons were probably seldom the ministers or officers of the kirk, but parishioners of wealth, standing and, no doubt, some taste. The Fyvie cup was presented by Alexander Seton, first Earl of Dunfermline, Chancellor and President of the Court of Session, whose arms are engraved on the bowl. It would appear that the gift of this cup commemorated a charter from the King to the Earl, conferring on him the patronage of the living of Fyvie, an event which took place in 1616.

Kirkwoode is also the author of Carnwath's beautiful pair of cups. They are

Pl.28.i
Pl.25.ii

84

in a style more like that of the Currie cups than Kirkwoode's usual mode, although the stem is reminiscent of the Forgue cups. This silversmith, however, with his usual inventiveness and taste, has contrived to turn the baluster form into something which recalls the outlines of an amphora, engraved with a calyx-like piece of decoration on its lower part. An identical form of decoration appears on the stems of the four cups of St. Cuthbert's, in Edinburgh, while the vase stems are also very similar and the foot has the same sharply-defined step and, on its upper edge, the same sort of modification of the decoration on the stem. The St. Cuthbert's cups have deep, bell-shaped bowls which were given their present form early in the nineteenth century and Burns deduced from the kirk-session records for 1619 that they originally resembled the bowls of the Currie and Carnwath cups.[1] Doubtless the maker's mark was on the bowls and has been obliterated, but in my view the design and taste of the cups make it highly probable they are the work of Kirkwoode. They are inscribed FOR THE VAST KIRK OVTVITH EDINBRVGHE and, round the centre of the bowl I · WIL · TAK · THE · COVP · OF · SALVATIOVNE · AND · CAL · VPON · THE · NAME · OF · THE · LORD, together with the date 1619 and, in the centre, 116 PSLM. They are exceptionally well documented, for the session records contain references to them over a period of three years. On 29th January, 1618, it is minuted that the Session 'tocht it maist meit that ther be fouir coups of silver to serve at the tabills', while the 'barrons, gentilmen, heritors and fewars' were to pay 400 marks and the town of Edinburgh and 'the fermars' 200 marks.[1]

Other fine cups of this type are the four at Dunfermline and the four at Inveresk. The Dunfermline group is by George Robertson, within George Craufurd's deaconate. Two are dated 1628 and two 1629. The bowl is unusually shallow, only $1\frac{3}{4}$ inches deep, and the stem is of the baluster shape seen in the Currie cups. Inveresk's cups have the vase stem of Carnwath's, but without engraving, and in this case George Craufurd is the maker and James Denneistoune the deacon.

The delicately-proportioned cups just described may possibly be prototypes of the heavier type which came into fashion about the middle of the century, a type represented at Dalkeith, Wemyss, Newbattle and elsewhere, and characteristic of the south-east of Scotland. Burns connects it with the mazers, with which it has several features in common; but there appears to be a continuous development from the Currie and Carnwath cups through those of Dunferm-

[1] Ibid., p. 210

85

PLATE 25

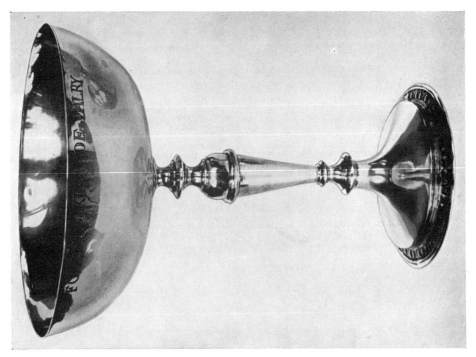

Communion Cup of Dalry: Edinburgh, 1617–19.
Maker: Gilbert Kirkwoode (*p.84*)

Baptismal Basin of St John's Kirk, Perth. Edinburgh, 1591. Maker: James Craufuird (*p.82*)

PLATE 26

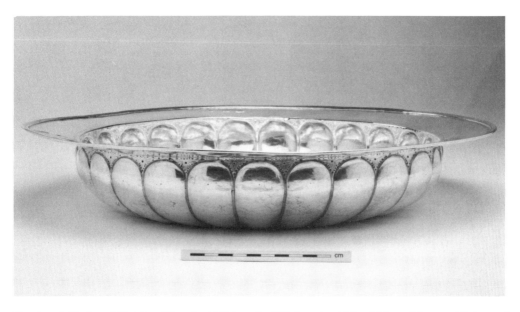

Baptismal Basin of Trinity Church, Edinburgh: Edinburgh, 1633. Maker: Thomas Kirkwood
(p.87)

Detail of the above, showing the inscribed central boss

PLATE 27

Bread-Plate of Trinity College, Edinburgh: Edinburgh, 1633–35. Maker: Thomas Kirkwood *(p.87)*

Laver and Basin of St Cuthbert's, Edinburgh: Edinburgh, 1700. Maker: Geo. Scott *(p.85)*

PLATE 28

Communion Cup, Dalkeith: Edinburgh, 1642. Maker: Patrick Borthwick (*p.86*)

Communion Cup of Balmagie known as the 'MacMillan' Cup: Edinburgh, 1617–19. Maker: Gilbert Kirkwoode (*p.84*)

line and Inveresk to the weightier if rather less elegant form adopted by some of the populous parishes of the Lothians and their vicinity.

Pl.28.ii The cups of the heavier type which seem most nearly related to the rare Currie type are those with some form of baluster stem. Four at Dalkeith are good examples. They were made during the decade 1650–60[1] when James Fairbairne, whose mark as deacon is on them all, had two terms of office. Three are by Robert Gibsoune, one by Patrick Borthwick. A massive, somewhat exaggerated baluster stem is their chief feature, and its plainness is varied by two cushion knops, which are engraved. Four cups at Newbattle are similar, although the sides of the bowl are vertical instead of outward-sloping. Each is by a different Edinburgh maker: Thomas Clyghorne, Adam Lamb, Andro Denneistoune and John Wardlaw. South Leith also has two cups of this kind, with the mark of Jon Scott both as maker and as deacon, which narrows the period of their manufacture to 1637–9 or 1646–8. The first is likely, as the cups are engraved with the date 1645. This is reinforced by an inscription recording that the donors, William Trotter and James Barnis, made their gift 'in tyme of pest', for the kirk-session records for that year refer to an outbreak of the pest 'in our new hospital called King James his hospital'.[2] Moreover, the records show the acquisition of a Communion cup on 30th March, 1643. No doubt by this time it was common practice to purchase cups from the silversmith's stock and have them suitably engraved. The Wemyss cups are rather later in date. The deacon's punch of James Symondstoune places them as seven or eight years earlier than the date of 1673 engraved on them. Their maker is Andrew Law. In this case the baluster stem is of an unusual and beautiful piriform variety, rising from a calyx. As with certain other cups, the bowl can be unscrewed, an arrangement which may have been to facilitate transport.

Another large-bowled type of Communion cup came into being about the same time. In place of the baluster stem is a simple waist with flattened knop, and there is a rather more liberal use of engraved decoration. This type, like the other, seems to be limited mainly to the south-eastern parishes. Edinburgh can show fine examples in Old Greyfriars, Trinity College and, above all, St. Giles'. Midcalder, Linlithgow, Yester, Dunblane, Stirling and Temple, among other places, also have cups of this sort. The four cups at St. Giles' are by Jon Scott and have the deacon's mark of John Fraser. They are exceptional in possessing hexagonal stems, accentuated by engraved panels, while the decora-

---

[1] Burns unaccountably dates one cup 1646   [2] Ibid., p. 216

tion round the foot is more elaborate than is usual. The lip of the bowl and parts of the knop and foot are gilt, and altogether the cups are massively handsome and worthy plate for the High Kirk of the Capital. A similar hexagonal stem marks the four Linlithgow cups. They are the work of Alexander Scott.

Under the Act of 1617 baptismal vessels also had to be provided, but they are not distinguished by the attractive variety of form found among Communion cups. Lavers and basins appear to have been modelled on the ewers and rose-water dishes in secular use about the beginning of the century, and no doubt secular pieces were transferred from the Kirk's use in the earlier days. Magnificent examples, not of Scottish make, are the basin and ewer of the Old Kirk, Edinburgh, which carry the London hall-marks for 1602–3. They are richly decorated in relief and flat chasing. Scottish-made examples are considerably later in date but follow the same general pattern, with little imaginative treatment. The Tron Kirk in Edinburgh possesses typical vessels. The laver bears the engraved date 1633, and as the maker is Thomas Kirkwood and the deacon George Craufuird this date is probably correct. A companion basin is of about fifty years later. Both pieces are without decoration and the plain surfaces are relieved only by inscriptions in lettering which admittedly is in itself decorative. Kirkwood also made the bread plate for Trinity College, Edinburgh. This is an exceptionally important and interesting piece, dating from the last deaconate of George Craufuird (1633–5). It has two inscriptions, duly recorded by Burns, as well as the engraved date 1633; but its most remarkable feature is the picture engraved in the centre. This is circular, and in a manner rather curiously medieval depicts Christ kneeling before the altar, or high table, which carries the elements of the Sacrament. It is clear that the cups and flagons depicted are intended to represent those of Trinity College itself, which bear London hall-marks, or vessels closely similar. Scarcity of early baptismal vessels, however, probably indicates that a great many were renewed in later times, as happened in the case of Old Greyfriars' vessels in Edinburgh. Greyfriars' basin is dated 1649, but the hall-marks are partly hammered out by a later modification of the piece, and its companion laver, dated 1707, may very well be an adaptation of a laver contemporary with the basin. An inscription on the South Leith basins refers specifically to such a renewal, for the original basins were apparently dated 1638, and the kirk-session records note[1] that on 30th January, 1718, the committee opined 'that the Bullion and forefaulted

Pl.27.i

[1] *Scot. Comm. Plate*, p. 217

pawns, etc., belonging to the Session be disposed of and applied to mending the Basons', and that one Charles Duncan be employed to renew the basins. One of the more handsome lavers belongs to the Canongate Kirk, Edinburgh, and it matches its basin in date, both having the mark of Edward Cleghorne. The bold lines of its handle and the lid fitted with double-ball thumb-piece clearly derive something from contemporary tankards, but there is dignity in the deep spout and the cabled decoration on lid, body and foot.

It is perhaps significant that there are only a few cups to represent the period from about 1620 to 1638. The Act of 1617 forced parishioners to supply within a year all that was necessary to administer the Sacraments, on pain of the minister 'lossing ane yeiris stepend', and the number of cups identified with this time is therefore comparatively great. But in the decades which followed the state of Scotland was grim. Charles I refused to countenance Presbyterian practices, although he hid his real sympathies behind a screen of anti-Catholic measures such as the administration of Communion to high officers of state. Wielding an Episcopalianism which was abhorrent to all Scotland except the north-eastern corner, he drove Presbyterianism underground, so that it took the form of Conventicles of increasing size while the churches emptied. Vast Communion gatherings took place, such as that at Shotts on 21st June, 1630, and soon there was general war against acceptance of the rites of Communion as laid down by the Five Articles of Perth. In such stern and bitter times, it mattered more how a minister used his vessels in the Sacrament than whether those vessels were rarely wrought. Whether the cup was of base metal or of silver mattered not at all, but whether a communicant received it kneeling or sitting betokened his loyalty to King or to Kirk and was therefore of the profoundest moment. The bare sprinkling of cups and lavers and basins from the years between the 1617 Act and the signing of the National Covenant, therefore, is no accident of survivals but a reflection of the troubled times.

Indeed it is probable goldsmiths and silversmiths were more often employed then in melting down plate than in making it. The Covenanters had no 'legitimate' source of revenue and their enemies were backed by all the resources of the state. Yet the great mass of the people were on the side of the Covenant, and there was pressure of numbers sufficient to requisition wealth where its possessors were not wholehearted in placing it at the disposal of the new, militant Kirk. Forced loans were resorted to, but not in any hasty or revengeful spirit. A detailed scheme was prepared, planned with what on the face of it appears to have been something like stern justice, and interest was allowed on the value of all wealth taken over. Possessors of plate were required to yield it up to the War Committee of their sheriffdom. I am indebted to Miss M. P. Ramsay for drawing my attention to the detailed instructions in the *Book of the War Committee of Kirkcudbright*. Instructions as to plate, laid down in 1640 by the Committee of Estates, apply of course to all Scotland.[1] Under Article 9, 'it is appoyntit, that all the silver worke and gold worke in Scotland, as weill to burgh as landwart, as weill noblemen, barrones and burgess, as uthers, of whatsomever degrie or qualitie they be, be given in to the Committie at Edinburgh'.

It is interesting to discover from the same source that the Covenanters were not as insensible to fine craftsmanship as some other movements in history which found themselves in similar straits. 'It is heirby declarit', the document records, 'that these quha hes any silver or gold worke quhich they crave raither to keip for thair ane use than delyver the samyn to be coinzed, shall have power to redeime the samyn at the prycess efter following, viz:—fiftie sex schillings for the unce of Scotts silver worke, fiftie aught schillings for every unce of Inglis silver worke, and xxxiiij lib. vjs. viiid. for everie unce of gold.' More discriminating still is a later provision: 'And, in case anie hath doubill gilt worke, and curious wrought worke, and cannot get monie to redeime thame, it is heirby declarit, that, the said gilt and curious worke being delyverit to the said Committie, shall not be melted nor disposit upon, befoire the term of Whitsounday next, betwixt and whilk time the owner thairof shall have power to redeime the samyn, at the prycess foiresaid, paying alwayes the annual rent thairof, sae lang as the samyn shall be unredemit.'

[1] p. 21

NOTES TO CHAPTER VIII

TRINITY CHURCH BAPTISMAL BASIN (pl.26)

The Baptismal Basin of Trinity Church, Edinburgh, was made by Thomas Kirkwood in 1633. It is almost 16″ in diameter. The central boss is engraved with the quotation:

> *"I indeed have baptized you with water but He shall baptize you with the Holy Ghost. Mark I.8".*

The underside is inscribed:

> *"Gifted to the North East Parish of Edenbrovh by John Trotter, Elder, Anno 1633".*

John Trotter was a merchant burgess of Edinburgh and laird of Mortounhall and was the father of Nicoll Trotter, goldsmith, who was not admitted to the Incorporation until two years after the presentation of the basin. (For the Laver made to match this Basin by Walter Scott in 1701-2, see p. 142:   PLATE 68,i.)

THE ST. CUTHBERT'S LAVER AND BASIN (pl.27,ii)

The Laver and Basin of Saint Cuthbert's Church, Edinburgh, were illustrated in the first edition of this work on the lower half of Plate 31 but were not discussed in the text. They were made in Edinburgh by George Scott and carry the date letter for 1700-01, although their form might suggest a date some fifty years earlier.

Chapter Nine

SECULAR PLATE
EARLY SEVENTEENTH CENTURY

THE levies of the war committees no doubt account for the disappearance of much secular plate, and it is remarkable how few pieces of silver not ecclesiastical have come down to us from the first half of the seventeenth century. Evidence, however, does not point to any slackening off among the goldsmiths. If great numbers of their more modest productions must have gone, the few more elaborate pieces which have survived suggest that, technically, they had built up considerable resources.

For example, one of the finest bell-headed maces in the United Kingdom is the mace of the City of Edinburgh, made by George Robertson in 1617. The decision to construct a worthy mace was taken by the Town Council on 18th December, 1616, when the Treasurer was instructed 'to mak ane fair Mase to be borne befoir the Proveist, of ten pund wecht of silver, and to caus mak the same partiall gilt, the samine to be maid by the advyse of David Aikenheid deyne of gild, and George Foulls, m^r of the Cunzie hous, and the expenses debursit thairupone sall be allowit to him in his compts'. It is surprising that the Commission went to Robertson, as he had only been admitted to the freedom of the Edinburgh Incorporation of Goldsmiths twelve days before this decision and it is hard to know what substantial proof of his ability can have been available. Yet he did indeed make a 'fair Mase'. It is to-day still 'borne befoir the Proveist' and has few rivals among other symbols of the kind. The City Treasurer's Accounts record that it weighed 159 ounces and that Robertson was paid £874 10s. for it. 3 ft. 2 ins. in length, it has a head surmounted by a crown with arches, orb and cross, the fillet of which is enriched by applied thistles, roses, harps and fleurs-de-lys. On the lower portion of the head are circles of threaded wire containing the royal cipher, IR, and the turreted castle of the city arms. Under the arches, the head is closed by a plate carrying the

Pl.29.i

arms of James VI. There is a shaft of baluster form with acanthus and other motives. It seems the mace was made to replace an older one of only about one quarter of its weight, for the Town Council records note that the city macer delivered this older emblem up to the Dean of Guild. Apparently earlier macers had the right to retain their maces on demitting office, as on appointment they were given money to purchase a mace[1]; but the sums given, which range only from £10 to £24, suggest that the symbol of office was customarily a very modest one, and that perhaps we have not lost a great deal by their subsequent disappearance. The present mace was carried in the ceremony of the Riding of the Parliament, that spectacular event in which the Honours of Scotland took a leading place up to the Union of 1707; although the drawing by John Sommers,[2] of about 1681, shows the mace as disproportionately large and exaggerates or even modifies certain features.

Pl.29.ii   The older of the two Aberdeen University maces follows the Edinburgh mace at an interval of about thirty years. It belongs to King's College. Walter Melvil's mark is on it, and it also carries the inscription WALTERUS MELVIL FECIT 1650. The staff is cylindrical and plain, enriched only by moulded and chased bands collared with acanthus leaves, but the head is of particular interest, for several reasons. Its bowl is embossed with the earliest cognisance of the University, the emblem of the Virgin, a pot with three lilies, and the arms of Bishop Elphinstone, who founded King's College. Cherubs worked in a manner characteristic of Scotland serve as supporters of these arms. The nature of the surmounting crown suggests that it is a free representation of the Crown of Scotland, for the fillet is embossed with 'gems' which imitate those on the royal crown. A plate closing the bowl bears the royal arms as they appeared until the end of Charles II's reign, and GOD SAVE THE KING is introduced in raised letters. Brook records[3] that it may have been made for one of Charles' visits to Aberdeen before his restoration in 1660, and that a sixteenth-century document in King's College refers to two earlier maces which have since disappeared. One of the most unusual features of this mace, however, is the inferior quality of the metal. The silver should be eleven-twelfths fine, but the decorated portions, and the staff even more, fall short of this. That Melvil, a deacon of the Hammermen in 1662 and master of the hospital in 1656–7, should have disregarded Parliament and the Edinburgh Goldsmiths' Incorpora-

[1] *P.S.A.S.*, Vol. XXVI, p. 484
[2] Chalmers Collection, Nat. Library of Scotland   [3] *P.S.A.S.*, Vol. XXVI, p. 495

tion in their attempts to stop this practice is perhaps evidence not so much of delinquency on the goldsmiths' part as of the consistent indifference of Aberdeen to practices accepted elsewhere.

Two of the maces of the Court of Session belong to the seventeenth century. The older has no hall-marks and no specific indication of date except the royal arms as used by the Stewarts from 1603 to 1688. There is a probability that it was made in Edinburgh at about the same time as Melvil made the King's College mace in Aberdeen. The blue enamel of the shield with the royal arms fixed to the top of the head is, as Brook states, crudely done; but the effect is good and the general appearance of the mace handsome. The second of the two seventeenth-century maces carries the punch of Edward Cleghorne as maker and the deacon's punch of Andro Burrell (1634–5 and 1659–61). Broadly, the features of this mace resemble those of the unmarked one, and it is obvious that the intention has been to keep the court maces uniform, for the other three, although later in date, conform. Only one of the silver court maces is quite different. This is the Lord President's, a tremendous and impressive piece, but of London make.

The protection apparently enjoyed to some extent by ecclesiastical and ceremonial plate during the greedy years of the mid-seventeenth century did not extend to domestic pieces or to ordinary secular wares. Spoons apart, so far as the first half of the century is concerned, survivors in the two categories might almost be numbered on the fingers of two hands.

Few pieces of early Scottish silver are better known than the cup known as the Loving Cup of George Heriot, which belongs to the Governors of George Heriot's Trust. The mounting in silver of coconuts, shells, ostrich-eggs and other odd receptacles of exotic origin was, of course, a popular practice. Relatively speaking, it seems to have been quite as common in Scotland as in England. In the north, such objects no doubt excited exceptional interest. The 'Heriot' cup consists of a nautilus shell, the incurving end of which is sheathed in silver, and the silver-mounted lip of which is connected by straps to a slender stem spreading into an engraved, trumpet-shaped foot. There is a very foreign look about the piece, which does not even follow English tradition, and actually seems to be, in greater part, a casting after a German pattern, unmodified by any chasing or engraving.[1] Brook has shown that for a long time it was a practice of Edinburgh goldsmiths to reproduce *repoussé* work by casting, as

Pl. 30

Pl. 31

Pl. 32.i

[1] *P.S.A.S.*, Vol. XXIV, p. 102

they did in the case of the Sword of State. The cup which for long was loosely attributed to George Heriot, goldsmith to James VI, has in addition to the Edinburgh hall-mark the maker's mark of Robert Denneistoune and a much-rubbed deacon's punch which has been identified as David Palmer's. This last dates the cup between 1611 and 1613. As a piece of old silver, it is more interesting than notable. There is competence in the silver sheathing, but the cast portions are somewhat dead in effect, as might be expected.

Pl.32.ii

Another unusual piece, which may be dated a year or two later, is an all-silver mazer by James Denneistoune. It has an unusually wide-spreading rim much everted, its lower edge deeply notched. Its sole decoration is some engraved coats-of-arms: in the interior, those of Inglis impaling Stewart, on the outside of the rim Bell impaling Inglis (C. P. Bell and his wife M. Inglis) and Bell impaling Campbell (C. P. M. Bell and his wife M. Campbell). The general form is that of the older mazers, but there is no reason to think this one ever possessed a wooden bowl.

Pl.21.ii

Early coconut cups are few and have neither the elegance nor the elaboration of Continental or even of English specimens, but their simple mounts have a beauty of their own. A cup which appears to be the earliest of the group has just come to light in a private collection in the north of Scotland, and as it is entirely unknown to collectors it is of special interest. It is a beautifully proportioned cup, with deep rim, four reeded straps and a bulbous stem faintly suggestive of the stems of some of the early seventeenth-century Communion cups such as Carnwath or St. Cuthbert's, Edinburgh. The maker's mark, stamped on the rim, is probably IH, and is unaccompanied by any other marks. It gives little clue to the origin of the cup, but is characteristically Scottish. The foot seems to be a replacement as it is quite different in feeling from the rest of the cup, and it has evidently been soldered on just below the bulb of the stem. It bears the inscription *Forss 1608* and carries the baffling key stamp which occurs sometimes alone and sometimes in association with a thistle on late eighteenth-century pieces. The focus of interest, however, lies in two coats-of-arms on the rim and the inscribed date '1588'. I should have been inclined to attribute the older part of the cup to the early seventeenth century; but the Lord Lyon, Sir Thomas Innes of Learney, has most kindly interpreted the arms for me in great detail and in such a way as to make it more than likely that the date engraved on the rim is correct. The larger arms are the undifferenced shield of the Sinclar Earls of Caithness, and the accompanying initials, GS, are

PLATE 29

Mace of the City of Edinburgh: Edinburgh, 1617. Maker: George Robertson (*pp.91-92*)

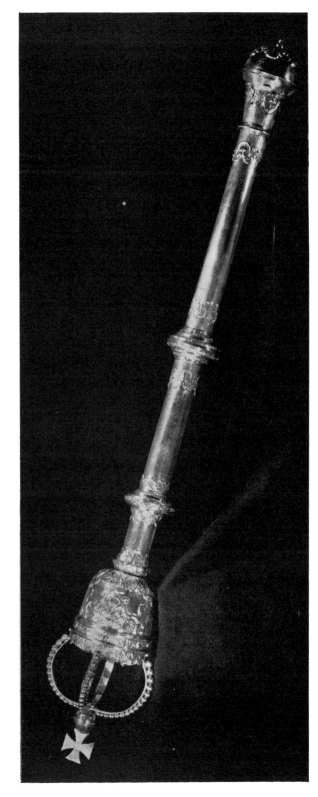

Mace of King's College, Aberdeen, about 1650. Maker: Walter Melvil (*p.92*)

PLATE 30

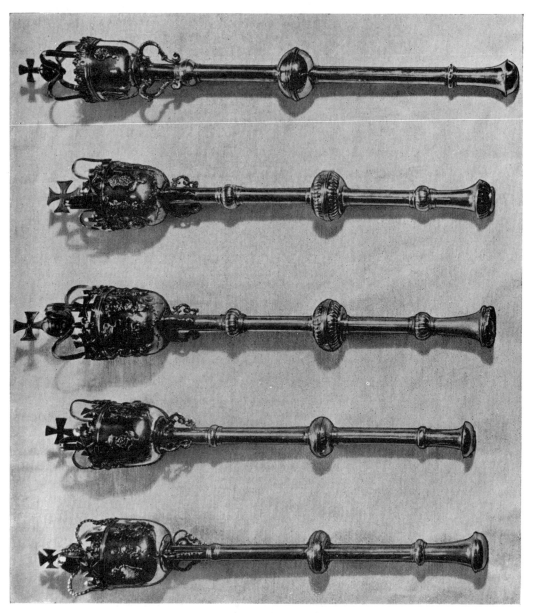

The Court of Session Maces: (1)? Edinburgh, dated 1760. Maker: W. S.; (2) Edinburgh, 1653–54 or 1659–61. Maker Edw. Cleghorn; (3) Edinburgh, dated 1815; (4) Edinburgh, 1704. Maker: Alex. Kincaid; (5)? Edinburgh, 17th century (p.93)

PLATE 31

Head of the earliest of the Court of Session Maces (No. 5 on Plate no. 30) *(p.93)*

PLATE 32

The Heriot Cup: Edinburgh, 1611-13. Maker: Robert Denneistoune *(pp.93-94)*; Wine Cup:
Edinburgh, about 1630. Maker: Thomas Cleghorne *(p.95)*

Bowl of mazer type: Edinburgh, 1617. Maker: James Denneistoune *(p.94)*

evidently those of the Hon. George Sinclair of Mey, 3rd son of the 4th Earl, and ancestor of the 12th and present Earls of Caithness, who received for his appanage fief the estate and Castle of Mey or Barrogill. This attribution is confirmed by the second coat-of-arms, with initials MF, for they relate to Margaret, sixth daughter of William, 7th Lord Forbes, who was the wife of George Sinclair. The Lord Lyon, therefore, regards the identity of the owners of the cup as 'completely settled', and thinks it may have been a gift or heirloom transmitted in connection with the marriage or investiture of his son, Sir William, which took place about 1600. The Lord Lyon adds that the Sinclairs of the fifteenth and sixteenth centuries, alike at Roslin, Girnigoe and Mey, were remarkable patrons of architecture and other arts. Two fine coconut cups by Dundee makers are in the Marquess of Bute's collection. One of them, by Thomas Lindsay, dates from about 1600 and is therefore almost as old as the Sinclair cup. The other, its lip engraved with the date 1612, is by Robert Gairdine. The earliest Edinburgh coconut cup is in the collection of Sir Malcolm MacGregor of MacGregor. It is, by comparison, elaborate, with a baluster-shaped stem and trumpet foot bordered by stamped decoration, and it is inscribed round the silver lip-band with EMS in monogram, NBES *mak . him . staker . Rob . Gib* ., while the foot is engraved with tulips, a motive which, as we shall see, became popular much later in the century with the engravers of quaichs. Andro Denneistoune is the maker of the cup and Jon Scott the deacon, which places it in the years 1637–9. Possibly the only simple wine cup of this time is a plain but elegant one by Thomas Cleghorne in the Marquess of Bute's collection. It is of course an Edinburgh piece and may be dated about 1630.

Pl.33.i

Pl.32.i

Commander How has remarked on the scarcity of Scottish silver spoons of this period, as compared with English spoons[1]; but the activities of the war committees are perhaps sufficient explanation, coupled with the likelihood that the Scots were mostly content with utensils of pewter or horn. Little hoards or caches of silver spoons such as those described by Dr. Callender[2] may well indicate successful steps taken to hide valuables from the agents of the committees. Two circumstances tend to increase the probability of this. In the first place, a pair of spoons found were in association with a silver-topped cane and a number of small silver coins which, by the dates of the latest, suggest that the

---

[1] *Connoisseur*, Vol. XCVIII, p. 341
[2] *P.S.A.S.*, Vol. LIX, pp. 120–126

hoard must have been laid away ten or fifteen years after Charles I came to the throne. Secondly, the place where this and another larger hoard were found is Irvine, in Ayrshire, once a stronghold of Covenanting activity.

The Scottish spoon of this period is quite distinctive. It has a round bowl, only slightly elongated, and a flat stem, sometimes very slender, sometimes broad, expanding to a disc-like end separated from the stem by notched or indented outlines. There is a short, stubby rat-tail on the back of the bowl. As a rule the spoons are more quaint than beautiful, although this is not always so, and How maintains that the type was introduced from Scotland into England, where it became the prototype of the Puritan spoon. How[1] incidentally corrects Sir Charles Jackson's inference that such spoons date only from about the second quarter of the seventeenth century when he shows there is no reason why the Canongate spoon in the National Museum of Antiquities should not be of the date inscribed on it, 1589. The type would seem, therefore, to have persisted from some time in the second half of the sixteenth century and to be in vogue a hundred years or more later, with gradual modifications. The Canongate spoon is the work of George Cunningham, Senior, and bears in their simplest forms all the features of its type, together with slight engraved ornament reminiscent of acanthus on the face of the stem, top and bottom.

Pl.33.ii

A set of fine Edinburgh spoons found at Irvine in 1865 and declared to be treasure trove are now also in the National Museum of Antiquities. They are long and slim in the stem, have small disc ends and show the notched assay-mark characteristic of Scots silver. They appear to have been made by Edward Hairt, with George Heriot, Senior, as deacon, which places them in the second half of the sixteenth century. Engraved on them are the initials IB and AC, and the second evidently point to a member of the Cuninghame family, as a Y-shaped device beside them has been identified as the shake-fork of the Cuninghames.[2] The Cuninghame shake-fork, with initials IC, also appears on the other Irvine find of a pair of spoons, as well as on the silver cane-top which came to light with them. These spoons have a broader and more elaborate head to the stem. The maker is Jon Scott and the deacon John Fraser who, however, was acting not as the regular deacon but as an interim officer, and the spoons must have been made in the 'twenties or 'thirties of the century. The cane-top provides rather more precise evidence of association with the Cuning-

[1] *Connoisseur*, Vol. XCVIII, p. 344
[2] *P.S.A.S.*, Vol. LIX, p. 126

hame family, for the arms engraved on it are the shake-fork between two garbs and a mullet-in-chief of Cuninghame of Cuninghamehead, in the parish of Dreghorn. In every case the crudity of the engraving of initials points to some local practitioner or handyman rather than to the Edinburgh silversmith who made the spoon. A group of similar spoons found on the Hill of Culrain in Ross-shire, and now in the National Museum, indicates that at this period even such simple domestic pieces were rather too ambitious for local craftsmen, for the Culrain spoons too are all of Edinburgh make. They have initials, but those have not been identified. Three of the spoons carry the incised date, 1617.

To complete the picture of the Scottish spoon of the seventeenth century, as given in this rapid sketch, a 'Puritan' type of spoon was found by workmen cutting a trench for water-pipes in Haddington. It has a tapering stem, slightly notched at the top and lightly engraved with foliaceous decoration and a heart. It has a wriggled assay-groove and is the work of David Bog during the deaconate of James Symonstoun, 1665–7. Before the end of the century the Scottish form of spoon gave place to the trifid-top, plainly borrowed from south of the Border since it is much commoner in England than in Scotland. The Scots, however, applied their own form of engraving to this spoon, directly borrowed from pieces of the Culrain type, as may be seen on the Ayr spoon attributed to Matthew Colquhoun.

Pl. 33. ii

In completion of this chapter, several curious items which fall into no category must be described.

The first two of those items are the 'Siller Guns' of Dumfries and Kirkcudbright. These little silver guns were presented to the incorporated trades of the two burghs by James VI, for annual competition in shooting: an inducement rather than the more usual injunction for the burghers to become more proficient as marksmen. An inscription on the Dumfries gun gives the date of presentation as 1598, but the event took place in 1617. In its present state the gun has the form of a barrel fitted with a comparatively modern gun-stock; but apparently it once possessed a wheeled carriage, also of silver, broken in 1808 by an individual who was fined £3 6s. 8d. for his act and banished from associating with his trade for twenty-one years. There are no hall-marks but it is reasonable to assume that the relic is of Scottish origin. The Hammermen Incorporation of Dumfries in a minute of 4th June, 1813, laid down detailed regulations for the shoot, which show that the craft was still carefully organised and disciplined at that late date, with powers to compel attendance under pain of fines. The Kirkcudbright Siller Gun is similar, and has a link and ring attachment fixed to a point about its centre of gravity. It bears the inscribed date 1587 and the initials *T. M. C.* with the arms of Sir Thomas MacLellan of Bombie, provost of the burgh at this time. Trophies of such a sort were no doubt numerous formerly, and some silver arrows used as archery prizes have also survived. Strangely enough, Charles I twice tried to enforce the use of the long-bow by special commissions under the Great Seal, and episcopalian Aberdeen produced silver arrow trophies for archery in the reigns of himself and of his son (1644 and 1679).

Pl.34.i   In the same miscellaneous category are the silver bells of Lanark and of Paisley. The story attached to the Lanark bell is that William the Lion gave it to the burgh. However, rather unexpectedly, it carries a maker's mark—Hugh Lindsay's—and the mark of Robert Denneistoune as deacon (1608–10). Traditionally, it has always been a prize for a horse-race. So are the Paisley bells. The larger of the Paisley bells is referred to in a minute of the Town Council for 27th April, 1608, requiring 'that one silver bell be made of 4 oz. weight with all diligence for one horse-race yearly'. A coat-of-arms appears on the bell. The smaller one is dated 1620, not 1820, as unaccountably recorded in the catalogue of the Palace of History in the Glasgow Exhibition of 1911. Neither bell carries any mark or even the assay-groove present on the Lanark bell. I am told that the only comparable English racing-bells are those belonging to Carlisle, dated 1599.

Col. Plate   Quite the most unusual, interesting and important of the unclassifiable pieces is the gold ampulla believed to have been used at the Scottish Coronation of Charles I at Holyroodhouse in 1633.[1] This little vial is pear-shaped, on a spreading base, and the lid, which screws on to the body, is fitted with a pair of diverging, horn-like tubes tapering to nozzles only .12 ins. in diameter. The height of the vessel is a mere 5 ins., its weight $3\frac{1}{2}$ oz. The foot is engraved with an egg-and-tongue pattern, rather crudely carried out; and indeed a certain crudity characterises the piece as a whole, and it conveys the impression of an almost functional vessel, a utensil rather than an ornament, either adapted or made in some haste and without the attention to craftsmanship which the dignity of the occasion and the preciousness of the metal would seem to have demanded. There is an inscription engraved on the side:

[1] *P.S.A.S.*, Vol. LXXXII, p. 237

AMPVLLA
AVREA SACRI olei
Receptaculum quo Carolvs
eius nominis primus Scotiæ
Angliæ Fran : et Hib : Rex
Edinburgi in Ecclesia
S:Crucis unctus fuit
Iunii xviii
1633

Nothing in the style of the inscription appears to be inconsistent with the date subscribed in it, and it is only unfortunate that there is no detailed contemporary description of the ampulla to support its claim. It is referred to in the records merely as a 'golden Ampule'. The form of the ceremony set down by Archbishop Laud's secretary stipulated a silver vessel to contain the oil, but the Lyon King of Arms, Sir James Balfour, who bore the ampulla at the coronation, left the record which describes it as of gold. The National Museum of Antiquities purchased it in London in 1948 from the Trustees of the late Sir George Grant Suttie, but it is not known how it came into the possession of the Sutties of Balgone, unless it was produced for the coronation by a certain George Suttie, then City Treasurer of Edinburgh, who retained it afterwards. Preparations for the ceremony were not the measured and leisurely ones usual on such occasions, for there was much changing of plans; and it may be the Capital tardily decided that a silver vessel would not be worthy of such an event and suddenly commissioned a gold one. This could account for the plainness and crudity of the vial, although it seems strange that a community with craft resources to produce the City Mace could not have created a vessel more in keeping with the solemn significance of the rite it served. Neither maker's nor deacon's mark appears on it, and there is no city mark. This is not altogether surprising as the vessel, if specially made, would be made without thought of its ever coming on the market, and it may be that a special dispensation covered such work. The Crown does not carry the punch of its known maker, John Mosman. There is no prescribed shape for an ampulla and the pair of horn-like nozzles may, as Mr. Stevenson suggests,[1] have some connexion with the Horn of Zadok mentioned in the Coronation sermon, but the practical need for an air-hole to render the flow of the oil easy no doubt played a major part in determining the form.

[1] *P.S.A.S.*, ibid., p. 239

Another unique piece is the silver-gilt case containing the seal attached to the Commission, issued by James VI and I on 13th December, 1604, appointing the 3rd Earl of Montrose Great Commissioner in Scotland. This is a sophisticated piece of work, a subtly-convex circular box, beautifully engraved, by George Cunningham, senior, of the Canongate, and now in the possession of the Duke of Montrose. It is briefly referred to later (p.171), and I described it fully in *The Burlington Magazine* (November, 1959). Apart from the evidence it provides of the standard of engraving at the time, its marks are of notable interest. It used to be thought that Canongate goldsmiths came under Royal patronage and were exempt from testing by a "tryar"; but the characteristic wriggled assay-groove is here present, although there is no assay-master's punch. Moreover, the stag's head town-mark has a discernible cross between the antlers, a cross which Jackson believed to be absent from the punch on Canongate plate. (See endpiece opposite page 262).

NOTES TO CHAPTER IX

WINE FUNNEL (pl.34,ii)
Edinburgh, c.1640, by Adam Lamb (maker's mark only). This is the only known seventeenth-century Scottish funnel. It is marked three times with the monogram of Adam Lamb, who became a freeman in 1619, and whose will was registered on 24 August 1647. From the fact that it is marked with the maker's mark only, it is quite likely that it dates from one of the periods when Adam Lamb was Deacon, in 1627-29, 1635-37, 1639-40 and 1644-46. It might be dated on stylistic grounds to any of these times. The idea that some seventeenth-century Deacons occasionally marked their own work with only their maker's mark has been suggested because it seems to fit the probable dates of a number of pieces so marked, including some that have an engraved date on them. This is not to say, however, that all pieces so marked date from the maker's deaconate.

Chapter Ten

SEVENTEENTH CENTURY PROVINCIAL WORK

ISOLATED examples of provincial silver have been noted, but by the close of the seventeenth century craftsmen were so firmly established in burghs other than the capital that some particular attention must be given to their work.

Dundee, already mentioned as a town which produced silver, must have been one of the earliest burghs to place the craft on an organised basis. Such small documentary evidence as there is may be found in the Locked Book of the Hammermen Trade. This had its beginning in 1587, but the statutes contained in it were already old. The rules of the craft show the usual concern both for the quality of the work and for the morals of the members. ('Gif it fortoun ony prenteis off the halm-men craft to comit adulterie or fornicatioun during the tyme of his prentischip, sall doubill his prentischip, and sall pay fourtie schillingis to ye puir, or ellis sall tyne ye libertie off his craft for ewir.') Two goldsmiths, Thomas Ramsay and Charles Ramsay, appear in a list of members at the beginning of the book, but from 1588 to 1650 there were only 5 goldsmiths as against 112 members of other trades, although in the next century the numbers rise to 11 as against 124. Some of the most interesting early pieces have the R.G. mark which appears on the Fergusson spoon, and although those range over more than one generation in time it is probable the makers all belong to the Gairdine or Gairdyne family. The latest of the group are the four[1] Communion cups at Brechin, with the engraved dates of 1631 (a pair), 1643 and 1648. The Brechin cups are splendid, simple pieces of silverwork, well-proportioned, although decoration is limited to the moulded foot. Alexander Lindsay is the author of two Communion cups at Kettins, rather more embellished with ornament, and of four exactly similar cups at Belhelvie. All are inscribed with the date 1636. Two of the Belhelvie cups were the gift of the

.38

---

[1] In *English and Scottish Silver Spoons* How referred to three (Vol. II, p. 313)

Rev. David Lyndesaye, minister of the parish from 1629 to 1667 and an active Covenanter, although for some unexplained reason he continued his ministry under Episcopal rule.

Gairdine also made the very beautiful and interesting cups presented to Monifieth in 1642 by William Durham and Jean Auchterlonie. The Durham family had owned the lands of Grange and Monifieth since 1322 and in the sixteenth century upheld Knox and the Reforming party, William Durham being a member of the Assembly of 1565 which abolished the Mass. Jean Auchterlonie, Lady Grange, however, in 1650 showed sympathy with Montrose after his capture at Assynt, and when his captors lodged him at Grange for the night she tried to effect his escape, but unsuccessfully, although the Committee of Estates evidently so admired her courage that they never called upon her to appear before them. She and her husband gave the parish an Edinburgh-made cup in 1638, similar in form to, although rather smaller than, the Gairdine cup. It is fairly clear that Gairdine copied the shape of the cup presented four years earlier, adding only an odd little notched flange at the foot of the stem. Both cups left Monifieth about 1816, for Lord Panmure exchanged them for new ones about this date. They were separated and the Dundee cup found its way to Exeter College, Oxford, in 1887, through the wife of the Rector who had received it as a wedding-present. This appears to be the cup which Jackson describes as of about 1648,[1] and which Commander How in 1953 continues to describe as at Exeter College, suggesting it may be much earlier than the date given it by Jackson.[2] In fact, however, the Dundee cup returned to Monifieth from Exeter College in 1922, rejoining its companion there. The travels of the two cups are fully described in a booklet published by the Rev. Gordon Quig, Minister of Monifieth, in 1938.[3]

The town-mark of Dundee was employed from early in the seventeenth century. It is the arms of the burgh: a two-handled pot with lilies. The 'pot' is of vase form, and it appears consistently and with little variation. The maker's initials are usually struck twice, once on either side of the town mark. There is nothing in the nature of a deacon's stamp.

A similar consistency cannot be claimed for Aberdeen, the town-marks of which vary in a perplexing manner. The letters AB or ABD occur from the

[1] *Engl. Goldsmiths and Their Marks*, p. 543
[2] *Engl. and Scot. Silver Spoons*, Vol. II, p. 313
[3] *The Romantic Adventures of two Old Monifieth Communion Cups*

seventeenth century onwards, and a castle stamped thrice, often, especially in later times, much resembling the letter X, is also common, with or without the groups of letters. There were two Aberdeens, the Old Town and the New, each having its own Incorporation of Hammermen which embraced the goldsmiths. The earliest known goldsmith of the New Town is David Theman, who took an apprentice called James Kemp in 1464. Not for nearly another two centuries, however, was the craft placed on a fully organised basis, for in 1649 the Town Council appointed William Anderson to be 'tryar of all gold and siluerwark', the quality of existing silver as usual being found insufficient. The record of his appointment[1] states that approved work had to be 'markit with the prob' and stamped with the town's mark. These two processes apparently are one, for Anderson was also appointed 'keiper of the town's mark' for the year. Brook was of the opinion that the office was not filled after Anderson vacated it, although the main evidence for this seems to be the great variety of town marks, suggesting that each maker employed his own. Documentary evidence about the state of the craft in the Old Town is of the scantiest. Brook lists Robert Cruickshank (admitted 1699) as the earliest name, although the Register of Burgesses gives, under the date October 17th, 1696, a Stephen Agate, 'frenchman, jeweller and goldsmith'.

A certain 'David Brois' (Bruce) is mentioned in the Town Register for 1508. In the Marquess of Bute's collection is a fine set of six disc-ended spoons inscribed with the date '1575' and stamped with the maker's mark, DB within a shield. There is no town-mark or assay-groove, but Commander How puts forward the theory that they are Scottish provincial, and that Aberdeen is the most probable town of origin.[2] Carrying his argument further, he considers that, since in Scotland Christian names were often passed on from father to son, the spoons may be the work of a grandson of David Brois. If they are indeed of Aberdeen origin they establish the high capability of the town's craftsmen at an early time, for they are beautiful spoons, admirably engraved with the usual leaf pattern.

Earliest among the Aberdeen makers who have left notable as well as definite evidence of what they could accomplish is Walter Melvil, admitted to the Incorporation in 1650. The outstanding piece from his bench is the mace of King's College, which has been described in a previous chapter. Another ex-

---

[1] *Town Council Register, 7/11/1649*
[2] *Engl. and Scot. Silver Spoons*, Vol. II, p. 334

PLATE 33

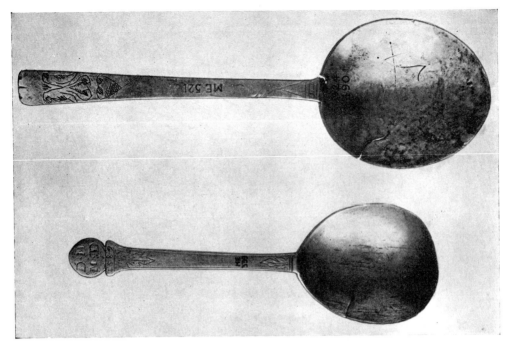

The Canongate Spoon, Canongate, c.1589. Maker: George Cunningham, sen. (pp.66 & 96) 'Puritan' type Spoon: Edinburgh, 1665-67. Maker: David Bog (p.97)

Holyrood Mass Bell: Edinburgh, 1686. Maker: Zacharius Mellinus (p.124); Edinburgh, 1637-39. Maker: Andro Denneistoune (p.95) Coconut Cup:

PLATE 34

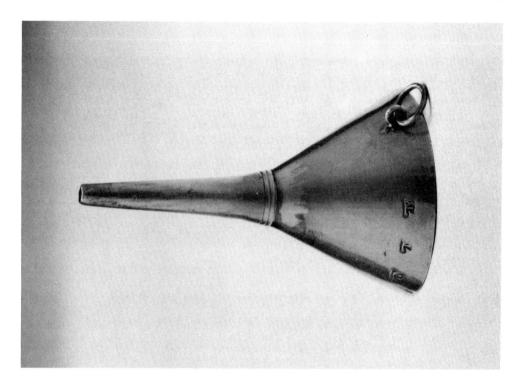

Wine Funnel: Edinburgh, c.1640. Maker's mark only
of Adam Lamb (*p.99*)

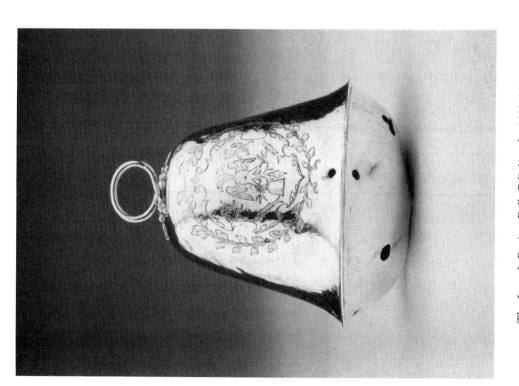

The Lanark Racing Bell: Edinburgh, 1608-10.
Maker: Hugh Lindsay (height 4″) (*p.98*)

PLATE 35

Pair of Communion Cups of the Parish of Bolton: Canongate, 1696. Maker: George Ziegler *(p.115)*

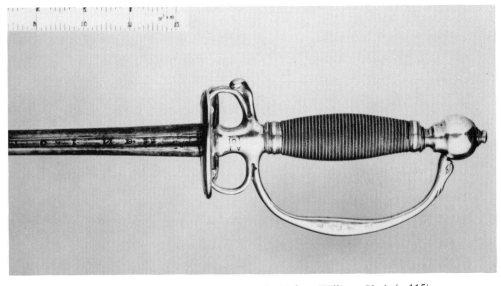

Silver Sword Hilt: Glasgow, 1698-99. Maker: William Clark *(p.115)*

PLATE 36

Pair of Wine Goblets: Dundee, c.1660. Maker: Robert Gairdyne *(p.115)*

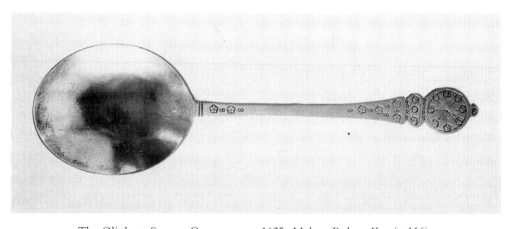

The Oliphant Spoon: Canongate, c.1625. Maker: Robert Ker *(p.116)*

PLATE 37

The Communion Basin of Dundee ('The Fiethie Salver'), presented by John Feithe: Dundee, c.1665.
Maker: Thomas Lindsay *(p.116)*

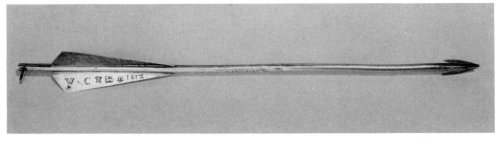

The Rattray Arrow: Perth, c.1612. Maker: Thomas Ramsay *(p.113)*

PLATE 38

Kettins Communion Cups: Dundee, about 1636. Maker: Alexander Lindsay *(p.101)*

PLATE 39

Communion Cup of Ellon: Aberdeen, c.1642.
Maker: Walter Melvil (p.104)

The Strathnaver Cup: Aberdeen, mid-17th century.
Maker: Walter Melvil (p.104)

PLATE 40

Tankard: Aberdeen, late 17th century. Maker: Robert Cruikshank *(p.103)*

Salt Cellar of St. Mary's College, St. Andrews: St. Andrews, about 1670.
Maker: Patrick Gairden *(p.107)*

PLATE 41

Coconut Cup: Aberdeen, c.1670. 1670
Maker: William Scott the Elder (p.106)

Beaker Communion Cup of Monymusk: Aberdeen, c.1691. ury
Maker: Geo. Walker (p.104)

PLATE 42

Communion Cup of Craig: Montrose, c.1682. Maker: Wm. Lyndsay *(p.106)*

PLATE 43

The Kinnoul Communion Cup: Perth, c.1680. Maker: Robert Gairdyne *(p.107)*

PLATE 44

The Innerpeffery Cups: Perth, c.1687. Maker: Robert Gairdyne *(p.113)*

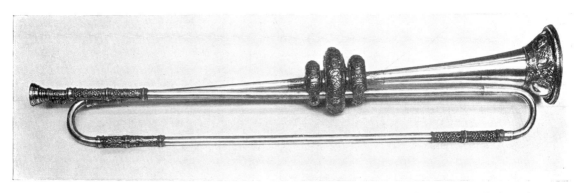

Trumpet, one of two: Glasgow, c.1680. Makers: Thomas Moncur and Robert Brock *(p.109)*

Pl.39.i ample of his work, in Marischal College, is the Strathnaver Cup,[1] of Com-
munion-cup form but lightly engraved with foliaceous scrolls. Its stem is unusual and particularly happy in design. The inscribed date of 1653 on the bowl
is probably near the date of the cup's manufacture. Melvil is also the maker of
Pl.39.ii one of the two beaker Communion cups at Ellon, which raises an issue of wide
interest because it involves the close economic and cultural ties between north-
east Scotland and the Low Countries. At first sight the Ellon cups are a pair.
Their upper parts are engraved with a pattern of strapwork, tendrils of foliage,
fruit and flowers. One, however, is more finely executed than the other, and
bears the inscription *Koft from Alexander Hayus Anno 1634* and the hall-mark of
Amsterdam. Melvil's cup is a copy of this one, and the date of its gift to Ellon
kirk is 1642. Secular drinking beakers of this type, a type common in Holland
and north Germany and not infrequently depicted in Dutch paintings, seem to
have found their way in considerable numbers to the Aberdeen district, and
Old Machar Church and King's College have foreign beakers with elaborate
decoration, including figures in the costume of the early seventeenth century.
The two King's College beakers were given by foreign students of the University in 1643, tangible evidence that the traffic of Scots students to Leiden was
by no means one-way. Most of the beaker cups in Scotland belong to north-
east coastal districts, and of the Scottish ones the great majority are by Aberdeen makers. This reflection of Netherlandish ideas is of course found in many
spheres, from words and surnames to the prevalence of Dutch gables and other
architectural features from the Firth of Forth northwards. Towards the end of
the century a number of good beaker cups were made by George Walker. His
Pl.41.i best achievement is the set of four cups at Monymusk, with their unusual outline marked by slight entasis. They are pleasingly engraved with strapwork and
floral decoration, although the work is not up to Continental standards. There
is an inscription recording that the cups were acquired in 1691, during the
ministry of John Burnett. The Kirk Session Records for the same year show
that the young laird of Monymusk, William Forbes, paid £125 2s. for the
cups, and that he was reimbursed by the treasurer.

It is a curious circumstance that those beaker cups, with a single exception,
are to be found north and east of the Tay. It is the more curious because, although most of them are of Aberdeen origin, a few were made in Edinburgh.
These last include the oldest of the type, the pair belonging to the little kirk of

[1] Noted by Jackson (*Engl. Goldsmiths*, p. 533) as the Strathnairn cup

Arbirlot, a hamlet a few miles inland from Arbroath, which were made by Gilbert Kirkwoode during Denneistoune's deaconate (1608–10), although dedicated for sacred use only in 1633. It would appear that in the north-east alone was this type of vessel popular, or even acceptable, which emphasises the strength of the link between the Low Countries and Aberdeen, as distinct from the rest of Scotland. Burns maintained,[1] on good grounds, that the cups were originally imported for secular use and that it was the shortage of plate after the Reformation which brought about their adaptation for sacred use. As already remarked, the style of decoration on several Communion cups proves the original purpose for which they were intended. Burns considers the beaker may have been in use in Scotland in the sixteenth century. It certainly was so abroad, and English goldsmiths also were producing the type before 1600; a number of them were adapted for church use, for example a London-made piece of 1593 at Haworth in Yorkshire.[2]

Two beakers at Elgin are undecorated and evidently are among those made specially for the Communion table. An inscription records that they were the gift of a provost of the burgh, William Cummen of Achray, in 1681. Burns thinks they may be the work of William Scott, the Elgin silversmith. Scott and his son were not admitted freemen of Elgin until 1701, but they, together with other silversmiths in the region, seem to have been peripatetic, for their names appear as following the trade in other towns. A William Scott was admitted a Hammerman of Aberdeen in 1666, and his initials are engraved—not punched—on two of the well-known series of medals of the Grammar School. He was also the maker of a set of six fine shield-top spoons of about 1700 in the Marquess of Bute's collection. Both Scotts, however, seem to have done a great deal of their work in Banff. The elder first appears there in 1688, the younger in 1699. Two years earlier the wife of the former died there, and he himself is reputed to have ended his days in the town in 1703. Forglen and Alvah both have beaker cups by Scott. Cullen also has a pair of cups with Scott's mark together with the town-mark ABC, which Brook assumes to be a Banff mark.[3] It is a strange variant of the BANF which is usual a little later, and Commander How's theory that it may be the town-mark of Aberchirder at least fits in with the practice of the district, as it does with the ubiquity of Scott himself, although no other piece with this mark exists and it is a little difficult to under-

[1] *Scot. Comm. Plate*, p. 291
[2] *Yorkshire Church Plate* (1915), Vol. II, plate 3   [3] *Scot. Comm. Plate*, p. 577

Pl.41.ii

stand why Scott should have used it. It was probably at Banff that Scott made the handsome coconut cup in the collection of Mr. W. S. Bell of Aberdeen, at a date around 1670, and another coconut cup, of about 1700, in the Bute collection.

Montrose is the place of origin of an important group of Communion cups, all from the hand of William Lyndsay. Two clock-makers earlier in the century are mentioned in the Town Records, and they may have practised as goldsmiths. Under the date 1687 there is also a David Ouchterlony. Lyndsay appears in the Records in 1688. In this year he was called upon by the Dean of Guild to become a Burgess, but refused on the argument that his father was a Burgess, presumably maintaining that he should receive the privilege by patrimony. The dispute went on for some months and he was fined 10 shillings Scots and subsequently imprisoned for not paying, but the cost of keeping him in prison was too much for the town to bear, so that he was freed. Later they made him a Burgess on condition that he would 'cutt ane new seal for the Toune's use'. He had been a member of the Town Council since 1672, representing the Blacksmiths, and this connection no doubt determined the design of his punch: his initials surmounted by hammer and crown. As Brook remarks,[1] Lyndsay's work, both technically and aesthetically, is, by Scottish standards at least, of a very high order. His Communion cups include those of

Pl.42

Forfar (1671), Bervie (1680), Craig (1682), Fordoun (1682), Aberlemno (1683) and Laurencekirk (1688). The decoration of these cups is of a comparatively sophisticated sort not often found on Scottish silver of the period. The Craig and Bervie cups, for example, have around the foot winged heads, presumably of angels, executed ably in *repoussé*, an exceptional method of treatment north of the Border. The proportions of the cups are very good and the inscriptions and engraving of arms on the bowls are likewise unusual in quality. Burns thinks that the cups at Glamis may also be Lyndsay's work,[2] although the maker's punch is gone, and the engraving of the Strathmore arms is certainly worthy of his hand. The Glamis cups (1676) have apparently had stem and foot renewed at a later date.

Silverware has been wrought in Perth since the sixteenth century, and the tradition goes back three centuries earlier still. As usual in the Scottish burghs, silversmiths were included in the Hammermen Incorporation, the records of which contain the only information about the early history of the craft in the

[1] *Scot. Comm. Plate*, p. 594   [2] Ibid., p. 396

town.[1] The first deacon of the craft to appear is Adam Denholme (1567), and the second is Thomas Ramsay (1604–12).[2] The earliest craftsman whose work has survived is Robert Gardiner. Commander How hints at a family connection between him and Robert Gairdyne of Dundee and a Patrick Gairden who worked at St. Andrews about the same time.[3] Gardiner may well have possessed some of the ubiquitous habits of William Scott and have been the same man as Robert Gairdyne or some other of the Gairdynes (for their period of working is long), since Coupar-Angus, in the fruit-growing district north-east of Dundee, has a pair of Communion cups by Gardiner with the Perth town-mark. They are dated 1687. At this time the Perth town-mark, later to become a double-headed eagle, was a lamb bearing the banner of St. Andrew—the device of St. Johnstone, the ancient name of Perth, as commemorated in St. John's Kirk. Gardiner's other surviving work includes a Communion cup at Muthill, a piece of date about 1669–74 in the Perth Museum, and the handsome Innerpefferay Cups c. 1687, in the collection of the Marquess of Bute. Some early Perth plate bearing the lamb mark is also struck with single gothic letters which have the appearance of date-letters, although there is no reason to think this is their significance.

The Patrick Gairden mentioned above is the only goldsmith whose name has been linked with St. Andrews. His initials, with a saltire cross, are found on three pieces in St Andrews: two Communion Cups of the Town Church dated 1671, and a salt-cellar in St. Mary's College. In addition, there is in the Marquess of Bute's collection a little coconut cup with squat foot and S-shaped handles.

Pl.40.ii

Much fuller investigation has been made into the history of the craft in Inverness,[4] through the zeal of Miss Margaret O. MacDougall, the County Librarian, to whom I am indebted for the greater part of my information on this subject. There appear to have been craft societies as early as 1566, but it was not until 1676 that the Sett of the Burgh recognised six crafts, among them the Hammermen. After that date several silversmiths settled in the town. A certain John Bayne appears to have been in business as a silversmith about 1668, as in that year he is charged with a debt for tobacco and 'broken silver'. The first to emerge clearly is Robert Elphinstone, who came about 1688 and was the first Deacon of the Hammermen Craft.

---

[1] *Perth Hammermen Book* (1518–68), Perth, 1899
[2] Not Robert, as Jackson, p. 552
[3] *Engl. and Scot. Silver Spoons*, Vol. II, p. 313
[4] See *Inverness Courier*, 24/1/47

Early Inverness silver is very rare. Jackson gives a quaich under the date 1640 and the Forres Communion cup as 1643; but the Forres cups in their present state in my view date from the early eighteenth century. They are very like the cup with an Inverness mark at Inverallan, Strathspey. Burns could not identify the maker's mark, M, on this cup, but Miss MacDougall has traced it to William McLean, who was apprenticed to Elphinstone. Some early Inverness silversmiths seem to have used only the initial or initials of their surname; so it is perhaps not unreasonable to identify the MK of the Forres cups and of the quaich mentioned by Jackson as Simon McKenzie, another apprentice of Elphinstone. He is probably also the maker of a charming little thistle cup in the Bute collection. Elphinstone himself has left little work behind him and his mark was until recently unidentified. How now attributes to him the fine set of six spoons with trefid tops in the Bute collection.[1] These, as he says, are indistinguishable from London-made spoons. With the marks is a letter H, which How considers may have been a date-letter for 1688 which, as we have seen, is approximately the start of Elphinstone's Inverness career. Miss MacDougall records that in that year he is mentioned in the Burgh Court books as a witness in an unsavoury case involving the music master! A second miniature thistle cup in the Bute collection, of about the same date, may also be his work. His name appears on the back of a draft of a letter,[2] written about 1687, preserved in the Minute Book of the Edinburgh Incorporation of Goldsmiths, a letter sent out when the Incorporation received its charter from James VII and II and addressed to goldsmiths in a number of Scottish burghs. The early silversmiths of Inverness were all admitted Burgess and Guild Brethren by the Town Council. A Guild Brother was a merchant who bought and sold goods, as distinct from a craft freeman, who only sold goods he himself produced and had to buy even the materials of his craft from a Guild Brother. Elphinstone and his successors were, therefore, both manufacturing and retailing goldsmiths and, no doubt, also jewellers.

In the fifteenth and sixteenth centuries Glasgow was a small and comparatively unimportant burgh, although it was of course a university town, and latterly the seat of an archbishop. If we are to judge by the goldsmiths—and perhaps they are no bad index—it was of less importance than Aberdeen or Dundee up to the middle of the seventeenth century, and it is only about the time of the letter of 1687 from the Edinburgh Incorporation, as mentioned in

[1] *Engl. and Scot. Silver Spoons*, Vol. II, p. 368   [2] *Scot. Comm. Plate*, p. 593

the note on Inverness, that the Glasgow craftsmen outstrip the Aberdeen ones by 5 to 3, Edinburgh at this time having about 25. The Hammermen of Glasgow were incorporated by Seal of Cause in 1536, some years later than the Aberdeen Hammermen. The earliest name mentioned in the minutes is John Kirkwood's, in 1616. Robert Brock, James Stirling, Thomas Cumming, George Luke and James Cumming are the five men to whom the Edinburgh letter was addressed in 1687. They were not, however, the sole representatives of their craft. Neither Burns' nor Jackson's books mention any Glasgow plate earlier than 1680, but the Bute collection contains a fine quaich of about 1670, by Thomas Moncur, admitted 1665, and a very remarkable pair of trumpets   Pl.44.ii
by Moncur and Robert Brock, which were formerly in Douglas Castle. These last are quite unique in Scotland.

Alexander Brook pointed an interesting contrast between the status of the Glasgow goldsmiths and that of their Edinburgh contemporaries,[1] a contrast which reflects outlooks still recognisable in the commercial attitudes of the two cities to-day. Edinburgh has always tended to be more pre-occupied with finance and administration, while Glasgow bent herself to productive industry. In the sixteenth and seventeenth centuries we find the Edinburgh goldsmiths much concerned with banking and money-lending, Heriot perhaps to the exclusion of his craft; but the Glasgow men had their eggs in many baskets, all industrial. The Lukes (or Louks) of Claythorn, most notable Glasgow goldsmiths of their time, were also partners in a soaperie, an ironwork, and in various shipping enterprises, among them the vessel in which cherry sacke was first imported into Glasgow. This sort of dabbling in other trades would have earned an Edinburgh goldsmith expulsion from his Incorporation. It did not, however, deter the Glasgow craftsmen from producing excellent work on their benches, and John Luke himself is the author of several fine pieces which have survived, including a quaich of about 1687 in the Bute collection. William Clark is a silversmith of much versatility. He is responsible for a piece which, at the other end of the scale in size, is as unique as the trumpets. This is the delightful little patch-box of delicate filigree in the collection of Mr. John Noble   Pl.45.i
of Ardkinglas. In the field of table silver, the Bute collection contains a set of five handsome trefid spoons of about 1689, by James Sterling, and—to overlap briefly into the next century—there is a superb hash-spoon of noble proportions, dating about 1705 and made by John Luke, in Lord Glentanar's collection.

[1] *Scot. Comm. Plate*, p. 584

References to conjectural and approximate dates draw attention to the fact that Glasgow silver of this time has frequently no date-mark, although the Glasgow craft began its date-letter system in the same year as Edinburgh did, 1681. In any case, Glasgow discontinued this device early in the eighteenth century. The town-mark is the burgh's arms: an oak-tree with a fish and a bell. Each silversmith appears to have had his own town-mark, and in the case of William Clark the surname actually appears on the stamp.

Only one other town is mentioned in the draft letter of 1687, and that is Ayr. The goldsmith named in the letter is Matthew Colquhoun. Little or nothing is known of Ayr silversmiths, but Brook and Jackson ascribed to Colquhoun a little quaich of the later seventeenth century having the maker's mark MC but no town-mark. Messrs. Wilson & Sharp of Edinburgh possess a beautiful

Pl. 45.ii

trefid-end spoon the form and decoration of which are typically Scottish, and this also carries the maker's mark MC, stamped twice. The town-mark is present in this case, but it is badly rubbed. It appears to be circular, with what might be a castle in one segment, but it is too indistinct to yield any marked points of resemblance to the triple-turreted castle which appears in the burgh arms of Ayr. The spoon, however, is of the right period and the circumstantial evidence reasonably good.

NOTES TO CHAPTER X

DUNDEE GOLDSMITHS (p.101, line 17)

The apparent shortage of Dundee goldsmiths in the early years of the seventeenth century is partly accounted for by the fact that around 1600 a disagreement occurred between the goldsmiths and the remaining hammermen, which resulted in the goldsmiths seeking, but not gaining, independence. During this hiatus there are only scattered references to goldsmiths in the Incorporation of Hammermen's records. It is thus possible that a goldsmith or goldsmiths could have started work in Dundee during the period of the split and never have been entered with the incorporation. The Town Council permitted the goldsmiths to organise their own affairs for a time, but they were expressly forbidden to attempt to elect their own deacon. After less than a decade the goldsmiths returned to the fold of the Hammermen's Incorporation.

ABERDEEN GOLDSMITHS (p.103, line 6)

In Aberdeen, several goldsmiths are known before the time of Theman Goldsmith, the earliest of whom is Martin Goldsmith, burgess, whose name appears in a charter dated 1281. (Reg. Episc. Aber. II,278)

WILLIAM ANDERSON "TRYAR" (p.103, line 8)

William Anderson's monogram is found as a tryer's mark on several pieces made in Aberdeen in the 1650s, including the mace of King's College and the Strathnaver Cup, both by Walter Melvil, and a wine taster by Thomas Moncur. His W is shaped like a V, as was usual at that date, and superimposed on the A it looks like XX, or "XX".

DISC-END SPOONS (p.103, line 21)

It seems unlikely that the set of spoons discussed in this paragraph were made in Aberdeen. Although out of period, it has been suggested to me that they may have been made by the Edinburgh goldsmith David Boog, although he was not admitted to the craft until 1653. They remain unascribed.

THE WILLIAM SCOTTS (p.105, lines 26-28)

A good deal of muddle has long persisted as to the dates and movements of the two William Scotts, found in Aberdeen, Banff and Elgin. Dr. James has done much to unscramble the situation in her *Goldsmiths of Aberdeen*. The original text of this chapter cannot be altered for typographical reasons, so the following up-date is inserted here. Note that there is still some ambiguity, since the elder Scott was already a member of the Banff Hammermen by 1688, though still resident in Aberdeen until at least 1689. This may have been a state of affairs somewhat analogous to his Elgin situation in 1701.

William Scott, elder.
    Aberdeen 1666-88. Banff 1688-c.1702. Elgin 1701-c.1702.

William Scott, younger.
    Aberdeen 1691-c.1699. Banff c.1699-1748. Elgin 1701-48.

Note that their admission in Elgin was in all probability for technical reasons, that is, to allow them to retail their work in that burgh in a booth of their own. It is unlikely that they dotted about between the two burghs and they were most certainly not "tinkers" or "itinerant smiths" as some people have branded them. It seems clear that they were living in Banff and had no residence of their own in Elgin at any time.

There remains the ABC mark found with the maker's mark of the elder William Scott, on the Cullen Communion Cups and elsewhere. It used to be thought that this represented yet another place where Scott plied his craft, and Aberchirder was suggested; but why should William Scott, then resident and working in Aberdeen, travel to Aberchirder (or anywhere else) to make the Communion Cups for the parish church of Cullen? Looking for another explanation we find the 1681 instruction of the Privy Council to all goldsmiths working in Scotland (not just those in Edinburgh) to mark their work with an annually changed date-letter. The wording of this order is that each goldsmith shall mark his work "*with the ABC*". It seems that William Scott, not understanding his instructions, took them literally and uncomprehendingly did just that! He must have discovered his mistake after a while but not before the ABC mark had appeared on a few more items. If this theory is correct it would accurately date the items in question to late 1681 or early 1682.

COCONUT CUP (p.106, line 1 & pl.41,i)

The late Mr. Bell's beautiful Coconut Cup was without question made in Aberdeen, not Banff, as may be seen by the revised dates of the elder William Scott's movements given above.

MONTROSE (p.106, line 6)

There were two William Lindsays in Montrose, father and son.

PERTH (pp.106–107)

The paragraph about Perth needs some amplification. Henry the Bald was royal goldsmith in Perth to William I, the Lyon, who died in 1214. Around that time there was a mint in Perth, some of whose workers also probably practised as goldsmiths. Also preserved in the records are the names of John Corin, a contemporary of Henry the Bald, William Goldsmith, c.1291, and John Goldsmith, c.1415. There were doubtless several others filling the gaps, whose names have not come down to us, or still lie undiscovered in forgotten archives. Andrew Lufe, goldsmith, founded the altar dedicated to St. Eloy in St. John's Kirk in 1431, and the Hammermen probably had a corporate identity from about that time onwards. Finlay Goldsmith made four chalices weighing a total of 63½oz. for the Bishop of Dunkeld in 1513, for the churches of Little Dunkeld, Alyth, Cargill and Strathmiglo.

Thomas Ramsay is the maker of the silver arrow of Rattray in 1612 (Pl.37,ii) and of a silver bowling trophy of the same year, both at present on loan to the museum in Perth. Both have medals pertaining to them, attached by successive winners. The bowl is in a deplorable condition. There was also once a silver curling stone at the same date but this has not been traced. The Rattray Arrow and Bowl are at present the earliest known pieces of Perth silver.

INNERPEFFRAY COMMUNION CUPS (p.107, line 15 & pl.44)

This pair of Communion Cups was made for the Church of Innerpeffray, not Kinnoull as stated in the first edition. The confusion doubtless arose because they were once in the possession of the late Earl of Kinnoull. The parish of Kinnoull also has a Communion Cup by Robert Gairdyne (pl.44,i) which is now in Perth City Museum.

ST. ANDREWS COMMUNION CUPS (p.107, second paragraph)

Saint Andrews possesses not *one* Communion Cup but a pair, by Patrick Gairden. There is still some doubt as to the identification of this man with the Patrick Gairdyne who was admitted to the Hammermen of Dundee in 1624. Evidence is still lacking to tie them together definitely, but it seems a good possibility. If so, he must have been about sixty-eight when he made the Communion Cups in 1671.

LETTER OF 1689 (p.108, line 20 *set seq*)

The date of the draft letter to the thirteen provincial goldsmiths is no longer in any real doubt. Mr. Stuart Maxwell appears to be the first authority to have pointed out that the expression "Their Majesties" contained in the letter points to its having been drafted in the reign of William and Mary, who were offered (and accepted) the Crown of Scotland on 11th May 1689. The letter almost certainly dates from later in the same year, since it goes on to speak of "Their Majesties' Mint being now open". It appears to be an amended version of an earlier directive first sent out in 1681. In that year, Deacon Edward Cleghorn was asked by the Privy Council to send out letters to the goldsmiths in the several burghs of the kingdom to send representatives to Edinburgh to be instructed in how to produce work up to the minimum standard finenes: of 11 dwt. fine. The letter, now somewhat damaged and partially illegible, appears to be from the Deacon and Incorporation in Edinburgh. Citing the act of the Privy Council, it reads in part:

> ". . . [we] require you (as we do all other goldsmiths of the kingdom) to send in to us your essay box of all work made by you since Michaelmas . . . to be tryed by our jurorprudence to the effect mentioned therein; which act obliges you so to do under confiscation thereof. We for our own econeratioune, and that ye may have no shaddow of ane Excouse, thought it fitt and dutyful to acquaint you by this line to do the same as the rest about ye . . ."

GLASGOW GOLDSMITHS (p.109, line 4)

At least nine goldsmiths are known to have worked in Glasgow before John Kirkwood, the earliest of whom is John Goldsmith, first mentioned in 1472. Another is Peter Lymeburner whose long career spanned more than forty years from the 1560s onwards, and possibly earlier. On 22 April 1567, he witnessed, in his own house, a document in favour of Ninian Bannatyne of Kames, the same man whose name is engraved on the rim of the Bute Mazer (Pl.15,i). Whether it is possible, given the slight discrepancy in dates, that Lymeburner may have actually made the rim and straps of the mazer is an intriguing speculation.

NEW ILLUSTRATIONS

THE BOLTON COMMUNION CUPS (pl.35,i) were made in Canongate by George Ziegler in 1696. Their form is very similar to the Monifeith Cups (see p.102).

The silver SWORD HILT (pl.35,ii) is surprisingly early, looking more eighteenth century than seventeenth.

The PAIR OF WINE CUPS (pl.36,i) by Robert Gairdyne of Dundee is a great rarity. Very few pieces of seventeenth century provincial domestic plate of this type have survived. They are engraved with the impaled arms of Sir James Mercer of Aldie and Jean Stewart, eldest daughter of Sir Thomas Stewart of Grantully. Their marriage took place in 1648, but the goblets are unlikely to date from before the Restoration in 1660, when the fortunes of both families took a turn for the better. Charles II stood godfather to their son and gave him, as a christening present, 80 ounces of gilt plate, some of which has survived in the hands of his descendants to this day. The maker of the cups is therefore in all probability the last of the Robert Gairdynes of Dundee, admitted to the Hammermen there in 1649 and continuing in the burgh for at least forty years. His father, who had become a burgess in 1624, died in 1656.

THE OLIPHANT SPOON (pl.36,ii) which, like the Mercer-Stewart wine cups, is in private hands, is at present the only known piece of work by Robert Ker of Canongate, and is most unusually decorated with cinquefoils.

THE COMMUNION BASIN OF DUNDEE, also known as the FEITHIE SALVER (pl.37,i) is a very remarkable and important piece by a skilled maker. Made by Thomas Lindsay, younger, in 1665, it was commissioned by a merchant burgess of Dundee named John Feithie and bears his coat of arms together with the inscription:

"Iohanes Fitheus in amoris tesseram ecclesiae Taodunensis ad sacram caenam celebrandam vas hoc argenteum dono dedit 1665".

The gift is recorded in the town council minutes on 28 March 1665:

"The said day ane silver bassone being giftit be John Feithy, merchand, for the use of the Communion Table, was deliverit to John Tarbet, kirkmaster . . ."

The basin, along with eight Communion cups, was saved from the fire which destroyed the church on the first Sunday morning of January 1841. It was afterwards lost sight of for many years until re-discovered in 1950, hidden at the bottom of an old tea-chest full of waste paper in Dundee City Museum. The discovery was accidental and the basin narrowly escaped being thrown out along with the wrappings.

Lindsay also made a fine PURITAN SPOON, now in the Royal Museum of Scotland, and one of the St. Andrews University archery medals, dated 1683. He was admitted to the Hammermen in Dundee in 1663 and continued there until at least 1688.

Chapter Eleven

THE LATER SEVENTEENTH CENTURY

By the beginning of the eighteenth century Scottish silversmiths had evolved and developed such characteristic forms and designs as they were to achieve. The Union of the Parliaments in 1707 might be said to mark the climax. After it, and perhaps to some extent because of it, decade by decade Scottish forms were merged with English forms and, although some of them survived, they survived only in deliberately perpetuated and self-conscious interpretations.

The Scottish standing mazer ended with the sixteenth century. As we have seen, in the first half of the seventeenth century the goldsmith produced many sacred vessels which are typically Scottish, but he seems to have done little with secular wares. Earliest of exclusively Scots secular vessels to emerge, and quite the most important, is the quaich; but this had had a long history before its possibilities were explored by the silversmiths in the second half of the seventeenth century.

No doubt the quaich began as a wooden or horn drinking cup. Its earlier stages are obscure. In the National Museum there is an example in marble. It has three lugs or handles and has been attributed to the late sixteenth or early seventeenth century, but two handles are the normal complement and the vessel usually described as a quaich is a shallow bowl with a pair of opposed handles jutting out horizontally from the lip, or just below the lip. 'Quaich' is derived from the Gaelic word *cuach*, which simply means a cup, and among the Celtic people was distinguished from two other primitive vessels, the *slioge*, or shell, and the *corn*, or drinking-horn. One writer claims a connexion with the Greek κυαθος and the Latin *cyathus*.[1] Three good early examples of quaichs carved from the solid were found in the rooftrees of a house in the Abbey Strand, Edinburgh, with papers dated 1690, and those probably represent the vessel in its basic form. At some period, probably quite early in the seventeenth century, the building-up of quaichs by the method of coopering took place,   Pl.46.i

[1] *Historical Catal. of 1911 Exhib.*, Glasgow, p. 688

and this method of construction continued to be popular for a very long time, not only with quaichs but with all the related 'bicker' family which includes cogs, coggies and luggies. In all but the plainest and most workaday examples, it was usual for the alternating wooden staves to be of different colours or even different materials. The woods employed are most often plane-tree, contrasting with the darker laburnum, mahogany or walnut. Coopered quaichs of ivory and ebony are known. Staves are beautifully 'feathered' to each other and call for much skill in construction. In nearly all such stave-constructed quaichs the handles conform closely to a pattern, for they are each part of the stave from which they project and have to be accommodated to the width and nature of it. They are therefore narrow in plan and deep in elevation and tend to fall away towards the ground with a marked droop.

It is during the seventeenth century that goldsmiths began to turn their attention to the quaich. In the first place, no doubt, they were called in to mount and embellish old wooden quaichs which had become favourites, and the usual mounts took the forms of rims, feet, plates fitted to the tops of the lugs, and sometimes hoops or bands replacing the cane or withy bindings. Very often the rims and lug-plates were scalloped and sometimes they were secured by pins run through the scallops, these in themselves forming a crude sort of decoration. Occasionally the interior was furnished with a silver boss, Pl. 46.ii or print. A walnut quaich which was in the possession of the late Mr. Moir Carnegie has a boss engraved with the inscription *K. Charles the 2nd 1660 Restauration AMEN*. Frequently lug-plates are engraved with initials which are doubtless those of man and wife. These silver-mounted quaichs, especially when the staves are variegated, are handsome pieces, and they range in size from 2 or 3 inches in diameter to 7 or 8 inches and more.

By the second half of the century quaichs were being executed entirely in silver. One lent to the Royal Academy Exhibition of Scottish Art in 1939 by Mr. George Henderson is an Aberdeen piece with a mark which appears to be Thomas Moncur's, which might refer it back almost to the middle years of the century. Such silver quaichs, and especially the earlier ones, are frequently engraved with lines in imitation of the joints of the staves. In addition, certain other engraved features are found again and again, notably a Tudor rose alternating with a tulip which no doubt points to the accession of the House of Orange. These flower motifs appear to have been copied in some instances at least quite mechanically, and comparisons between pieces separated by a generation or two show the smallest details to have been slavishly repeated. This association of rose and tulip is also found on Scottish pistols of the time and irresistably suggests a judicious blend of Orange and Jacobite. As a rule thistles do not appear, although a somewhat curious bowl-quaich of Aberdeen origin, shown in the 1931 Scottish Exhibition in London, bore thistles, roses and foliage in *repoussé*. I have not examined this example, which was dated about 1700, but the possibility occurs that the *repoussé* work was done later. A Banff quaich of about 1680 lent to the 1939 exhibition by Major H. N. Robertson had decoration of flowers and birds. Such silver quaichs vary much in form. A quaich is essentially wide and rather shallow, with no very great capacity, a shape determined largely by the earlier wooden types, and the best of the silver ones perpetuate this. A good example was the piece by Robert Cruickshank of Old Aberdeen, which was in the collection of the late Major J. Milne-Davidson. Gradually the bowl tends to deepen until the object ceases to be a quaich and becomes a bowl with handles, and nearly all modern reproductions repeat this error which results in stiffness and inelegance. Goldsmiths for some reason also seldom imitated the type of handle or lug common to the wood-stave quaichs, but substituted a pair of rather clumsy horizontal handles dropped at the ends. These are usually engraved with the initials of the original owner.

Several quaichs have found their way into the possession of the Church of Scotland. They are Edinburgh pieces. One is at Alvah in Aberdeenshire. It is nearly 6½ inches in diameter and bears the initials of Sir Alexander Urquhart of Cromarty, and it was made during one of the deaconates of Patrick Borthwick (1661–63, 1683–84), the maker being Edward Cleghorne. An inventory of 1745 suggests that it was used for the collection of money at the Sacrament, and Burns believes it to have been used for Communion purposes,[1] but its present use is as a baptismal basin. The four Ayr quaichs are handsome pieces, although later in date. On one lug is engraved '1722', and since this is the work of Charles Dickson it is probably close to the actual date. They are still used for Communion purposes and therefore have the distinction of being the only quaichs so employed.

The normal secular uses of the quaich were many and various. It is probable that the large ones served for companies on special occasions, as the mazers did in monasteries in the middle ages; and no doubt they were also made use of for such foods as porridge. The placing of the lugs suggests the act of handing on

Pl. 48.i

---

[1] *Scot. Comm. Plate*, p. 401

PLATE 45

Patch Box: Glasgow, 1695.
Maker: William Clark *(p.109)*

The Ayr Spoon: possible Ayr, late 17th century.
Maker's mark: M.C. *(pp.110 & 123)*

Postman's Blazon, St. Andrews University: probably 17th century

PLATE 46

Silver-mounted Quaich: second half 17th century *(pp.117-118)*

Silver-mounted Quaich of walnut bound with willow: about 1660 *(p.118)*

PLATE 47

Quaich: Glasgow, c.1709. Maker: William Clark

Quaich: Edinburgh, 1685-86. Maker: James Penman

PLATE 48

Quaich used as a Communion Cup, Alvah: Edinburgh, 1663-84. Maker: Edward Cleghorne *(p.119)*

Mug of 'thistle' type: Edinburgh, 1696-97. Maker: Alexander Forbes *(p.120)*

PLATE 49

Tankard: Edinburgh, 1700–01. Maker: Edward Penman (*p.132*)

Peg Tankard: Edinburgh, 1663–81. Maker: Edward Cleghorne (*p.121*)

PLATE 50

Pair of Tankards: Edinburgh, 1685-86. Maker: James Cockburn (*p.121*)

PLATE 51

Castor: Edinburgh, 1694–95. Maker: George Yorstoune *(p.122)*

Salver on foot, or Tazza: Edinburgh, about 1670. Maker: William Law

PLATE 52

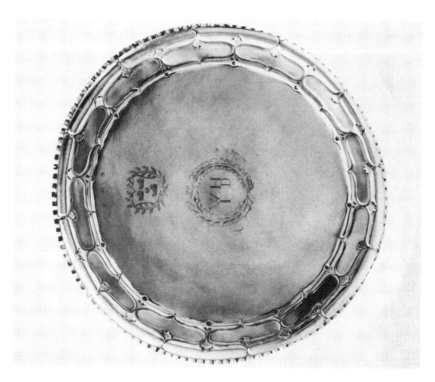

Salver on foot: Edinburgh, c.1675(?)
Maker: probably William Law (p.127)

The Strathmore Salver: Edinburgh, c.1670.
Maker: Alexander Scott (p.127)

the cup, just as do the projecting handles of offertory bags. Clearly, small quaichs were meant to contain more potent drinks such as brandy or whisky or possibly even the mead or mead-like beverages which must sometimes have been brewed from the dregs in straining heather honey, but certainly not ale, as has sometimes been suggested, for there were tankards and mugs in great variety and of more generous capacity for malted liquors. The number of quaichs associated with historic personages, such as those linked with the name of Prince Charles Edward or the quaich made from the Wallace oak at Torwood, Stirlingshire, make it obvious that this type of vessel was held in particular regard and had a special significance in Scottish social ritual. In the seventeenth and eighteenth centuries men no doubt carried small quaichs in their pockets as they carried knives, spoons and snuff-boxes. That their primary purpose was to contain drink rather than food is suggested by some of the mottoes which are engraved on them, such as the Gaelic *squab ase*, the meaning of which is 'sweep it up'.

Another form of cup peculiar to Scotland, and probably common at one time although now unknown to most, is the beautiful little mug which has come to be known as a thistle-cup. Its essential features are a markedly everted lip, an S-shaped ribbon handle usually with beaded decoration, a waist-fillet, and a calyx of *appliqué* lobes rising from the foot towards the waist. Such cups are unusually pleasing and it is surprising that nothing like them occurs beyond the borders of Scotland. They were made in many sizes ranging from the proportions of a tea-cup, or even a breakfast-cup, down to miniatures which could only have been used for dolls' tea-parties. The Royal Scottish Museum possesses two, one of them an Edinburgh cup of 1696 and the other made in Glasgow in 1705. The Edinburgh cup, by Alexander Forbes, has a specially graceful form and several refinements, as for example the embellishments of the handle and the notching of waist-band and foot. Thistle-cups were also made in other centres. Fine Aberdeen ones of about 1695 are in the collections of Mr. C. H. King and Mr. John Noble, and the Bute collection contains two attractive miniature pieces made in Inverness, one by Elphinstone about 1690 and the other of about 1700 with the MK mark which I think probably signifies Simon Mackenzie. Lord Bute also has a Canongate thistle cup of about 1694 bearing a punch which is probably Walter Graham's. It seems likely that these little mugs came into fashion towards the close of Charles II's reign, for the earliest of which I have records are one by Andrew Law of Edinburgh, 1682,

Pl.48.ii
Pl.81.ii

in the Bute collection, and the two which are dated 1685 in the possession of George Heriot's Trust.

For the rest, it is simpler to say what is not typical than it is to point to markedly Scottish types or features. Those delightful little wine-cups, strawberry dishes and other vessels of thin metal with beaten and engraved designs, which in England were made in great numbers during the Commonwealth and Protectorate, have no parallel in Scotland; and there is also little of that exuberant sort of silver which followed the Restoration in England. Among the few highly-decorated pieces is the beautiful porringer with cover in Mr. John Noble's collection. It is ornamented with acanthus leaves in *repoussé* and surmounted by a strawberry finial. Quite exceptional among Scottish goldsmiths' work, this is an Edinburgh piece of 1682 by Alexander Reid, John Borthwick being the assay-master. It is a pity that little of Reid's work has survived. The tankards which are among the glories of Charles II's reign in England are in Scotland fortunately matched by some fine pieces, although beer and ale drinking were not so general as they were in the south. One of the earliest and finest is an Edinburgh peg-tankard of 1663–80, by Edward Cleghorne, in Sir John Stirling Maxwell's collection. It has three vigorous claw-and-ball feet and much elaborate floral design in *repoussé* embellished with engraving. This type of tankard has a foreign appearance and no doubt was introduced from Scandinavia, with which Scotland had many links, military and economic, in the seventeenth century. It is significant that in England these footed tankards are found only with Hull, Newcastle and York marks and Mr. Oman states that they are derived from Denmark.[1] The peg-measures appear also on the Newcastle tankard in Boston. A superb pair of tankards of very un-Scottish appearance, with lion thumb-pieces recalling the tankard illustrated by Jackson (Vol. II, fig. 990), was lent anonymously to the exhibition of Scottish silver at the Royal Scottish Museum in 1948. They were Edinburgh pieces of 1685, by James Cockburn. Lord Bute owns handsome tankards more akin to the usual English model, both of Edinburgh origin, one of 1698 by John Seatoun and one of 1701 by Thomas Ker. Edward Penman is both maker and assay-master of a big tankard in perfect condition, of date 1700, in the collection of the Duke of Buccleuch. Its gadrooned foot matches the edge of the lid, and the finial is mounted on an attractive device of cut-card work.

The large, cylindrical 'lighthouse' sugar-casters found in England before

Pl.60.ii

Pl.49.i

Pl.50

---

[1] *English Domestic Silver*, p. 143

1700 also occur in Scotland, and to the casual eye there is little to distinguish the Scottish ones except perhaps that the detail is rather less sophisticated. In Scotland, the earlier casters are perhaps flatter on the top than they are in England. A massive one bequeathed by J. Cathcart White to the Royal Scottish Museum has more of the gadrooning or roping so often found on English casters of the period, but the finial is mounted on a pretty piece of cut-card work. It is an Edinburgh piece of 1690, by James Penman. Bayonet clasps are usual on this type of caster. Lord Bute's collection contains several very attractive examples, including one with splayed sides and another which is transitional between this type and the vase-shaped caster of the eighteenth century.

Pl.51.i A fine Edinburgh 'lighthouse' caster of 1694, by George Yorstoune, belongs to the Lady Vivien Younger. The sets of three, common in England, do not appear to have come into general use in Scotland until after 1700.

Because of its name and supposed origin in a 'fantastical Scot' who wore a scalloped cloak, the monteith might be expected to have been more common in Scotland, but in fact it must have been excessively rare. I know of only three examples, all of outstanding quality. The rarity of this sort of punch-bowl is matched by the rarity of Scottish silver punch-bowls of all sorts. Punch-bowls of earthenware are found in some numbers north of the Tweed. From this it might be deduced that in Scotland punch was indulged in mainly in the humbler homes, were it not for occasional contradictions such as the big, handsome bowl made in Edinburgh in 1692 by John Borthwick and lent to the Royal Academy exhibition of 1939 by Mrs. Stewart Stevenson. Claret was, of course, the national drink so far as the nobility and probably also the middle classes were concerned, and this held true until the convivial link with the Auld Alliance was supplanted by the native-brewed whisky early in the nineteenth century. The earlier of the two monteiths which I have examined[1] belongs to

Pl.57 Lieut.-Colonel J. N. Price Wood. It is a massive thing of fine design, made in Edinburgh in 1698 by Colin McKenzie. The great monteith belonging to the

Pl.63.ii Royal Company of Archers, the Queen's Bodyguard for Scotland, is comparatively late. Also an Edinburgh piece, it came from the workshop of William Ged and is inscribed with the date 20th June, 1720, and to the effect that the bowl was furnished by the Royal Company 'to be shot for as ane annuall pryze at Rovers by the said Company'. The simplicity and fine lines of the

[1] A third is listed in a *Catalogue of a Loan Exhibition of Scottish Art and Antiquities*, London, 1931, p. 5

bowl are difficult to appreciate because of the rows of gold medals attached, now covering three tiers of the plinth as well as the sides of the bowl. There is a handsome and appropriately massive punch-ladle.

One may recognise as Scottish most of the domestic and table silver made in Scotland towards the end of the seventeenth century, although it has no obvious national characteristics. It is as a rule fairly weighty, but ornament and decoration are at a minimum and are often executed without that assurance and sophisticated skill which would be expected in English or foreign silver of the time. The heavy embossing and representational ornament which were borrowed from the Dutch by goldsmiths further south during Charles II's reign are hardly ever imitated in Scotland, and then generally with a crudity of execution which, while it may in its ingenuousness have much charm for modern collectors, reveals the total lack of any tradition of ornamental work among the imitators. The *chinoiserie* which became so popular in England must have been excessively rare in Scotland, no doubt because she had no trade direct with the East, but James Cockburn of Edinburgh about 1685 made a small tea caddy simply engraved in this spirit. When the trefid type   Pl.53.ii
of spoon came to Scotland, perhaps in the 'sixties, it drove out the native disc-end, but Scottish trefids are frequently recognisable, without any very close scrutiny, because of small variations in form or proportion or, as in the case of the Ayr spoon, by the engraving. Col. Price Wood possesses what must be the   Pl.45.ii
earliest set of four such trefids, made probably in the 'seventies. How noted that Edinburgh and Glasgow trefids are usually more markedly Scottish than those made further north.[1] The broad splay of the ends of Glasgow trefids, mentioned by How, is very clear in the case of the beautifully-marked set of six by Robert Brook, lent to the Glasgow Exhibition of 1938 by Mr. John R. Campbell. Mr. John Noble has a set of six fine dinner-knives made in Edinburgh about 1684 by George Yorstoune, but it would be difficult to point to any markedly Scottish feature in them.

The extinction of the Scottish Parliament in the early eighteenth century must have involved the noble families of Scotland in comparatively frequent visits to London, and there is small doubt they must have bought much of their domestic plate from London goldsmiths. This would certainly apply to elaborate groups of articles such as toilet-services. So far as my knowledge goes, only one complete Scottish toilet-set has survived, that lent by Mr. William Stirling   Pl.62

[1] *Engl. and Scot. Silver Spoons*, Vol. II, p. 361

PLATE 53

Trefid Spoons, from set of our earliest known: Edinburgh, 1665–80. Maker: Alexander Reid
(p.123)

Tea Caddy: Edinburgh, c.1685.
Maker: James Cockburn *(p.123)*

PLATE 54

Writing Equipage of Nicol Sommervell, unscrewed to show its various parts: Edinburgh, 1674.
Maker: Thomas Cleghorn *(p.127)*

Pair of Chamber Candlesticks: Edinburgh, 1693-94. Maker: James Penman *(p.128)*

PLATE 55

The Forsyth Chalice and Paten: Edinburgh, c.1688. Maker: Zacharius Mellinus *(p.128)*

Two-handled Porringer: Edinburgh, 1675-77. Maker: William Law *(p.128)*

PLATE 56

Wall-Sconce, one of pair: Edinburgh, 1698-99. Maker: James Penman *(p.124)*

PLATE 57

Monteith Bowl: Edinburgh, 1698-99. Maker: Colin McKenzie (p. 122)

PLATE 58

Communion Cup of Trinity Church, Edinburgh: Edinburgh, 1698-99.
Maker: Thomas Ker (*p.128*)

Tankard showing cut-card work and beaded rat-tail: Edinburgh,
1697-98. Maker: Robert Bruce (*p.128*)

PLATE 59

Oval Box: Glasgow, 1685–86, Maker: Robert Brock *(p.128)*

Wine Taster: Edinburgh, 1637–39 or 1646–48. Maker: Thomas Cleghorn *(p.128)*

PLATE 60

Covered Porringer: Edinburgh, 1682–83. Maker: Alexander Reid (*p.121*)

Covered Cup: Edinburgh, 1693–94. Maker: James Penman

to the Royal Academy in 1938. It is an Edinburgh product of 1703, by Colin McKenzie. It includes mirror, brushes and whisks, bottles, bowls, a large oblong box and four circular ones, two candlesticks and a pincushion, all of which have a functional austerity expected in Scottish pieces. The only decoration is the engraved cartouche on each piece. It is interesting that the set belonged to the Hon. Marion Stewart, daughter of the fifth Lord Blantyre, who married James Stirling of Keir in 1704, because it was this Lord Blantyre who inherited from his second cousin, 'La Belle Stewart', the Duchess of Richmond and Lennox, a French toilet-set which is perhaps the finest thing of its kind in existence, discovered in an attic in one of the towers of Lennoxlove about fifty years ago. Foreign indeed to Scottish silversmiths was the sort of elegance sought by purchasers of those ornaments of the boudoir. I know of only one other Scottish toilet article. Thomas Ker of Edinburgh in 1706 contributed a large, oblong box to a toilet set by Anthony Nelme which was formerly at Hopetoun House but changed hands at Sotheby's in 1953. At the same sale Hopetoun lost a pair of wall-sconces which are probably unique among Scottish silver. They are Edinburgh work of 1698 by James Penman. The oval, convex mirror-surface is surrounded by intricate *repoussé* decoration comprising *amorini* with fruit and scrolls, a most unusual departure in design for any Scottish craftsman of the time. Another unusual pair of lighting appliances are the charming bedroom candlesticks with octagonal bases and roped edges belonging to Mr. John Noble. They are by James Penman, and of date 1693.

Pl.64.ii

Pl.56

Pl.54.ii

There remains still to be mentioned in this chapter two notable and unique pieces of the seventeenth century. The first of the two, and the better-known, is the pretty little Mass bell in the possession of the Bishop of Aberdeen. James VII, while Duke of York, took up residence in the Palace of Holyroodhouse and in the chapel celebrated Mass for his Catholic subjects. After the landing of William of Orange and the defeat of James at the Battle of the Boyne the Edinburgh mob, supported by six hundred of the Town Guard, invaded the Palace and sacked the chapel. Some sacred vessels, with them the Mass bell, were preserved by the chaplain, Father David Burnett. The bell is a simple little article with a baluster handle, engraved with the initials JR, crowned. It has the assay-master's punch of John Borthwick and was made in Edinburgh in 1686, evidently specially for the Palace. The maker's mark, ZM, is curiously given as unknown in the catalogue of the 1939 exhibition, but is

Pl.33.i

clearly the mark of Zacharias Mellinus. Mr. Oman draws my attention to the probability that this bell was part of the set mentioned in the inventory of the goods of the King.[1] The second piece—at the time of writing, at least—has a less happy history. It is the baton of the Master of the Household, until recently   Pl.61
preserved by the Duke of Argyll at Inveraray Castle. In 1953 this valuable relic was stolen from the castle together with other plate, and no traces of it have as yet been found. The baton was described in the inventory as 'seventeenth-century Scottish', and a brief examination persuaded me of the probability of this. No maker's mark or other punch appeared anywhere on the piece, but the execution suggested a native craftsman. The baton consists, or consisted, of a wooden staff of octagonal section about 3 feet long covered with crimson velvet with applied thistles of silver gilt, completed by a silver-gilt head comprising crown, orb and cross surmounted by a lion sejant. Unhappily the robbers seemed to be people of little discrimination or even shrewdness, for they dropped at least one fine thing on their flight, and since the baton is of little intrinsic value they may have disposed of it in a summary way, unaware of its historical and artistic importance. It has not been possible to secure a good direct photograph, but the Duke of Argyll has kindly drawn my attention to representations of this relic in several family portraits, and that shown in the picture of the 4th Duke, now in the Scottish National Portrait Gallery, is reproduced.

[1] *Archaeologia*, XVIII, p. 233.

NOTES TO CHAPTER XI

CUP AND COVER OR PORRINGER (p.121, line 10 & pl.60,ii)

The collection of the late Mr. John Noble of Ardkinglas has now been dispersed. The two-handled cup and cover or porringer by Alexander Reid from that collection, made famous by its use as the illustration on the dust cover of the first edition of this book, is now in the Royal Museum of Scotland.

MONTEITHS (p.120, second paragraph)

At least ten Scottish Monteiths are known and there are probably more in private hands. All date between 1698 and 1746, the latter being much later than the general run of English examples. Aberdeen City Museum has one of 1746-7, which they acquired recently after the Reviewing Committee on the Export of Works of Art had recommended an export stop. The Monteith which once belonged to Lieutenant-Colonel Wood (Pl.57) also came up for an export licence before the same committee, in 1969, and was eventually bought by the Edinburgh City Museum, Huntly House, where it now reposes.

COURT AND PARLIAMENT (p.123, line 30)

This whole paragraph more properly belongs to Chapter XII. The first line is a slip of the pen; the Court had passed south a century earlier in 1603. It was the Parliament of Scotland that ceased to function in 1707 and this is the event to which Mr. Finlay had intended to refer.

BATON OF THE MASTER OF THE HOUSEHOLD (p.125, end, & pl.61)

The present Duke of Argyll has had a replacement baton made by Messrs. Hamilton and Inches of Edinburgh, copied partly from the portrait of the 4th Duke.

NEW ILLUSTRATIONS

Ten pieces of late seventeenth-century silver are newly illustrated in this chapter, all of them either belonging to, or on loan to, the Royal Museum of Scotland:

THE STRATHMORE SALVER (pl.52,i) Edinburgh 1667-9, by Alexander Scott. The rim is decorated with acanthus foliage and raised embossed ovals; the print is engraved (slightly later) with the arms of Patrick Lyon, 1st Earl of Strathmore. The earl set about rebuilding the family fortunes after the Restoration and assembled a quantity of plate in the process. He noted in his *Book of Records* that in 1684 he bought £3,000 Scots worth of new and second-hand plate from James Cockburn, goldsmith in Edinburgh. Cockburn agreed to remove the existing armorials from the second-hand items and engrave the Strathmore arms in their place. This is a valuable piece of evidence pointing to the practice of buying and selling second-hand plate, rather than melting it down and starting afresh. The fact that the salver was only some fifteen years old when it changed hands should make one more aware of the importance of paying close attention to the arms and other engraving found on silver. It is rather too glib to dismiss an object just because its arms can be shown not to be exactly contemporary with its manufacture. In this instance, that fact is not only part of the legitimate history of the piece, it is arguably the most interesting part.

SALVER ON FOOT (pl.52,ii), Edinburgh c.1675. Maker probably William Law. The engraved coat of arms, initials and wreath are all of later date. This is another instance of something which must have changed owners not all that long after it was made.

WRITING EQUIPAGE OF NICOL SOMMERVELL (pl.54,i), Edinburgh 1674, by Thomas Cleghorn. This entertaining piece is inscribed round the rim of the sand box:

"Giftit be the Goldsmiths of Edr to Nicol Sommervell their clerk anno 1674".

Sommervell was Clerk to the Incorporation from 1674 until 1706 and the minutes during these years are written in his hand. When the five parts (sander, candle holder, ink well, seal and quill holder) are screwed together they form the shape of a table bell with a cylindrical handle.

PAIR OF CHAMBER CANDLESTICKS on octagonal bases (pl.54,ii) Edinburgh 1693-4 by James Penman. This pair is referred to in the text as being in the Noble Collection, and is now in the Royal Museum of Scotland.

THE FORSYTH CHALICE AND PATEN (pl.55,i), Edinburgh 1688, by Zacharias Mellinus. Height 7¾". This Chalice and the Holyrood Sanctus Bell are the only two known pieces by Mellinus. The Chalice and Paten were made for Fr. Henry Forsyth, SJ, who worked among the Gaelic-speaking catholics around Braemar on Deeside for some twenty years until his death on 8 November 1708. His initials and the date 1688 are scratched on both Chalice and Paten. More is said about them in the *Innes Review*, Vol. XVIII, p.145 (1967). An examination of the Chalice shows that originally it was made in three parts, designed to unscrew above and below the knopped stem, so as to be more easily hidden and transported. It has since been altered so that it no longer comes apart. In use at Presham in Banffshire until about twenty-five years ago, it is now on loan from the Scottish Catholic Hierarchy to the Royal Museum of Scotland.

TWO-HANDLED PORRINGER (pl.55,ii), Edinburgh 1675-7, by William Law. This type of porringer is a rarity in Scotland. It probably once had a lid.

TANKARD (pl.58,i), Edinburgh 1697-8, by Robert Bruce. This is illustrated in order to show a fine example of Scottish cut-card work, a technique not much practised north of the border.

COMMUNION CUP OF TRINITY CHURCH, Edinburgh (pl.58,ii), Edinburgh 1698-9, by Thomas Ker.

OVAL TOBACCO BOX (pl.59,i), Glasgow 1698-9, by Robert Brock.

WINE TASTER (pl.59,ii), Edinburgh 1637-9 or 1646-8, by Thomas Cleghorn. Only one other Scottish wine taster has come to my attention; it is by Thomas Moncur of Aberdeen and belongs to Messrs. Jamieson and Carry, jewellers of that city.

Chapter Twelve

EDINBURGH—THE GOLDEN AGE

I T might be claimed that the Scottish goldsmiths attained their peak, technically and aesthetically, in the years following 1700, and this period reflects a dramatic contrast of poverty and riches. These two states were, in Scotland, more entangled perhaps than in most other countries. Social status was not demarcated as in England, far less as in France. But the contrast of extremes was violent. About this time the number of poor is said to have doubled and vagrants reached the figure of 200,000; yet at the other end of the scale the nobility and gentry indulged in extravagant habits and welcomed occasions for pomp and pageantry. They staged colourful state entries and solemn funeral processions which progressed for great distances across the country, and in eating and drinking especially they spared no expense. A MS. household book of the Duchess of Buccleuch,[1] compiled at Dalkeith in 1701 and 1702, reveals interesting examples of everyday fare, such as the following:

Dinner: first course, haunch of venison boiled; roast mutton; veal collops; boiled fish; pidgeon pye; brown fricasee of rabbits; whiting pottage. Second course: roasted wild fowl; roasted chickens; eggs in gravy; fried floundres; collard pig; buttered crabs; tarts.

The *menu* is perhaps more substantial than discriminating. One can understand how Lauder of Fountainhall, when in France, greeted the substitution of frogs' legs for pullets' with 'such damned cheats be all the French!' But gross though the feeding may often have been, one must assume certain standards of display if not of elegance at table. No doubt meat and game were dished in a style which did credit to the house. It must be remembered, too, that in those days when coin was so scarce that 'siller' became synonymous with money a man invested much of his wealth in plate as good as he could buy. In public life, too, there was a liking for display, and the Edinburgh goldsmiths must have profited by the sycophantic attitude of their civic authorities towards the later Stewart kings, a contemptible pose that owed nothing to loyalty and which in due course was easily transferred to 'Dutch William'. Again and again the city

[1] Hugo Arnot: *The History of Edinburgh*, (1788), p.199

129

fathers arranged costly feasts and processions. An entertainment given to James VII is said to have cost £1,400 sterling.

There is curiously little evidence of the import of fine plate from abroad. Lading lists in, for example, the Port of Leith mention neither silver nor jewellery among a great variety of merchandise. The national balance of trade was yet too adverse. Some superb foreign wares there must have been in the larger houses, brought in by those who had travelled abroad or lived in the south: as, for example, the magnificent silver-gilt toilet service of Frances Stewart, Duchess of Richmond and Lennox— 'La Belle Stewart', the coy and frivolous favourite of Charles II—mentioned in the last chapter. At a humbler level there must have been fairly good custom for Scottish craftsmen, especially for those of Edinburgh. The Edinburgh goldsmiths were men of standing.[1] They were the *élite* of the city's tradesmen and strutted on the plainstanes in cocked hats, with scarlet cloaks and gold-mounted canes. It is claimed that down to the year 1780 there was not a goldsmith in Edinburgh who did not labour at his bench. Their shops were clustered in or near Parliament Close, where Goldsmiths' Hall was then situated. These shops were small—George Heriot's, at the beginning of the seventeenth century, is reputed to have been no more than seven feet square!—but they appear to have done a big trade in domestic pieces. Country couples went to them for their wedding-rings and silver spoons, all of which had to be ordered long beforehand since the goldsmiths kept little in stock. To complete the deal, it was usual for craftsman and customer to adjourn to the Baijen Hole, a baker's shop, or to John's Coffee House, a famous *howff* in the north-east corner of Parliament Close.

There is not a great deal of evidence relating to the prices asked by the goldsmiths, or to the manner in which they conducted their businesses, but quite recently an account-book of one of them has been discovered.[2] It belonged to John Rollo. Rollo later became the 6th Baron Rollo: an instance of how, in Scotland, sons of the nobility sometimes engaged in trade. He was apprenticed to Harry Beathune in 1724 and was admitted to the Incorporation in 1731, in June of which year he opened this account-book, entitling it 'Ledger No. A'. The last entry is for 1737, and many blank pages follow, so that the business would appear to have ceased in that year. Entries are detailed. For example:

[1] Grant: *Old and New Edinburgh*, Vol. I, p. 174
[2] MS. Ledger, Central Library, Edinburgh

To 2 silver jugs, wt. 11 oz. 12 dr. £3. 2. 8d.
To making ditto 10. 0d.
To Duty 5. 10½d.

The total cost of two candlesticks, weight 14 oz., is £5 13s. A 'teapott' of 21 oz. costs eight guineas, with an additional 8s. for 'engraving round the mouth'. A salver of 50 oz. costs £20 7s. 7d.; a tankard of 39 oz., £14 17s. 3d.; a tea-kettle of 65 oz. with engraving, £28 2s. 8d.; a coffee-pot of 62 oz., £24 16s. 8d.; a punch-bowl of 45 oz., £18. In the big majority of cases orders are for small items such as tea-spoons, tea-tongs, buckles, and even for cleaning and mending watches. There are one or two sword-hilts, including a broadsword-hilt for the Duke of Perth at £11 11s. 8d., and it is interesting to remember that the man to whom Rollo was apprenticed, Beathune, made a silver basket-hilt for such a sword, which has survived. There are two other unusual entries. One is for a box for a burgess-ticket, at £12 10s. 11d., executed for 'the good Toun of Edinburgh', as the account has it. The other, for the same patron, is a 'gold coop' of 18 oz., engraved with the Royal Arms and having two ebony handles. The total cost is £95 17s. Is this a race-trophy, like the gold teapots and the large gold cups, to be discussed below? Rollo had a wide variety of clients, ranging between the nobility and the smaller merchants. The largest single account is Lord Ruthven's, amounting in all to £322 19s. 10½d. between 1731 and 1735. It is paid up in full. Also paid in full is Lord Rollo's account, but it has a domestic look and includes such alien things as stockings, shoes, books and 'smouthing irons'.

Pl. 77. ii

The repeated mention in this ledger of duty paid calls attention to Act 6, George I, cap. 11, imposing a duty of 6d. per ounce on all plate made in Great Britain. In conformity with it, on 1st June, 1720, the Scottish standard was raised from 11 oz. fine to 11 oz. 2 dwt. fine, the English standard. It will be recalled that in England, from 1696 until 1720, the standard was raised to 11 oz. 10 dwts. to prevent coin of the realm from being melted down and converted into plate. This is known as Britannia standard. After 1720 goldsmiths had the option of reverting to the old standard or of making plate of the Britannia standard. After the Union Scottish craftsmen were, of course, entitled to make wares of Britannia standard, but, so far as my knowledge goes, they never did so.

Because of the large domestic trade of a humble sort, Scottish styles in silver-ware were particularly sober and depended for their beauty on sheer craftsmanship and elegant line. Brief outbursts of exuberance under Charles II, such as

Mr. Noble's porringer, Sir J. Stirling-Maxwell's peg tankard, or the sconces formerly in Hopetoun House, leave one with a feeling the maker was doing something far out of his usual sphere. Nothing illustrates more vividly the distance in spirit between the capital which had cradled the Stewart dynasty and the capital in which that dynasty dissipated its declining years. Not that a similar sobriety is uncommon in English silver of the late seventeenth century, but there it is perhaps due mainly to the impact of Huguenot workers who came, many of them, from the French provinces. This influx of refugees after the Revocation of the Edict of Nantes was bitterly resented in London. Huguenots came to Scotland in some numbers, but silversmiths do not appear to have been among them.

Notable examples of the fine, simple domestic pieces which are typical of the earliest years of the eighteenth century are of their kind unsurpassed in any country. There is for example the barber's bowl of 1702, by Thomas Ker, in the Earl of Haddington's collection. It is a costly vessel to be employed for everyday purposes, but was clearly made for private use. Ker is also the author of a handsome jug in Lord Bute's collection, a year earlier in date, and of a fine domed tankard, heavily gadrooned, in the same collection. He was apprenticed to James Penman in 1685 and appears to have been at the height of his powers just after 1700. Another apprentice of Penman, who booked his indentures in 1688, is Colin—or Colline, according to the Apprentice Roll—McKenzie, whose father seems to have come from Pluscarden, in Morayshire. McKenzie's work will be considered presently, as most surviving examples date around 1714. John Seatoun was a maker of massive, simple things with fine lines. Lord Rosebery has a splendid tazza by him, of 1708; and the great two-handled covered cup of the following year in Lord Haddington's collection is equally impressive. It is instructive to compare this last with similar types of cup made in England about the same time, many of which are elaborately ornamented with embossing, gadrooning and, before 1700 at least, with intricate cut-card work. Lord Bute also has a handsome tankard by Seatoun. There is an equally impressive one by Edward Penman, of date 1704, in the Royal Scottish Museum. Broadly, Scottish tankards follow the same lines of development as English, the domed or stepped lid appearing early in the reign of Queen Anne, possibly with a finial of acorn type such as the one surmounting Lord Glentanar's peg tankard of 1709, by James Tait. It may be that the bulbous or baluster form of body appeared earlier in Scotland than it did in

Pl.64.i

Pl.60.i

Pl.49.ii

the south, where it is usually given to the middle of the eighteenth century or after, since a fully-developed example of this kind with the Edinburgh date-stamp for 1709 was recently acquired by the Royal Scottish Museum with the aid of the National Art-Collections Fund. This fine tankard has a moulded, domed cover with flattened top and a finial, as well as a thumb-piece of leaf-and-scroll type, while an armorial crest of Macpherson Grant of Ballindalloch is engraved on the body. The maker is Colin McKenzie.

McKenzie's name at once suggests the subject of tea and coffee services, articles in the making of which this craftsman excelled. He is responsible for one of the two earliest known Scottish teapots. Made in 1714, it is in the Bute collection. Jackson illustrates an Edinburgh teapot claimed to be hall-marked 1708,[1] but How scouts the date and places it as not earlier than 1718,[2] and on the evidence of the illustration alone my own inclination would be to date it not earlier than 1725. The earliest recorded English teapot is one of 1670 in the Victoria & Albert Museum, presented by George Lord Berkeley to the Committee of the East India Company. It is of tapering cylinder form and has a handle at right angles to the straight spout. This type does not seem to have been made in Scotland. Indulgence in tea-drinking in England began during Charles II's reign, and Pepys tasted his first cup in 1660; but Scotland does not appear to have been affected by the habit for another thirty or forty years. In Edinburgh, tea was first imported towards the end of the century.[3] A receipt existed, and may still exist, from the East India Company to an Edinburgh merchant for a chest of Bohea at 15s. per pound, the order amounting to a total value of £225 15s. In 1705 the price of Bohea seems to have doubled, and green tea then fetched 16s. per pound. There is little contemporary evidence on the use of tea, coffee or chocolate in Scotland at this time, the normal potations of a well-to-do household being 'claret, sack, canary, mum-beer, herb ale, warm wine and ale'.[4] Meat and drink were taken more often in the taverns than at the family board, a custom which tea itself must have played a major part in altering. Scotland, then, must have passed over the tapering cylindrical, and the pear forms of teapot which occurred in England between about 1680 and 1720 and adopted at once the delightfully functional 'bullet' teapots of which the McKenzie piece mentioned is a fine example.

Those early Scottish teapots are among the most perfectly designed of all

---

[1] *History of English Plate*, Fig. 1270   [2] *Antique Collector*, May, 1939, p. 108
[3] *Old and New Edinburgh*, III, p. 276   [4] Sir J. Foulis of Ravelston: *Account Book*, (1671–1707)

PLATE 61

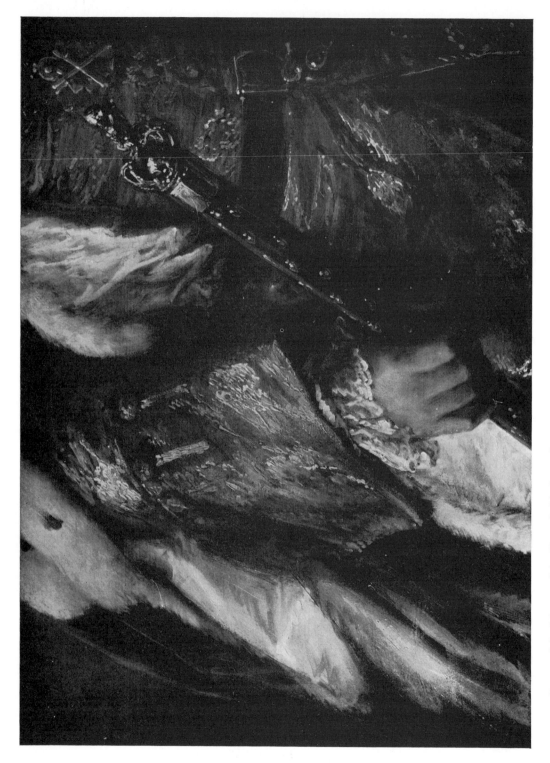

Baton of the Master of the Household, formerly at Inverary Castle. From portrait of 4th Duke of Argyll (p.125)

PLATE 62

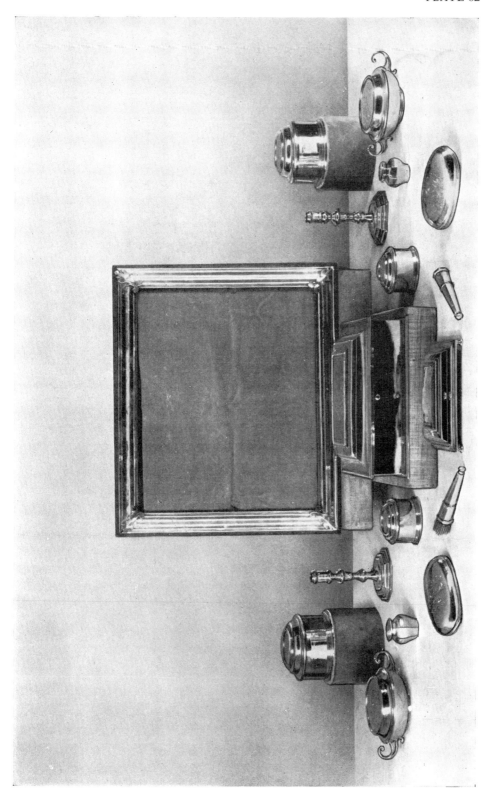

Toilet Set which belonged to the Hon. Marion Stewart, daughter of 5th Lord Blantyre, who married James Stirling of Keir in 1704: Edinburgh, 1703–04. Maker: Colin McKenzie (*p.123*)

PLATE 63

Monteith Bowl: Edinburgh, 1702–03. Maker: James Cockburn (Notes, Ch.12)

Monteith Bowl of the Royal Company of Archers: Edinburgh, 1719–20. Maker: William Ged
(p.122)

PLATE 64

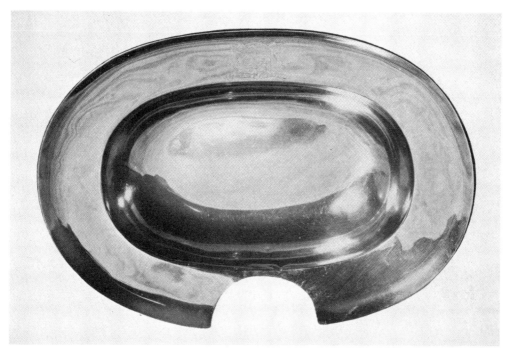

Barber's Bowl: Edinburgh, 1702-03. Maker: Thomas Ker *(p.132)*

Basin, Ewer and Casket: Edinburgh, 1706-07. Maker: Thomas Ker (Notes, Ch.12)

PLATE 65

Three-lugged Quaich: Edinburgh, c.1735. Maker's mark only of Edward Lothian (Notes, Ch.12)

The Hopetoun Spout-cup: Edinburgh, 1707-08. Maker: Walter Scott (Notes, Ch.12)

PLATE 66

Deep Tazza or Fruit Dish: Edinburgh, 1708–09. Maker: John Seatoun *(p.132)*

Two-handled Cup: Edinburgh, 1709–10. Maker: John Seatoun *(p.132)*

PLATE 67

Tankard: Edinburgh, 1709-10. Maker: Colin McKenzie

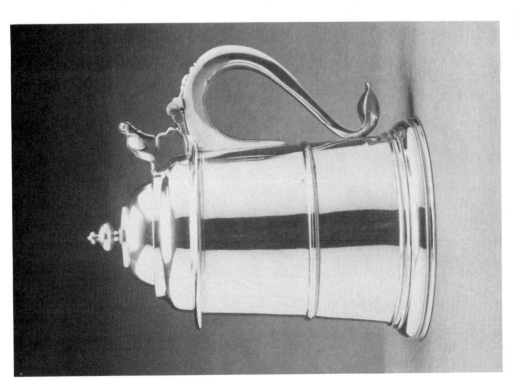

Tankard: Edinburgh, 1705-06. Maker: Alexander Forbes (Notes, Ch.12)

PLATE 68

The Selkirk Chocolate pot, probably a race prize: Edinburgh, 1720–21. Maker: Patrick Murray (Notes, Ch.12)

Laver of Trinity College, Edinburgh: Edinburgh, 1701–02. Maker: Walter Scott (Notes, Ch.12)

PLATE 69

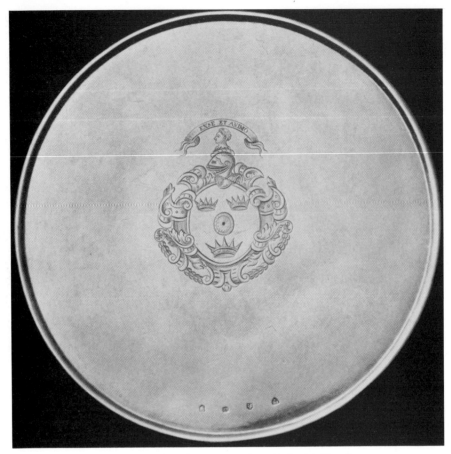

Tazza: Edinburgh, 1710. Maker: Colin McKenzie

Double-lipped Sauceboat: Edinburgh, 1738-39. Maker: John Main (Notes, Ch.12)

PLATE 70

Bowl of silver gilt: Edinburgh, 1736–37. Maker: Dougal Ged

Set of Casters: Edinburgh, 1703–04. Maker (tallest): I. H. Others by John Seatoun

PLATE 71

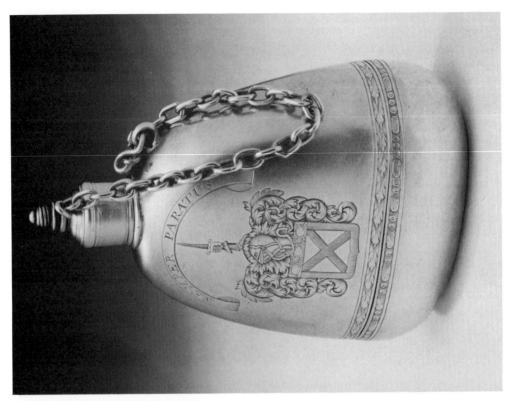

Spirit Flask '1716': Edinburgh, c.1716. Maker's mark only of Alexander Kincaid (Notes, Ch.12)

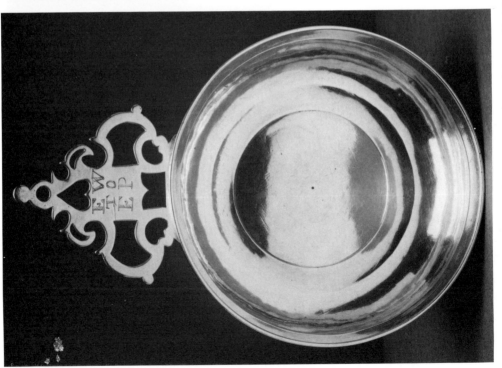

Porringer: Edinburgh, 1722–23. Maker: Henry Bethune (Notes, Ch.12)

PLATE 72

Travelling Canteen of Prince Charles Edward Stewart: Edinburgh, 1740–41. Maker: Ebenezer Oliphant (Notes, Ch.12)

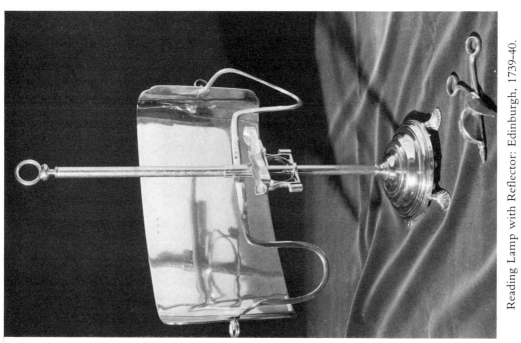

Reading Lamp with Reflector: Edinburgh, 1739–40. Maker: William Aytoun (Notes, Ch.12)

articles of domestic silverware, for their functional shapes anticipate the Bauhaus, yet they incorporate just enough of the element of the purely decorative to give them a spare elegance which is peculiarly appealing. There are two principal forms: a spherical teapot on a moulded foot, and a teapot of elongated bullet type with a flattened base. McKenzie made both types. Spouts are straight, although McKenzie's are very slightly shaped. Lids are flush with the body, small, and usually beautifully hinged. A teapot by McKenzie of 1719, in the Ivory collection, is equipped with a plain, flat stand dating from the previous year. Such stands are characteristic, and may well have been standard accompaniments to the teapots at this time. The first type of teapot is not, in its early stages, a perfect sphere, for it is rather melon shaped, which lends it a certain poise and stability of its own. The flamboyant curve of the handle is a fine foil to the severely simple lines of the pot. By English standards, early Scottish teapots tend to be great in capacity.

Refinement of the lines and balance of these teapots develops steadily throughout the 'twenties. After about 1725 the body becomes something like a perfect sphere. As McKenzie is the chief exponent of the earlier teapots, if we are to judge by survivals, so James Ker is the prince of Edinburgh teapot makers when this article attains its zenith in the late 'twenties and early 'thirties. We know little about him, as a man. Probably he was the son of Thomas Ker, who has been mentioned earlier. The Burgess Roll records that a *jeweller* of the name of James Ker[1] became burgess in 1723 by right of freedom of Thomas Ker, the goldsmith, and the date fits in with what we know of his work, which is eloquent testimony to his talent. A particular elegance touches all he has done. One teapot of 1725 from his bench, of elongated bullet type, has the flanged foot which one looks for in an English teapot[2]; but the proportions and relationships of the parts, as well as the form of the body, are for subtlety worthy of the finest Chinese potters of Ching-te-Chên. His taste is equally impeccable when he designs spherical teapots. Among his masterpieces is a tea-set of 1727 consisting of teapot and stand, sugar bowl and helmet cream-jug, and here he introduces delicately an element of decoration, limited to an engraved band round the lid, while the edges of stand, jug and sugar basin are moulded. Ker's work typifies what is Scottish, and especially what is Edinburgh. Such Scottish teapots could

[1] A London teapot by René Pillean, 1736, has the maker's mark overpunched by James Ker, who may have bought and sold silver. *Connoisseur*, Aug. 1953

[2] Cf. Jackson, fig. 1272 and Oman, Pl. XVI, fig. 66

never be mistaken for English ones. Among the most distinctive Scottish features are the simplicity and near-absence of decoration, the small, close-fitting lid, and perhaps above all the severe, conical form of the straight spout, jutting uncompromisingly from the belly of the teapot without any sort of moulding.

Several of Ker's spherical teapots dating from the 'thirties have survived. Notable among them are two made, not of silver, but of gold, linked not only by authorship but also by the fact that they were evidently given as prizes for the winners of horse-races. One, dating from 1736, is the property of Mr. Michael Noble, and was formerly in the collection of Mr. Anthony de Rothschild. It is engraved on one side with the Royal Arms and on the other with a representation of a jockey on horseback above the inscription *Legacy, 1736*, the horse Legacy having been owned by an ancestor of Mr. de Rothschild. Around the lid there is a certain amount of light engraving.

The other teapot, just a year later in date, belongs to Lord Rosebery. It closely resembles Mr. Noble's, but the chasing round the lid is more elaborate and deeply cut, in a design of flowers and rococo scrolls mingled with shells, while in this case the supporters of the Royal Arms bear standards, one with the cross of St. Andrew and the other with the St. George's cross. Both teapots are 5 inches in diameter. Mr. Noble's weighs $20\frac{3}{4}$ ounces, Lord Rosebery's about the same. Clearly, both were awarded as trophies in Royal races, and there has been much speculation about the identities of the races. The late Mr. E. Alfred Jones assumed that the first was the King's Plate for mares, which Legacy won at Newmarket in April, 1736, and this assumption was perpetuated in the catalogue of the Scottish Exhibition at Burlington House in 1939, although the silver catalogue of the Glasgow Empire Exhibition of the previous year had given Edinburgh as the location of the race won by Legacy. Mr. A. G. Grimwade asserts,[1] I think rightly, that both teapots were prizes for a Royal Plate race in or near Edinburgh, with which he also associates the two splendid gold covered cups of the 'fifties, to be described later. It is, on the face of it, most unlikely that these Edinburgh pieces would have been made for important races in the south, at a time when there were numerous able goldsmiths in London. It seems probable that similar gold trophies were made and presented over a lengthy period covering the years 1736 and 1755, dates of the earliest and latest of the surviving trophies, and it is provoking to realise how much splendid plate must have disappeared. That James Ker should have been ap-

Pl.76.ii

---

[1] *Connoisseur*, Vol. CXXVIII, p. 16

pointed to make the two teapots underlines his position of eminence among Scottish goldsmiths of his day.

The other adjuncts of tea drinking appeared, in Scotland as in England, later than the teapot itself. It must be assumed, therefore, that at first tea was taken in the oriental manner: that is, without sugar, cream or other addition. The earliest English cream jugs date from the beginning of the eighteenth century, though they are very rare. Scotland may have been slightly later in adopting them, but a baluster-shaped jug by Colin McKenzie in the Ivory collection belongs to the year 1719. A helmet type came somewhat later. Also in the Ivory collection is a helmet cream jug of 1732 with an upstanding open scroll handle which might be called of a Scottish type. Its author is William Aytoun. From him too comes the still more unusual spherical, covered cream jug of 1730, recently presented to the Royal Scottish Museum by Sir Eric Miller through the National Art-Collections Fund. Another such cream jug is one

Pl.74   of the items in the magnificent tea service by the same maker, of the year 1733 formerly in the Girdwood collection. Covered sugar bowls are not unknown—there is an Aberdeen example in the Countess of Southesk's collection—but the usual basin is open. A favourite form of sugar basin in the 'thirties was hemispherical with a foot and a flat, everted rim with shaped edge. Two examples are in the Royal Scottish Museum, almost precisely similar although by different makers. Tea caddies seem to have been made seldom at this time, although Mr. W. S. Bell has a simple and most pleasing one by George Cooper of Aberdeen. Silver tea cups are unknown in Scotland— they were soon discarded in England for their heat-conducting qualities— unless the so-called thistle cups were ever put to this use.

Coffee-houses became in Scotland as much the centres of gossip and intrigue as they did in England, yet the practice of coffee-drinking must have spread northwards rather later than did the drinking of tea. The early tapering, cylindrical form of coffee-pot does not appear to have existed in Scotland. On the

Pl.73.i   other hand, there must have been predecessors to the magnificent piece made by Colin McKenzie in 1713, now in Lord Haddington's collection. Very simple in design, this is one of the most beautiful coffee-pots in the United Kingdom. It is of tapering octagonal form with a domed top and a slender, curved spout with a small, hinged cover. The only decoration is an engraved crest. Like most Scottish silverware of the Queen Anne period, it is weighty. In the same collection, and of the same year, is a fine octagonal, baluster-shaped hot-milk jug by McKenzie in the family tradition of pure, functional form. An early coffee-urn, made by Hugh Gordon in 1729, is in Mr. John Noble's collection. Chocolate-drinking cannot have been popular in Scotland, as there are no chocolate pots until a much later date.

Pl.73.i

There is a rather curious scarcity of smaller table silver at this period. After the set of six dinner knives of about 1684, by George Yorstoune, in Mr. Noble's possession, the only considerable group of cutlery is a dessert service of 1709 by Robert Bruce. It now comprises twelve forks, three spoons and eight knives, and belongs to the Marquess of Bute. As regards salts, the form used appears to have been the trencher, and the forms of condiment receptacle characteristic of the Scots table do not appear until much later. Pepper-casters were not really common in either kingdom until well into the eighteenth century, although some Elizabethan bell-salts had receptacles for pepper. The Earl of Moray has a pepper-pot made by Colin McKenzie about the end of the seventeenth century, and Mr. Noble has one by John Seatoune, made in 1723. In Scotland, the sugar-caster is the only type which has survived in any numbers from the early years of the eighteenth century. Some attractive forms appeared after the passing of the cylindrical caster of the late seventeenth century. There is, for instance, the caster with its upper portion cylindrical and tapering and its lower part bulbous. In some of them, notably those in the Bute and the Strathmore collections, the piercing of the apertures is particularly elegant. Such casters are quite distinct from English sorts and are recognisable as Scottish at a glance. They retain the character of the older cylindrical caster and add to it sophistication with an air which is more than a little foreign.

Lighting appliances largely follow the same line of development as they do in England. From about 1700 onwards they are normally of baluster shape, heavily moulded, with fixed nozzles. Several sets fortunately survive. In the Cathcart White collection bequeathed to the Royal Scottish Museum is a fine group of four, of date 1707, by James Simpson, and Mr. John Noble has four of 1725, by James Taitt. One of the most remarkable sets of all belonged to the Marquess of Linlithgow. It consisted of four table candlesticks and a pair of three-light branches to fit. The baluster stems were octagonal in section and the moulded bases were engraved with a crest. They were made by Colin McKenzie in 1710. The branches were also of octagonal section and were gracefully curved and were engraved with the same crest. They were made in 1728 and marked on arms and wax-pans by James Ker. In both cases James Penman was

Pl.79.i

PLATE 73

Coffee-Pot and Hot Milk Jug: Edinburgh, 1713-14. Maker: Colin McKenzie *(pp.136 & 137)*

Covered Sugar Bowl: Edinburgh, 1724-25. Maker: James Ker (Notes, Ch. 12)

PLATE 74

Tea Service: Edinburgh, 1733-34. Maker: William Aytoun *(p. 136)*

PLATE 75

Tea Pot: Edinburgh, 1719-20. Maker: Henry Bethune (Notes, Ch.12)

Tea Pot: Edinburgh, 1719-20. Maker: Colin McKenzie

PLATE 76

Tea Pot: Edinburgh, 1722-23. Maker: James Mitchellsone

Gold Tea Pot: Edinburgh, 1737. Maker: James Ker *(p.135)*

PLATE 77

Dish: Edinburgh, 1731-32. Maker: John Main

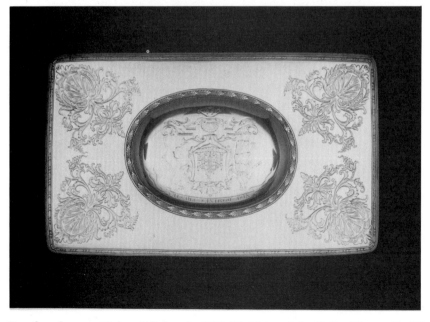

Box for a burgess Ticket: Edinburgh, 1736-37. Maker: John Rollo (Notes, Ch.12)

PLATE 78

Salver: Edinburgh, 1741–42. Maker: Dougal Ged

PLATE 79

Candlesticks with Branches: Edinburgh, 1710-11 and 1728-29 (branches). Maker: Colin McKenzie, Branches by James Ker *(p.137)*

Set of Candlesticks: Edinburgh, 1748-49. Maker: William Aytoun

PLATE 80

Cream Jug: Edinburgh, 1719-20.
Maker: Mungo Yorstoun

Cream Jug: Edinburgh,1730-31.
Maker: William Aytoun (Notes, Ch.12)

Silver gilt Mug: Edinburgh, 1744-45.
Maker: Lawrence Oliphant (Notes, Ch.12)

Covered Cream Jug: Edinburgh, 1744-45.
Maker: William Dempster (Notes, Ch.12)

PLATE 81

Cake-basket: Edinburgh, 1747–48. Maker: William Dempster (Notes, Ch.12)

Tea Pot: Edinburgh, 1758–59. Maker: Robert Gordon; Mug of 'thistle' type: Glasgow, c.1705.
Maker: John Luke *(p.120)*

PLATE 82

Golf-Club and Balls of the Royal and Ancient Golf Club, St. Andrews: mid-18th century onwards
(p.165)

Coffee Pot: Edinburgh, 1750–51. Maker: Edward Lothian

PLATE 83

Coffee Urn: Edinburgh, 1729-30. Maker: Hugh Gordon

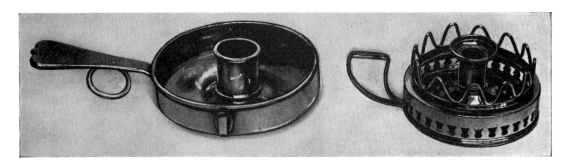

Hand Candlestick: Edinburgh, 1789-90. Maker: IB; Taper Stick: Edinburgh, 1809-10. Maker: Cunningham and Simpson

PLATE 84

Kettle and Stand: Edinburgh, 1753–54. Maker: William Gilchrist *(p.158)*

assay-master. These superb pieces weighed in all 101 ounces and were sold at Sotheby's in 1953 for £1,300. A charming pair of chamber candlesticks of 1693 is in Mr. John Noble's collection. The base is octagonal and flat, with roped border, and there is a pleasing finger-ring handle. They are by James Penman.

The massive, functional simplicity of Scottish silver of the Queen Anne and early Georgian periods should be considered carefully against the social and economic conditions of that time. At first appearance it seems to belie the depressing effect on trade which we know to have been the immediate result of the Union. The Kers, McKenzie, Aytoun and other goldsmiths of the capital city developed their skills at a time when coinage was so scarce that it was often difficult enough to find silver to cover a pound note. Glasgow was soon to win certain benefits from the Union; but the Edinburgh which was and which continued to be the centre of the goldsmiths' craft faced the brunt of a political measure which deprived her, in effect, of her status and of most of the profits which are the perquisites of a capital. Her assets, always largely of the invisible kind, became invisible in quite another sense. For instance, she was the stronghold of the Scottish legal system, yet after the Union the salaries of high law officers were sometimes twelve months in arrears. It has been said that, linked with the poverty of Scotland at this time, went a corresponding deadness of the mind; but one is tempted to see in the sterling workmanship and functional beauty of McKenzie's coffee-pots and Ker's and Aytoun's teapots the qualities which produced the great revival, agricultural, industrial and finally cultural, which transformed Scotland in the second half of the century. One may see in them also the legacy of the seventeenth century. Their pureness of form is due neither to any lack of capacity to decorate, nor to any absence of the graces in patrons who caused them to be made. The austerity of the Kirk of the Covenant was a grim and forbidding thing, while it lasted, but it shrived and bared the national character and for a generation or two safeguarded it from the tendency to don airs and graces imitated from foreign ways of life. The strength and logic of purpose which Kipling long after was to detect as a link between Calvin and the Glasgow marine engineer's creations in the nineteenth and twentieth centuries perhaps also informs the silverware of Scotland in the first half of the eighteenth century.

It is a matter for regret that none of the goldsmiths of this time stands out as a personality. So much sumptuous plate was produced, especially in Edinburgh, that one cannot help wishing to know more about the men who made it. However, one interesting document throws light among them, dim though it be. This is an *Information for Charles Duncan, Deacon of the Goldsmiths of Edinburgh, against Archibald Ure, Goldsmith there*, and is dated December 3, 1728. Duncan and Ure had been candidates for the deaconate. The first had secured 11 votes, the second 10; but an objection was made by the supporters of Ure that John Penman's vote, cast for Duncan, should not count, since Penman had for some time received charity from the Corporation, and that, since the existing Deacon's vote had been given to Ure and should count as a casting vote, Ure should be Deacon-elect. The issue is not material here. The document, on the other hand, contains some illuminating points. Against the retirement of Penman it is maintained that Ure himself 'has no Shop nor Forge going, and has not now for a very long Time brought one Bit of Work to the Essay-master'. Jackson, it is amusing to note, records a table-spoon by Ure for 1725–6[1]; but, whatever the interpretation of 'a very long time', it is quite true that work by Ure must be excessively rare. Yet to be just to Ure, I am not acquainted with a single example of a piece of work by the rival contestant, Duncan. It would seem that even in the early eighteenth century there were those who prefer serving on committees to producing the goods! Archibald Ure, as it happens, secured the office of assay-master in 1729.

In this connection it will be remembered that, until 1681, it was the Deacon of the Incorporation who was responsible for assaying silver and for setting his punch upon what he approved. The list of deacons given by Jackson ends at 1681 and may give the impression that after this date the office of assay-master somehow superseded that of deacon. This, of course, is not so. The assay-master, who set his stamp on all proved silver from 1681 (the year when the date-letter was introduced for Edinburgh silver) until 1759, had a limited function, and the principal officer of the Incorporation continued to be the Deacon. The Deacon it was who represented the Incorporation in the Town Council, as a member of that body. The document quoted above refers to the method of election. The first step was the preparation of a long leit or list of six persons to be presented to the Council, 'out of which the Council strike out any three whom they think fit, and return the remaining three, in what is called a short leit to the Corporation, who make a Choise of that Number for their Deacon, and present him to the Council, by whom he is admitted, if duly elected, and posted as Ordinary or Extraordinary Member of the Council, as they shall think fit.'

[1] *English Goldsmiths and Their Marks*, p. 501

NOTES TO CHAPTER XII

JOHN SEATOUN and JAMES SYMPSONE (p.132, line 24, etc.)

Jackson ascribed the circular mark with the monogrammed IS to James Sympsone and the later "eyebrows" mark to John Seatoun, and Mr. Finlay has followed him in this. I am now able to state that *both* marks pertain to John Seatoun. This is not an arbitrary judgement but is based principally on the entries of the two men in the *Assay Master's Accounts*. The accounts show that Sympsone sent only very little silver to be assayed, thirty-two parcels to be exact, between the assay-year 1686-7 (when he became a freeman) and 1696-7 when his name appears for the last time. The most he ever sent in one assay-year was 197 oz. in 1690-1, while in 1693-4 he only sent a single parcel of plate weighing 9 oz and in the previous year he had sent nothing at all. His total output during his ten-year working period amounted only to 696 oz. It is clearly impossible for him to have been the maker of all the fine silver previously ascribed to him, which includes the Communion Cups of Benholm, Kirriemuir, Dunbarney and St. Cyrus besides all the large pieces mentioned in this book.

Turning to the only other goldsmith with the same initials working in Edinburgh at this time, we find a very different story with John Seatoun. Admitted in 1688, he sent work for assay every year until the account books cease in 1701-2. (Subsequent volumes were burnt in the fire which destroyed the Goldsmiths' Hall, the Assay Office and all that it contained in 1796 and records were not resumed again until December 1799.) Seatoun's largest weight of silver to be assayed in any one recorded year was 1,770 oz. in 1700-1. Altogether in the fourteen years during which he appears in the accounts he sent in 259 parcels of plate with a total weight of 14,320 oz. He made the Corstorphine Communion Cup in 1717 and was still an active member of the Incorporation in 1728. There is no doubt that Seatoun was the maker of all the known plate marked with the initials IS during this period. No work by James Sympsone has yet been identified. Seatoun appears to have changed his maker's mark in about 1708-10; the earlier mark is composed of a monogram of his initials in a circular punch; the later one is more conventional, showing his initials side by side with an "eye-brow" over each.

STANDARD OF METAL (p.131, second paragraph)

The paragraph concerning the standard of wrought silver in Scotland during the eighteenth century needs a little clarification. The fact that the law required Sterling Standard to be used does not mean that this in fact happened. On the contrary, it is clear from their minutes that the goldsmiths continued with the Old Scots Standard of 11 dwt. fine until 1759. The Incorporation raised its standard to that of Sterling on 1 September 1759 and on 15th of the same month, when Hugh Gordon was re-elected Assay Master, he was required to strike the Saxon letter E.

> "to be put on the plate said year with the stamp or impression of a Scots thistle in place of the initial letters of the assay master's name".

The change to the use of the thistle mark therefore indicates a change from the Old Scots Standard to Sterling. The story is not quite so simple as that, however, because on 3 August 1771, when Robert Low was sworn in as Assay Master in place of the deceased Hugh Gordon, he was required to take trial "by copal assay, and the said Robert Low, finding the same to be of the fineness of eleven penny fine, . . ." shall stamp it accordingly. Not until the nineteenth century was Sterling standard established on a permanent basis.

NEW ILLUSTRATIONS

MONTEITH (pl.63,i), Edinburgh 1702-3, by James Cockburn. More is said about Monteiths in my notes to the previous chapter (p.n).

BASIN, EWER AND CASKET (pl.64,ii), Edinburgh 1706-7, by Thomas Ker. These three superb pieces were made for Charles Hope, 1st Earl of Hopetoun, (1681-1742) and are engraved with his coronet and initials. They supplemented the large toilet service already made for him by the London goldsmith Anthony Nelme in 1691-2.

THREE-LUGGED QUAICH (pl.65,i), Edinburgh c.1735, by Edward Lothian (maker's mark only). This quaich is extremely unusual in having three lugs instead of the usual two. It was in danger of going to a private collector in America but in January 1969 the Reviewing Committee on the Export of Works of Art recommended that a licence be withheld for one month. The National Museum of Antiquities of Scotland was able to buy it within the stated period for £2,020.

THE HOPETOUN SPOUT CUP (pl.65,ii), Edinburgh 1707-8 by Walter Scott. Spout Cups, sometimes also called posset cups, are a great rarity. The only other Scottish example which I have seen is by Charles Blair of Edinburgh and was made in 1724-5. This example was made for the 1st Earl of Hopetoun.

TANKARD (pl.67,i), Edinburgh 1705-6, by Alexander Forbes. This is of typical Scottish form with its domed lid, finial and thumb piece.

LAVER OF TRINITY CHURCH, EDINBURGH (pl.68,i), Edinburgh 1701-2, by Walter Scott. The Laver was made to match an earlier Basin (see pl.26) which had been made by Thomas Kirkwood in 1633. (See my note, p.90.)

THE SELKIRK CHOCOLATE POT (pl.68,ii), Edinburgh 1720-1, by Patrick Murray. This pot is engraved below the lip with the arms of the Burgh of Selkirk and appears to have been made as a prize for horse racing. The lid is detachable.

DOUBLE-LIPPED SAUCE BOAT (pl.69,ii), Edinburgh 1738-9, by John Main. A common enough form in England but unusual in Scotland.

SPIRIT FLASK (pl.71,ii), Edinburgh c.1716, by Alexander Kincaid. This lovely heavy-quality flask is engraved with the date "1716" and is marked with the maker's mark only. The bottom detaches to form a beaker in the usual way.

PORRINGER (pl.71,ii), Edinburgh 1722-3, by Henry Bethune. The handle is engraved with the lettering "EW to EP" showing that it was a gift.

LIBRARY LAMP (pl.72,i), Edinburgh 1739-40, by William Aytoun. This object is unique in my experience and was perhaps a special one-off commission. It is fitted to take two candles and the reflector can be raised, lowered and tilted to direct the light where the reader wishes. There is also a pair of snuffers with a built-in tray to hold them.

THE TRAVELLING CANTEEN OF PRINCE CHARLES EDWARD STUART (pl.72,ii and illustrated on front cover) Edinburgh 1740-1, by Ebenezer Oliphant. The Canteen comprises a set of two beakers, two knives, two forks and two spoons, a teaspoon-cum-marrow scoop, a nutmeg-grater-cum-corkscrew, a salt box and a dram dish, all fitted neatly into an outer case. The case has a hinged lid and is chased with bands of linked thistles, flowers and foliage. It is a fine and rare example of all-over Rococo work which was not often done in Scotland except for a special commission such as this one. James Mitchellson, Ebenezer Oliphant's master, had earlier been noted as the only goldsmith in Scotland able to execute the difficult deep chasing technique used on such pieces. Oliphant learned his craft well, as this piece shows, and continued his master's tradition. Despite his well-known Jacobite sympathies he escaped government censure after the '45. By 1753 his business had prospered so well that he was able to help his family to buy back their forfeited estate of Gask, in Perthshire. The Canteen appears to have been made as a twenty-first birthday present for the Prince. The rather stiff bands of linked thistles represent the collar of the Order of the Thistle while the lid bears the Saint Andrew Medal of that order. The frontal cartouche is engraved with the Prince of Wales's Feathers. Charles was created Prince of Wales at his birth and a knight of the Thistle and the Garter shortly afterwards.

The Canteen was captured by the Hanoverians along with much else at Culloden in 1746 and fell into the hands of the Duke of Cumberland. Later that day he presented it to his aid-de-camp, George Keppel, Lord Bury, later Earl of Albermarle, in whose family it descended until it was sold in 1963. In 1984 it came up for sale again and, with the intervention of the Reviewing Committee on the Export of Works of Art and by dint of a successful public appeal and generous donations from the National Heritage Memorial Fund and a whisky company, it was bought by the National Museum of Antiquities of Scotland.

COFFEE-POT AND HOT MILK-JUG (pl.73,i), Edinburgh 1713-4, by Colin McKenzie (see pp.136-37). Mr. Stuart Maxwell found both the pot and the jug referred to in Lady Grizell Baillie's *Household Books* (the manuscript but not the printed version) under the date January 1714, as follows:

"To McKenzie Gold Smith to workmanship of the silver Coffee pot and Milk pot at 2s.2d per ounce, and there was some odds in the weight of plate I gave him to make them off; They weigh 50 unce 12 drop; and three handles cost 17/-. Total £6.8s.3d".

In the last years of her life this formidable lady claimed to possess 4,000 ounces of plate, which was the same as amount as was admitted to by the

Duke of Buccleuch for plate tax purposes, and more than all but one or two of the Scottish nobility.

COVERED SUGAR BOWL (pl.73,ii), Edinburgh 1724-5, by James Ker. This is illustrated to show the beauty that can be created by utter simplicity; the bowl needs no adornment other than its own shape.

TEA-POT (pl.75,i), Edinburgh 1719-20, by Henry Bethune. Notice that this is the same date as the quite different pot by Colin McKenzie in Plate 75,ii.

BOX FOR A BURGESS TICKET (pl.77,ii), Edinburgh 1736-7, by John Rollo. On page 123 is mentioned "a box for a burgess-ticket at £12.10s.11d". In March 1958 this very box turned up in auction at Sotheby's and was subsequently bought by the Royal Scottish Museum with the aid of a grant from the National Art-Collections Fund. It is well documented, for the town council minutes record that it contained the burgess ticket of the Hon. Sir John Barnard, MP for the city of London and later Lord Mayor:

> "Nota: This ticket was sent up in a Silver Box with the seal of the Town of the date of the Act of Council for Sir John's eminent appearance for preserving the rights and privileges of the City [of Edinburgh] in the Bill brought into Parliament against the Treasurer and Provost, 15th June 1737".

This Bill was:

> "to disable Alexander Wilson Esquire [the Provost] from taking, holding or enjoying any office or place of magistracy in the City of Edinburgh or elsewhere in Great Britain; and for imprisoning the said Alexander Wilson; and for abolishing the Guard kept up in the said City commonly called the Town Guard; and for taking away the gates of the Nether Bow Port of the said City and keeping open the same".

This vindictive measure was brought in to penalise the City of Edinburgh and its chief magistrate for the hanging of Captain Porteous by the mob in 1737. Porteous, in charge of the Guard at the execution of a smuggler, had ordered his men to fire on the mob when it showed itself in ugly mood. Smugglers of liquor were popular in the Scotland of those days, less because of their trade than because they represented defiance of a government which, by a majority, had been regarded ever since the Union of Parliaments in 1707 as an imposition upon the northern partner. The Bill passed the Lords; In the Commons, however, the Scottish members opposed it fiercely, and they were supported by numerous English members who saw its foolishness. The Bill was denuded of nearly all its objectionable clauses when at last it was passed. Its leading English opponent was Sir John Barnard, whom the Scottish Capital at once rewarded by bestowing the Freedom of the City upon him. The original Burgess Ticket still reposes in the box which is a superb example of its kind, engraved with the City's arms (at a cost of £2:2/-)

CREAM-JUG (pl.80,ii), Edinburgh 1730-1, by William Aytoun. This jug is very similar to the one from the tea service by the same maker, dated 1733-4 (pl.74).

SILVER-GILT MUG (pl.80,ii), Edinburgh 1744-5, by Lawrence Oliphant. This superb little mug is of the highest quality and is completely covered in heavily chased flowers and foliage in the rococo manner, somewhat reminiscent of the Prince Charles Edward Canteen. Given the date of the piece and the Jacobite connections of its maker, one might be tempted to wonder if it were not intended as a gift for the same recipient.

COVERED CREAM-JUG (pl.80,iv), Edinburgh 1744-5, by William Dempster. This piece shows typically Scottish flat-chasing around the body and lid.

CAKE BASKET (pl.81,i), Edinburgh 1744-5, by William Dempster. Mr. Finlay wrote about this basket in *Country Life* in 1963, commenting wryly that:

> "it is so loaded with marine motifs that one wonders if its function was not to contain sea-food of some kind".

The shell bowl is 13½″ across, the three legs are formed as fish and the handle is a sea horse.

Chapter Thirteen

HIGHLAND JEWELLERY AND WEAPONS

IT is perhaps unusual to include jewellery and weapons in an account of gold and silver wares, but it is impossible here to avoid discussing the silverworkers of the Highlands in the eighteenth century, because their crafts contribute the last chapter to the long history of Celtic metal-working which has been considered earlier. The isolation of the Highland community had no parallel elsewhere in these islands. Partly because of geographical factors, to a less degree because of language, the Highland clans retained a way of life of their own until the 'pacification' which followed the Jacobite rising in the middle of the century. It was a way of life largely unaffected by the broad social changes which were occurring throughout the rest of western Europe, and it might be said that the Edinburgh of Queen Anne's day had, culturally, much more in common with Paris, far less London, than it had with villages and townships within a hundred miles to the north-west of it. By comparison, the scattered Highland communities were poverty-stricken, materially speaking, as descriptions by travellers such as Martin, or even Boswell in the second half of the century, make clear; but the same writers make it equally clear that the Highlands were still animated by consciousness of a rich tradition of their own and that they were full of things of interest to the stranger.

The inaccessibility and no doubt also the poverty of the Highland communities developed their self-sufficiency. The Rev. John Lane Buchanan,[1] writing as late as the 1780's, notes the technical precociousness of the average Gael. 'It is very common', he writes, 'to find men who are taylors, shoemakers, stocking-weavers, coopers, carpenters, and sawyers of timber. Some of them employ the plane, the saw, the adze, the wimble, and they even groove the deals for chests. They make hooks for fishing, cast metal buckles, brooches and rings for their favourite females.' Martin, seventy years earlier, had remarked on 'the mechanical genius and quickness of apprehension' of the Highlanders

------

[1] *Travels in the Western Hebrides*, pp. 83, 87

and referred to their ability to engrave various natural forms on bone, horn or wood with the simplest tools.

The metal plaid brooches of the seventeenth and eighteenth centuries are derived undoubtedly, if remotely, from the brooches of a thousand years before, and more directly from the medieval brooches which have been described in Chapter IV. Strangely, the later brooches show a much more marked feeling for the Celtic tradition than do the medieval brooches, which exhibit no Celtic features except perhaps the grotesque animals and the use of *niello*. Grotesque animals also appear on some of the first of the later brooches and, in addition, the triquetra and other forms of knotwork are to be found on nearly all specimens. Although we are primarily concerned with the silver brooches it is impossible to segregate them completely from the brass brooches, which are closely related to them and obviously carried out by the same class of craftsmen. As a rule, the brass brooches are rather larger than the silver, no doubt because the metal was more easily obtainable. It has been claimed that brass brooches were worn by men and silver by women, and this is a reasonable theory as the brass are larger and the silver more dainty, although it must be kept in mind that brass brooches occurred earlier than silver. It has also been claimed that the circular brooch as a whole was worn by the women and not by the men, who usually employed a pin for their plaids.[1] It is not likely, however, that women wore the larger brass brooches, some of which are as large as small plates.

Brass brooches should be described briefly in the first place, for as a type they seem to have preceded silver brooches of similar, annular design. They are usually made from bars or ingots of brass bent around into a circle and hammered flat. The pin is also of brass and swivels in a slot which breaks the circle. Iron pins are not uncommon, but they are later replacements. Decoration is effected by deep engraving. It consists of four or five circular *paterae* or medallions commonly infilled with knotwork, the panels between being occupied by foliage or by grotesque monsters which represent deer, wild cats and other animals more dubious, such as the griffon. In the best, and usually earliest examples, the creatures are sometimes quite in the style of the bestiaries, and it is hard to know how the craftsman arrived at his concept. Later, decoration more commonly consists of chevron-like panels containing triquetras. The knotwork within the circles is never repetitious. This may be a fairly good

Pl. 86

[1] Scottish Exhibition, Glasgow, 1911, *Historical Catalogue*, p. 135

index of the creative vitality and horror of uniformity which have always marked the Celt. To some extent the age of a brooch may be judged by the treatment of the knotwork, which as time passes is clearly executed in a more
Pl. 86
perfunctory manner. The seventeenth century is the period of the best of these brooches, which in size range from about 3 inches in diameter up to 7 inches, the commonest sizes lying between $3\frac{1}{2}$ and $4\frac{1}{2}$ inches. Technically, these brooches are of no very high standard, but they exhibit a well-developed sense of design and most excellent taste, and the ancient Celt's unfailing ability to fill a given space with appropriate and vital decoration. Those brooches which are dated belong to the later years of the seventeenth century. Some of the best come from Aberdeenshire and neighbouring counties of the north-east.

There appears to be a wide gap in time between the passing of the medieval silver brooches, with their black-letter inscriptions, and the appearance of the circular silver brooches. There is some doubt about when these brooches came into being, but it must have been within a decade of 1700, either way. Certainly there are no silver brooches of this type in the period of the earlier brass brooches. Generally, the decoration of the silver ones is less spontaneous, less vital, and is in some degree derivative. One of the largest and best of them shows, for example, the feature of alternate circles and chevrons typical of the later brass brooches. Yet the knotwork of many of the silver brooches is well-devised and executed, and this may be taken broadly as a good test of the quality of decoration in the Celtic tradition.

In the Highlands all fine metalwork, and much of the stone-carving and other craft work of good quality, has been attributed to the class of artificers known as *ceardan*. *Ceard* (or *caird*, as it is pronounced) is a curious word. While its significance is 'artificer', the *ceard* was, in earlier times at least, more than a mechanic in the ordinary sense, and it is possible that the ancient Highlander, essentially a warrior, looked down on manual work as a trade, much as the Montenegrins have done in more recent times, and left all such work to the tinkers or gypsies—again as the Montenegrins did. 'Tinker' is one of the dictionary meanings given for *ceard*. These *ceardan* formed a caste of their own.[1] In their way, they were artists. They had a great tradition of story-telling. By word of mouth they passed on much lore about supernatural smiths. It is not unreasonable to trace the preoccupation of the *ceardan* with metalwork as far back as the late La Tène period, and one authority refers to a quantity of frag-

[1] *Journal of the Gypsy Lore Society*, Vol. I, p. 355

mentary paalstaves, celts and other metal articles found at Lisnacroghera as the material of a *ceard* 'whose aim was to use the metal in the manufacture of new weapons, instruments or ornaments'.[1] This authority avers that many of our crannogs may at one time have been occupied by the *ceardan*. An interesting attempt has been made to identify this caste with the Picts, although it seems to do little more than establish the possibility that the Shelta language spoken by these people is Celtic in origin.

To-day the *ceard* is represented by those tinkers or gypsies whose camps are to be seen all over the Highlands during the summer months. They appear to have forgotten the skills of their predecessors, but it is not so long since they made brooches. A writer at the end of last century mentions one of the name of Ross, still remembered by older people in central Perthshire not so many years before.[2] The same writer states that he met an old woman in Killin wearing a silver brooch, now in the National Museum of Antiquities, and this brooch she said had been made in Glenlyon for the marriage of her grandmother, whose initials appear with her husband's, and the date 1714, on the reverse of the brooch.

These plaid brooches, brass and silver, may generally be classified under three groups. First, there is the oldest type, in which the circumference is divided into compartments by circles or medallions, the compartments frequently being filled with animal or plant forms. Invariably this type is of brass. Second, there is the later type in which the chevron motif is introduced, with or without medallions. This may be either of brass or of silver. Third, there is a group of brooches with a wide variety of designs. Most of them show an obvious aesthetic and technical deterioration, and they belong to the final phase. Effects are usually achieved by use of the chevron or zig-zag dividing up the surface, which is covered with hatched lines or some similar perfunctory device. In this phase the thistle makes its appearance. Type 1 may be attributed to the seventeenth century. Examples of type 2 range between 1700 and the 'Forty-five, or perhaps a little later. Silver brooches, whether in type 2 or type 3, all seem to be betrothal tokens, for they carry two sets of initials in association and are dated. Known examples cover a period from 1713 to 1770.

Many of the silver brooches depend largely on the use of *niello* for effect.   Pl.87
Niello has been referred to briefly in an earlier chapter; but in view of the con-

---

[1] *Journal of the Royal Historical and Archaeological Association of Ireland*, Vol. IX, p. 99
[2] *P.S.A.S.*, XXXIII, pp. 61, 67

tention that such brooches are the work of wanderng *ceardan* it should perhaps be explained here that the technique of *niello* is by no means beyond the capacity of such craftsmen. *Niello* is not strictly an enamel: that is, it is not vitreous but metallic. Being metallic, it is malleable; and indeed in Russia it is regarded as a test of the excellence of the inlay if a silver plate decorated with *niello* can be hammered out cold to twice its original size without the *niello* cracking.[1] Preparation involves melting in a crucible certain quantities of silver, copper, lead and sulphur at a temperature of about 1200° C. A reaction takes place resulting in the complete fusion of all ingredients. The solid amalgam must be ground to a suitable size of grain—Cellini recommends a grain the size of millet seed—or granulated by pouring the molten compound into water. When the surface of the silver prepared for inlay has been cleaned, it is moistened with a solution of borax. The *niello* is spread evenly over the surface and the metal heated in an oven until the *niello* melts and flows into the lines of the engraving. Finally, the excess material is filed away and the surface finished by polishing and burnishing. There are, it is true, various technical difficulties in preparing and applying the amalgam, but they are not such tremendous difficulties as face the enameller, and there is no reason why an ingenious *ceard* should have been baffled by them. Possibly the actual preparation of the *niello* may have been left to certain specially skilled persons, for the prepared material is said to have been stored for use in goose-quills. The quality of the inlay, while sometimes very good, cannot compare with similar work done by more sophisticated craftsmen, judged purely on a technical level. In this group of Highland brooches *niello* is rarely applied to any metal except silver. Occasionally it appears on brass pieces—there is a good example in the National Museum of Antiquities—but, apart from the obvious fact that it is less effective on yellow metal, it runs less well on brass than it does on silver.

At one time there must have been very large numbers of Highland brooches of this period, for they were something more than mere ornaments. They had an essential function. The *breacan-feile*, or belted plaid, could not be secured without one; and when the place of this garment was taken by the *feile-beag*, or kilt as we know it to-day, a development of the early eighteenth century, a brooch was required to fix the separate plaid. Women also wore the plaid, drawing it round the shoulders and adapting it as a hood in cold or wet weather, and for this too the brooch was essential. No doubt pins or crudely-

[1] *Studies in Conservation*, Vol. I, No. 2

contrived brooches were employed widely, articles like the brooches of copper or even zinc made in St. Kilda in more recent times; but even the crudest pieces often had their engraving, and it is probable there was a certain amount of discrimination among the poorest clansmen. Brooches made by Inverness and Glasgow goldsmiths from the last quarter of the eighteenth century onwards were designed in imitation of the older brooches, but although technically the imitations may often be the better their decoration is without vitality or spontaneity. The old practice of inscribing initials of betrothed couples continued.

Highland metalworkers also practised their arts in the decoration of weapons, which in the glens were implements of everyday use. I do not propose to discuss weapons as such, but it would be almost as pointed an omission to pass over Highland weapons in an account of Scottish gold and silverware as to pass over the Highlands in an account of Scottish history. It is typical of the Gael that his craftsmen should have used their very considerable abilities to embellish weapons and personal ornaments rather than to devise elegant domestic pieces. A. J. S. Brooke remarked on the fact that he had noted only four Highland artificers whose names eventually appeared in the lists of city goldsmiths. To trace such men is difficult, and whether Brook included in his group anyone such as Colin McKenzie, for example, who came of a Morayshire family, is not recorded; but one might hazard a guess that as a rule the temperament of those who made the brooches, or of those who decorated the weapons, would not find the same satisfaction in making teapots or salvers.

I have implied a distinction as between the makers of brooches and the decorators of weapons. Possibly there is no justification for this. Many a *ceard* may have tried his hand at beautifying the weapons with which he was familiar. But all that we know about the conditions under which weapons were wrought suggests that they were the work of a different class of craftsmen. In most cases a weapon is evidently decorated by the man who made it, and he is usually a clan armourer or a craftsman working in a particular centre under conditions very different from those of the gypsy life of the *ceard*.

We may dismiss briefly the only branch of armoury in which it seems likely that the *ceard* may have played an important part. This is the making of the round targes or targets which the clansmen carried as late as the eighteenth century. Decoration principally consists in the embossing of the leather, very often with Celtic designs of a simple sort but of considerable beauty, and in studding the surfaces with bosses and round-headed nails which are part-func-

PLATE 85

Gold Race Cup: Edinburgh, c.1755. Maker: Ker and Dempster *(p.159)*

Gold Race Cup: Edinburgh, 1752-53. Maker: William Gilchrist *(p.158)*

PLATE 86

Brass Brooch: 17th century *(pp.147-148)*

PLATE 87

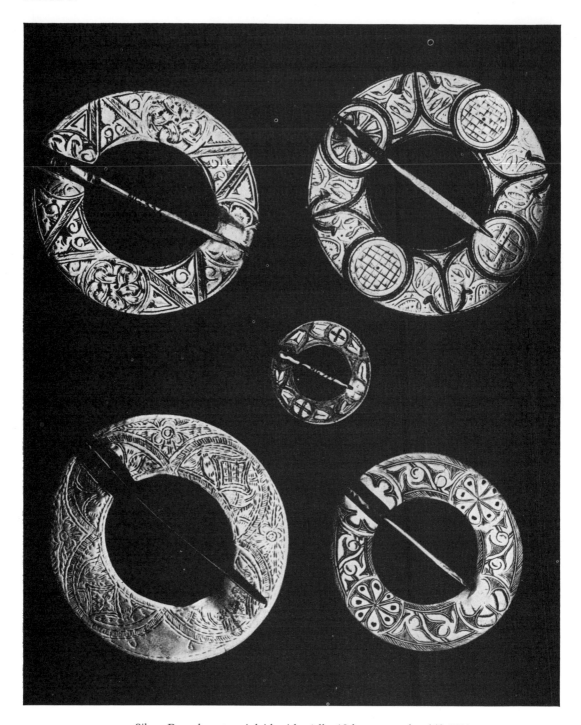

Silver Brooches, two inlaid with *niello*: 18th century *(pp.149-150)*

PLATE 88

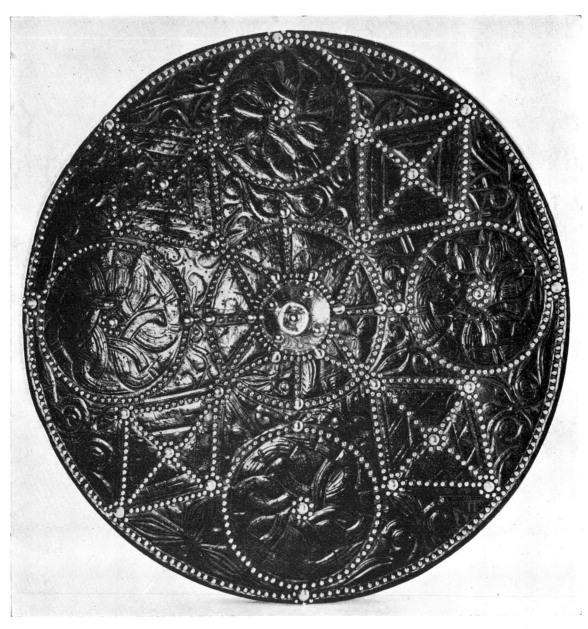

Targe, silver mounted: early 18th century. Formerly belonging to Duke of Richmond and Gordon ɔn
(p.152)

PLATE 89

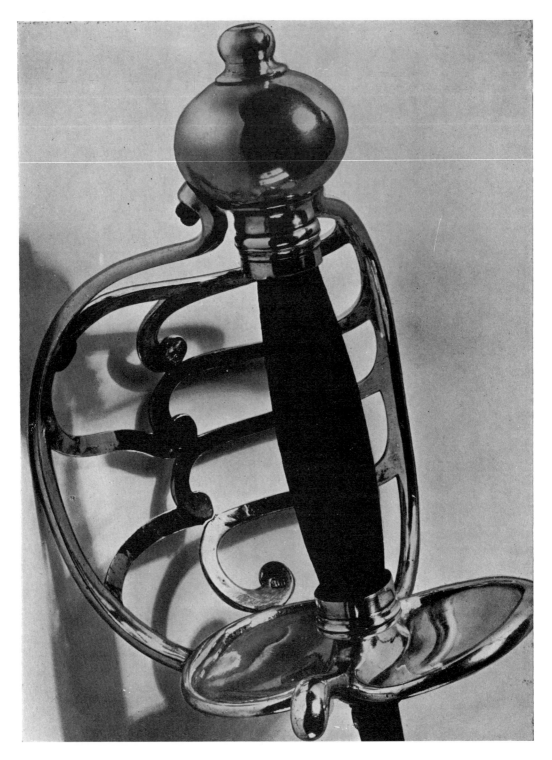

Silver Sword-Hilt: Edinburgh, c.1715. Maker: Harry Beauthune *(p.152)*

PLATE 90

Sword-Hilts inlaid with silver: first half 18th century (That on right by John Allan of Stirling as described in text) *(p.152)*

tional and partly for effect. There is undoubtedly some similarity between the patterns adopted on the targes and those of the brooches, so that sometimes the same hand may have been at work. Studs and bosses are usually brass-headed, but silver fittings are not unknown. Of the targes so decorated, quite the finest Pl.90 with which I am familiar is that which once belonged to the fifth Duke of Gordon, purchased from the Duke of Richmond and Gordon by the late Major J. Milne-Davidson and after his death acquired by the National Museum of Antiquities. Its dark, almost black leather enhances superbly the pattern of silver studs radiating from a boss which bears some light engraving.

The makers and decorators of sword-hilts had no close association with the Highlands at all, except for the fact that, in the main, their products were destined for use there. An Edinburgh goldsmith, Harry Beathune, made at Pl.89 least one such hilt, a massive creation of solid silver formerly in the Milne-Davidson collection and now in the National Museum of Antiquities. This is not a Highland type of hilt at all, and quite possibly has no association with Highlanders except that its date, which must be around 1715, suggests that it may have been carried in the Jacobite army. It bears the maker's punch, but no hall-mark. Perhaps the only other example of such a piece by a known goldsmith is the hilt of the magnificent broadsword by William Scott of Elgin in the collection of Her Majesty the Queen. William Scott the Elder worked in the late seventeenth and early eighteenth century. Her Majesty possesses a silver-hilted backsword of about the same period which may also have been hilted by a domestic goldsmith rather than by an armourer, but it is without hall-mark or punch of any kind.

The most celebrated makers of hilts worked mainly in Stirling and in Glasgow, both places well situated for easy communication with the clans. These men rarely used silver, and they never used it as the material for the hilt as a whole. Usually the introduction of silver was limited to the attachment of two or more small thistles cut out from sheet metal and rather crudely engraved, additions which look tawdry by comparison with the magnificent workmanship of the basket-hilt itself. Of all the pieces by these hilt-makers, possibly the Pl.88 finest on which silver is employed to any important extent is a striking one by John Allan of Stirling in the Clanranald Bequest in the National Museum of Antiquities. The engraving is crude, but effective, and the silver inlay consists of a chain-link pattern and a shape like a sword with simple quillons.

However, the most interesting class of Highland weapons on which precious metals were used for decoration is that of pistols. The Highland pistol has a history covering an unbroken period of two and a half centuries, and only during the last fifty years of this does it fail to rise to the level of a masterpiece of its kind. The study of these pistols is very much a field for the specialist and has been covered in a scholarly if all too brief section by the late Charles White-law in *European Hand Firearms of the XVIth, XVIIth and XVIIIth Centuries*. The amount of goldsmithing done by the gunsmiths who made the weapons is perhaps not very great, but the employment of the precious metals is vital to the effects obtained, so that we must concede to these men a degree of skill and taste which sets them beside the more sophisticated craftsmen of the cities.

In the sixteenth century, when the characteristic Scottish pistol was taking shape, the gunsmith was known as a dag-maker. The dag-maker of this period does not appear to be a clan armourer, for the fish-tailed weapons he makes are far from crude, and their general appearance and decoration are at first glance foreign, even faintly oriental. Butts and stocks are sometimes of wood, some-times of brass. Rarely—although indeed all such pistols are rare—silver is em-ployed in mounting the heel of the wooden butt, as well as in decorating the barrel. The sheet silver used for the butt-mount is engraved delicately, and with considerable taste and knowledge. A stylised rose and flowery tendrils are the motifs, applied to the brass as well as to the silver mounts of the more elegant wooden-stocked pistols. I find these last weapons baffling. There are very few of them, and they have an exotic look. The strangely sophisticated rose design used on them appears also on the lemon-shaped butt of the brass pistol belonging to Aberdeen University, and on Scottish pistols in London, Stockholm and elsewhere, so they were probably made in Scotland; but they may have been produced by, or under the direction of, some foreign gunsmith working in a Scottish town. Whitelaw hints at Dutch models. However, by the middle of the seventeenth century the form of the pistol had changed and gunsmiths who were Scots, without any doubt, were employing silver exten-sively on the distinctive arms which they were producing.

A temporary digression to the Lowlands becomes necessary. Gunsmiths in Lowland towns, especially along the east coast, did in the second half of the seventeenth century evolve a type of pistol peculiar to Scotland in the decora-tion of which silver plays a part. This type is usually long-barrelled, but its distinguishing feature is a heart-shaped butt. The pistol is of steel, lock, stock and barrel. There is little engraving on the surface. Evidently the hardness proved too much for any urge which the gunsmiths may have had to decorate their handiwork in this way, and the blueing of the surface would in any case have rendered the engraving ineffective. Bands and plates of silver were, however, inlaid on butt and barrel, and the softer nature of the silver encouraged a certain amount of decoration. The inlay is generally fairly crude, although in its way effective enough, and in artistry does not compare with the work lavished on the Highland pistols to be described. Undoubtedly the finest of these heart-butt weapons is a dag 20½ inches long in the Royal Scottish Museum. Its inlays are executed in brass as well as in silver, and they are done with more than the usual amount of taste. On the barrel are the normal raised cross-mouldings with engraved bands of silver, but in the compartments between twine stems of brass linking rosettes, thistles and tulips of silver inlay. The butt is decorated in similar style. Fence and belt-hook are each ornamented with a brass ring which encloses a very beautiful rosette in delicate openwork filigree. This introduction of the Dutch tulip in company with the rose and the thistle marks, of course, the reign of William of Orange. It will be remembered that the tulip also appears on silver quaichs of the same period. An inscription on the stock reads: EX DONO IA D DE HAMILTON · PAT LUNDIN · JAMES LUNDIN . *James Grahame his noball arm given to him by . . . Daneile esquire.* James, Duke of Hamilton, succeeded to the title in 1698.

Pl.91.i

The true Highland pistol is a development of the weapon with fish-tail butt, described earlier, and in its finest form is associated mainly, if not entirely, with the village of Doune in Perthshire. Its butt terminates in a double scroll or 'ram's-horn' device. The weapon is of steel, stock, butt and barrel, and the best examples are ornamented with precious metals. Its period ranges over a century, from 1700 or a few years earlier until about 1790, when the *Statistical Account of Scotland* records that the last of the Doune gunsmiths was still at work. Earlier Doune pistols are somewhat crude. In the museum at Montrose there is a piece by Thomas Caddell which Whitelaw dated about 1700, and on it the silver plaques and inlaid bands are no more elegant than the enrichments of many heart-butt pistols. But as the pistols improved in grace of outline so did their embellishments improve. By 1725 an intricate pattern of links and scrolls and circles had been evolved, covering stock and butt, and much of this pattern was inlaid in silver with considerable skill. It has been compared with early Celtic work by several writers, including the present author; but it is a comparison which must be made with caution, for on mature consideration it clearly becomes difficult to derive one from the other with any assurance, although the degree of taste and skill shown certainly suggest the inheritance of some special ability for dealing with metals.

It is a curious fact that the beauty of Doune pistols continues to grow until the third quarter of the century: that is, until long after the imposition of the Disarming Act which followed Culloden. Similar legislation passed after the incident of the 'Fifteen had proved impotent, and even dangerous, since only old and useless weapons were surrendered, and because the clans which surrendered them were those which were loyal to the established government. The Act of 1746 was enforced with powers of search and with heavy penalties. A general proscription of things Highland was not relaxed until 1782.[1] Yet in the years between those two dates the master-gunsmiths of Doune were perfecting their art and producing arms which were reckoned worthy to be sent as gifts to the courts of German princes and even to Louis XVI. There is a close parallel between this flowering of craftsmanship and the great renaissance of Gaelic poetry which flourished during the same period. The poets sang of past glories, as Celtic bards have done habitually, and drew from Jacobitism a great store of tender imagery and rousing rhythms. The Doune gunsmiths made weapons patterned with similar lyric loveliness, and weapons which were as efficient as they were fair to look at.

Decoration adopted by those gunsmiths conformed to the same general pattern over a generation or more. It was, both in design and execution, refined until at the height of their fame the gunsmiths were making pistols which seemed to be encased in lacework. Engraving is married to inlaid tracery so fine, so sensitive and so true that in some cases the lines appear to have been drawn with a pen dipped in silver, although in fact they are formed by thin silver strips packed into grooves with undercut edges. Oval silver medallions are inlaid on the butts, and are intended for the arms of the owner, or for his initials. The terminals of trigger and pricker are also of silver. In the best instances they are formed by joining two hemispheres, the resulting ball being mounted on an iron tang. They, too, are delicately engraved. It should be said that the steel of such pistols was originally blued, to discourage rusting, and this made a fine foil for silver inlays and mounts.

In a very few cases the inlays and mounts are not of silver, but of gold. A superb pair of gold-mounted pistols by John Campbell of Doune was formerly   Pl.91.ii

[1] 1 & 2 George II, cap. 62

in the Colville Collection in Edinburgh Castle, but evidently disappeared during some systematic thieving before 1939. I had the good fortune to photograph these pistols before their loss, and it is to be hoped they will yet come to light in some part of the world. Another magnificent pistol, which Whitelaw described as 'the finest piece of Scottish gunsmith work extant', is in the Royal Armoury at Windsor. Here the stock is actually of silver, inlaid with gold. A gold escutcheon is inserted on either side of the butt, one bearing the Royal Arms, the other the Royal cypher of George III. Trigger and pricker terminals are of gold. The pistol is signed JOHN CHRISTIE, STIRLING: probably the man of the same name who is associated with Doune.

The final phase of this singular Celtic revival belongs to the first quarter of the nineteenth century. Highland dress entered a phase of renewed popularity after the law prohibiting it was revoked, even more so after the influence of the Waverley Novels began to make itself felt. Brooches and other accoutrements were made in large numbers by goldsmiths and jewellers, who paid scant attention to traditional forms. This is the hey-day of the massively-mounted cairngorm stone, of the exploitation of the thistle as the emblem of Scotland. Commercialism set its stamp on everything that was done and the taste and restraint of the *ceardan* and the clan-armourers were forgotten under a welter of vulgar ornament concocted to satisfy and flatter romantic notions. Highland chieftains themselves seem to have had small power of discrimination between genuine and false. Macdonell of Glengarry, a quarrelsome and conceited young man believed to have been the original of Fergus MacIvor in *Waverley*, is shown in the portrait by Raeburn in the National Gallery of Scotland in the Highland costume affected at the beginning of the nineteenth century. His dirk, powder-horn and pistols survive. Gorgeous is perhaps the adjective best applicable to them, but only very superficially do they conform to traditional pattern. The pistols, like a similar pair in the Clanranald Collection in the National Museum of Antiquities, are at first glance of the 'ram's-horn' type; but the gilding and enamel work, while slickly professional in finish, are crude aesthetically beside the work of the Doune masters of fifty years before. In short, the craftsmen of the Highlands had lost their trade in competition with the huge, organised gunsmith industry of Birmingham, the proof-marks of which appear on the barrels of the Macdonell pistols.

Chapter Fourteen

EDINBURGH—THE LATER EIGHTEENTH CENTURY

IF the ornaments and decorated weapons of the Highlands during the eighteenth century are socially significant, the silverware produced in Edinburgh from 1750 until the end of the century is equally so. Excellent as were the Edinburgh goldsmiths during this period, much of what they made is, to the student, unrewarding if their social circumstances are forgotten.

Unlike Glasgow, Edinburgh has been little affected by the ebullient genius of the Celt. Her contribution to the national character has been stern and austere. It was by no accident of place that Knox preached in her High Kirk, for here in the south-east the Reformer found the essential uncompromising element he needed for the core of his movement. Here is the flint on which Scotland has struck fire to raise the torch in her most critical times. Here the Divine Right of Kings proved impotent in the face of a covenanted religion; and here, a century and a half later, the church defied an invasion of its prerogatives by another secular tyrant, this time the State. In the middle of the eighteenth century, however, conformity and compliance prevailed. The Kirk was still, perhaps, the leader. But the Kirk was in the hands of the Moderates, who had small use for the covenanting spirit, though scholarship was held in high esteem by leading divines and the city building up into a formidable stronghold of learning. In intellectual circles national issues were of less moment than European movements. Men of the arts like Ramsay and, later, Raeburn and Robert Adam, scholars like Hume, even professional men such as Boswell went to the Continent as a matter of course to complete their education, and continental fashions made impacts almost as swiftly on Edinburgh as they did on London.

It is significant that by 1750 forms peculiar to Scotland had fallen quite out of fashion with the Edinburgh goldsmiths. The thistle cup had been abandoned by 1700, which suggests that in some way it may have been functionally unsatisfactory; but we might expect that the quaich would have survived in its

PLATE 91

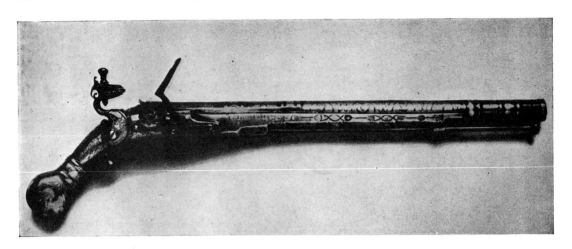

Steel Pistol inlaid with silver: later 17th century *(p.154)*

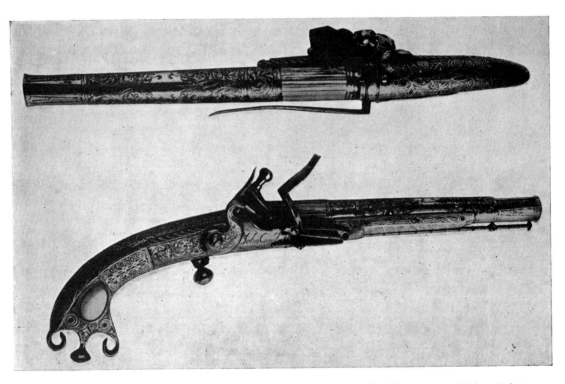

Pair of steel Pistols inlaid and mounted with gold: Doune, mid–18th century. Maker: John Campbell *(pp.155-156)*

PLATE 92

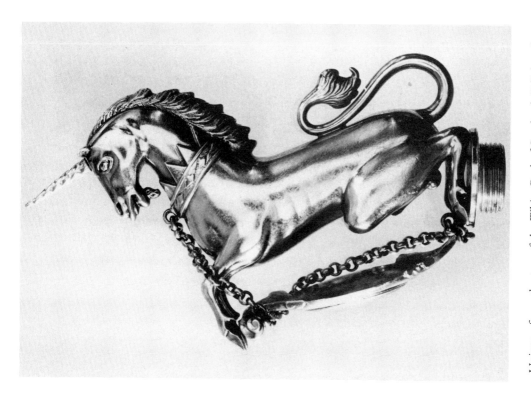

Unicorn from the top of the White Rod of Scotland: Edinburgh, 1758-59. Maker: John Clark (see frontispiece) (Notes, Ch.14)

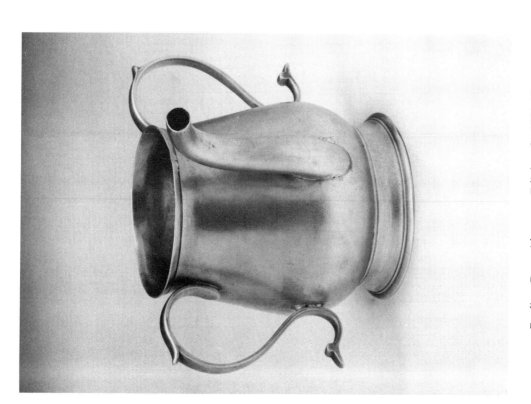

Feeding Cup with spout: Edinburgh, 1764-65. Maker: Alexander Gairdner

silver form, since the other members of the bicker family continued in practical use in country places right through the century. I have seen a silver-mounted quaich stamped with a mark which looked like John Gilsland's, which would place it about 1745; but, so far as Edinburgh is concerned at least, the all-silver quaich would seem to have gone out of favour in the 'thirties. A big one by John Blair in the Royal Scottish Museum shows signs of stiffening into that rigidity which renders most recent reproductions of this graceful type of vessel no better than bowls with handles on. The old tradition of functional simplicity does persist, nevertheless, here and there. One or two of the more long-lived craftsmen continued with little alteration in their style, among them James Ker. Ker, who began his career in the early 'twenties, was still active in the middle of the century, and a cream-ewer of 1748 in Sir John Stirling-Maxwell's collection reveals that he was then still a master of pure line. Aytoun runs him close with about 25 years of activity. But on the whole rapid changes of fashion were favoured by the comparatively short careers of most of the goldsmiths, if we are to judge by the time-ranges covered by their surviving works.

In England, from the 'thirties onwards, the dominant styles in furnishings took their inspiration from the France of Louis XV. So far as the decorative arts were concerned, this France was effete. The *régime* tottered towards its end surrounded by fripperies and conceits, and the meaningless scrolls and garlands and pretty foolishnesses were translated in England into a style both dignified and elegant by Thomas Chippendale and his contemporaries. His rococo scrolls and shells and garlands before the middle of the century began to affect Scottish silverware. A teapot of 1740 in the Royal Scottish Museum retains, fundamentally, the bullet form and fine lines of earlier teapots, but the restrained engraving which surrounded their lids has here begun to show signs of flamboyance, while the vigour of the straight spout has surrendered to the seductions of the curve. By 1753 James Weems had made a coffee-pot covered with a rash of scrolls and counter-scrolls, repeated in the handle and in the weak, rather ridiculous spout with zoomorphic lip; and in the same year Robert Gordon produced a kettle, well-proportioned but decked with scrollwork and surmounted by a bird, set on a stand quite French in its manner, a group once in the possession of the Haigs of Bemersyde. William Gilchrist is the maker of Pl.84 a similar rococo kettle and stand in Sir J. Stirling-Maxwell's collection, of date 1753.

Pl.85.i   Gilchrist is the author of one of the two remarkable gold race cups which have survived from this time.[1] It is a tall piece—10½ inches—and weighs 22 ozs. 7 dwts. The year is 1752. It is one of the most elaborate cups of its kind made in the United Kingdom, and the surface is almost entirely covered with rococo scrolls, acanthus leaves and sprays of flowers. The double-scroll handles are of ebony, socketed at the top under gold acanthus leaves and at the foot in volutes. Cartouches on the body are engraved with the arms of Edinburgh and with the crest and motto of George II. This cup is now in America. The other is by Ker & Dempster. Its decoration is much more restrained, being confined to floral chasing on the cover and on the upper portion of the body. A cartouche in this floral setting carries the arms of Edinburgh and, beneath it, a finely-engraved Royal coat-of-arms. The cup has been conservatively dated at about 1755, on the ground of the maker's mark, although it is admitted that the plainness suggests a considerably earlier date. This cup is rather smaller than the other: 8¼ inches high, weighing 21 ozs. 3 dwts. The two cups, taken in conjunction with the gold teapots by James Ker described in an earlier chapter, are evidence of an important annual race-meeting in or near Edinburgh.

Pl.85.ii

Florid and even grotesque rococo work persisted until far into the third quarter of the century. The outline of a coffee-pot of 1769 by Patrick Robertson, in the Royal Scottish Museum, is distorted by its surface decoration, although this consists mainly of scrolls in the Chippendale manner. Yet call it taste or native caution as one chooses, nearly always there is a sense of restraint, withholding the maker from the wilder orgies of ornament. The engraver's tools tend to bite more deeply as the years pass, and the fringe of light decoration round the lids of teapots which is such a pleasing feature in the 'thirties is much too timid for the 'fifties. On the other hand, I know of no attempts at realistic reproduction like the English teapot by Wirgman illustrated by Mr. Oman.[2] *Chinoiserie* occurs hardly at all. There is a faint reflection of it in the engraving on a salver by Lothian & Robertson in the Royal Scottish Museum, of date 1751. Here a 'Chinese' figure is introduced, with parasol, feathers in hat, and shoes with turned-up toes of a rather blatantly oriental kind, but the notion appears to be derived at second- or third-hand from some English tea-caddy. It is odd that the Chinese taste was so little cultivated by Scottish goldsmiths, for there were Scots enough in foreign trade. Many Scots families had their specially-painted services of Chinese armorial porcelain, and the Chinese porcelain painters produced at least one series of plates depicting their notion of

Pl.95

[1] *The Connoisseur*, Vol. CXXVIII, p. 85   [2] *English Domestic Silver*, Pl. XVI, No. 67

kilted Highlanders. Extravaganza either did not appeal to the Scots or taxed too much the craftsmen's powers of design.

Nearly always a fine sense of form shows itself, even in the phases of elaboration. For example, from 1750 onwards there appeared a great many admirable trays and salvers. An unusual rectangular salver with openwork border, bearing the Dunlop crest, was lent to the Glasgow Exhibition of 1938 and is illustrated in the catalogue (No. 48). It is by Lothian & Robertson, of date 1759. On most salvers and trays of this time the engraving is of good quality, although conventional in design. Cake-baskets and sweetmeat-baskets follow the usual patterns also. Ker and Dempster are the authors of a particularly handsome cake-basket of 1752 lent to the Glasgow Exhibition by the Trustees of the late Sir Charles Jackson. The piercing is crisp and spirited, the handle and feet are massive. A charming little sweetmeat-basket is in the Cathcart White collection in the Royal Scottish Museum, also by Ker & Dempster, but of the year 1766. Also in the Museum is an article peculiar to Scotland, Pl.97.ii   although very rare—a bannock-rack, formed like an immense toast-rack to carry thick oatmeal bannocks hot from the girdle. Condiment articles as a rule follow the usual lines, but the late Queen Mary lent to the Glasgow Exhibition an exceptional set of four salt-cellars of 1755, by James Gilsland, with triple feet of shell form and embossed decoration. And even at this late date we find pure forms, untouched by ornament of any sort, such as the teapot and kettle by Robert Gordon, 1758, in Lord Haddington's collection.

Urns, both for coffee and for tea, were made throughout most of the century, and seem to have come into use in Scotland before they did in England. Until the later decades of the century they are egg-shaped, with snake handles and three feet curved in cabriole style. Possibly the earliest is the coffee-urn of 1724 in Lord Bute's collection. It is by James Mitchellsone. James Ker made urns as well as teapots, and did it with his usual distinctive touch. In Scotland, as in England, this sort of vessel lent itself peculiarly well to the classical designs of the Adam style. Most striking of all classical tea-urns is the big one in the Royal Scottish Museum, a piece of much dignity, well adapted to fit into the rooms in the great houses of the New Town of Edinburgh, then emerging from the plans of Craig and, in certain cases, of Robert Adam himself. This Pl.96   urn is 19½ inches high and weighs 116 ozs. It is beautifully conceived and executed, the faceted body and lofty, sweeping handles lending it an architectural quality and the characteristic *garrya* pendants and classical finials supplying interesting detail. Its year is 1778, and it is the work of Patrick Robertson, maker of the rococo coffee-pot in the same museum.

A vast amount of table ware and what is known in the trade as 'flat silver' must have been made in this period, for as early as 1731 John Rollo's ledger shows the high proportion of the goldsmith's time given to these small necessities. Such smaller articles, and especially spoons, forks and knives, tend to disappear, and they are often not fully marked. Provincial Scottish spoons are particularly inadequately marked, a subject of which further mention will be made in the next chapter, but Edinburgh spoons are also often remiss in this respect. There are, however, subtle differences in form which distinguish Scottish from English spoons of this time, and anyone who has handled numbers of them will recognise the differences. Many handsome serving spoons, soup ladles and toddy ladles have survived. There is a fish-slice by William Robertson of as early a date as 1752 in Sir Charles D. Hope-Dunbar's collection. An unusual piece in this category is the cream-scoop in Mr. John Noble's collection. It has a handle of pebble. It was made in 1790, but the maker's mark, RS, is unidentified. As far as the Canongate is concerned—still a separate burgh until the nineteenth century—spoons and small domestic articles appear to have been all that the goldsmiths were producing in the latter half of the eighteenth century, and it is doubtful if they produced many pieces more ambitious in the first half. The Canongate bowl, dating from early in the century, and the Communion cups of Auchtertool (1763), are exceptional in their importance. Men such as Adam Davis, M. Hinchcliffe and David Greig have left their marks only on spoons. Grant states[1] that the profits on spoons and forks were so small that their manufacture soon passed into the hands of English makers, and the prices quoted in Rollo's ledger support this, for they seem to be little more than the value of the silver itself.

Pl.104.i

The second half of the eighteenth century produced no church plate that is remarkable. The period begins, at the time of the 'Forty-five, with yet another phase of heavy losses in old plate.[2] In some places—the Church of St. Nicholas in Aberdeen is an instance—spoliation on behalf of the Jacobites was disastrous, but the Royalists themselves came out of the incident with no high repute. Such losses apart, even at this late period the Kirk was most inadequately supplied with Communion vessels, and the old practice of borrowing and lending these continued. Some Edinburgh goldsmiths must have been occupied steadily

---

[1] *Old and New Edinburgh*, Vol. I, p. 376   [2] *Scottish Communion Plate*, p. 109

PLATE 93

Tea Pot: Edinburgh, 1753-54. Makers: Lothian and Robertson

Tea Pot: Edinburgh, 1758-59. Makers: Lothian and Robertson

PLATE 94

Pair of Candlesticks: Edinburgh, 1759-60. Makers: Lothian and Robertson

Cake Basket made for the 2nd Earl of Hopetoun: Edinburgh, 1757-58. Maker: William Dempster

PLATE 95

Coffee Pot: Edinbrugh, 1769–70. Maker: Patrick Robertson *(p.159)*

PLATE 96

Tea Urn: Edinburgh, 1778-79. Maker: Patrick Robertson *(p.160)*

PLATE 97

Tea Pot: Edinburgh, 1776–77. Maker: James Gillieland

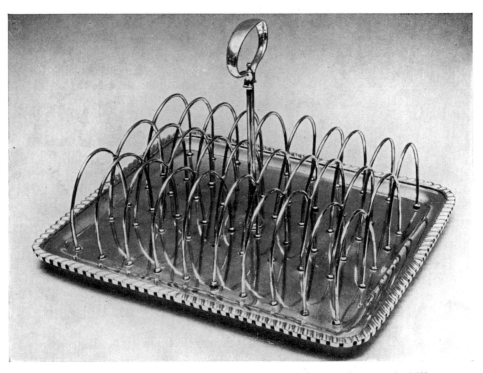

Bannock Rack: Edinburgh, 1773–74. Maker: Patrick Robertson *(p.160)*

PLATE 98

Four-piece Tea Set: Edinburgh, 1791-92. Maker: William Robertson

Octagonal Tea Pot: Edinburgh, 1789-90. Maker: Patrick Robertson

PLATE 99

Cup and Cover: Edinburgh, 1771-72. Maker: Lothian and Robertson

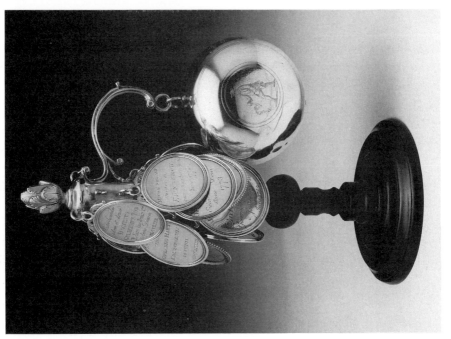

Bowling Trophy with Winner's Medals, presented 1771.
Unmarked

PLATE 100

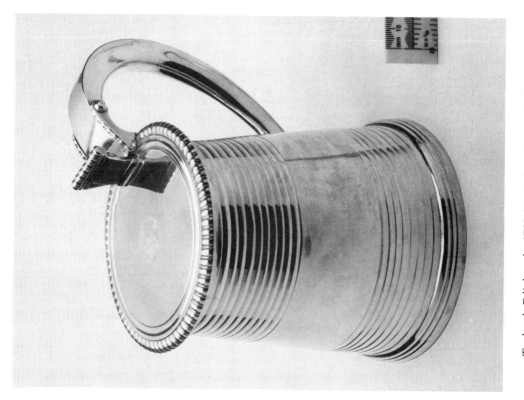

Tankard: Edinburgh, 1785-86. Maker: Patrick Robertson

Ink Pot and Sander: Edinburgh, 1785-86. Maker: William Davie

in supplying the want. By the late 'thirties and the 'forties the shape of the
Communion cup had virtually become uniform in that it adhered to the goblet
type, with baluster stem and stepped, moulded foot. There are of course variations within the limits of the type. James Mackenzie made an elegant pair of
cups for Old Cumnock in 1755, with deep bowl and slightly everted lip, the
bowl nicely engraved with the arms of the donor, the whole being more than
a little reminiscent of James Ker's cups made for Auchinleck in 1733, presented
by Lady Elizabeth Boswell.

Such marked character is rare after 1750. Indeed, there began a tendency
among some makers to fix on a pattern and to reproduce it with what is almost
shameless persistence. Lothian & Robertson, for instance, who seem to have
had many commissions to remake cups to conform with new requirements,
modified the Tron cups in Edinburgh, giving them bowls not unlike those of
the Cumnock cups. The original cups were made in 1633, no doubt resembling
the Old Greyfriars cups in the same city, and they were renewed by the Town
Council in 1756. Murroes Parish Church in Dundee and New Abbey church
both have cups of the same pattern, by the same maker. There is little point in
multiplying examples of the cups of the period for, by comparison with seventeenth-century vessels, it is so rarely they deviate appreciably from the dull
norm. The Moderatism which prevailed in the Kirk, with its rebuttal of the
fiery evangelism of earlier times, may perhaps help to explain the dull, the
almost casual conformity of the cups of the 'fifties and 'sixties; yet on the other
hand one might have expected of the intellectually inclined and good-living
Moderates vessels more indicative of the taste and talents of contemporary
goldsmiths. It is an interesting problem for those who maintain that the spirit
of Calvin was inimical to art. In the very decades when Communion plate
declined aesthetically almost to the monotonous level of mass-production the
Church had relaxed its traditional severity, surrendered on point after point of
discipline, compromised on what had formerly been relentless penalties. By
the fourth quarter of the century the minister no longer ruled his kirk-session,[1]
and the zeal of the sessions themselves was tempered by worldly considerations
which deemed fines in the poor-box on the whole more useful than public
penances in the kirk.

Between about 1790 and 1820 much admirable silver came out of Edinburgh, although the period is not yet become a fashionable one with collectors.

[1] Ibid., p. 119

The restless ornament of the rococo had largely disappeared and the grandiose tastes of the Regency had thrown no shadows before them. There were, for example, some beautiful teapots. One of these, given to the Royal Scottish Museum by Mrs. E. H. D. Marjoribanks, has all the functional as well as the aesthetic virtues, with its deep-set, straight spout, capacious body and generously-proportioned handle. Its lightly-engraved ornament is typical. Made by William Robertson, the teapot and its stand are both of the year 1796. A pleasant sugar basin and cream jug of eight years later, also given by Mrs. Marjoribanks, are by Cunningham & Simpson. Like a kettle sold in London in December, 1953, the teapot bears a Marjoribanks crest which links it with the family of a former Lord Provost of Edinburgh, so that such quiet, elegant pieces may be accepted as characteristic of the best silverware made at the time.

Such domestic work apart, the Edinburgh goldsmiths of the day seem to have confined themselves on the whole to rather unambitious and even pedestrian things. There was a certain trade in presentation silver, as for example the fine punch-bowl made in 1809 for Lieut.-Colonel George Brown of Capelrig, Commandant of the Renfrewshire Volunteer Infantry. A few simple Communion cups were still commissioned, and the quaich began to make its appearance again, perhaps recreated by the romanticism of the era of the Waverley Novels. But there was no Paul Storr among the Edinburgh goldsmiths. Not that the technical skills had decayed, for the latest of the five Court of Session maces is of date 1815, although it is modelled closely on the form of the mace of 1704. The mace of the University of Edinburgh is also a late one, for it was made in 1789 to replace an older mace which had been stolen. It follows the usual pattern of bell-headed maces, and carries the mark of William Davie. An inscription in Latin records that it was presented to the University by William Creech, the College Bailie, who did this in the name of the Lord Provost, Magistrates and Council. The reason for the gift seems to have been that there was a widespread belief that the theft of the old mace could be attributed to the notorious Deacon Brodie, executed in 1788 for robberies committed over a term of years while he posed as a respectable citizen. Since Brodie had been a patron of the College he had every opportunity to be the thief, and the Town Council was evidently only too ready to close the matter by presenting a new mace.

One branch of silverware, the manufacture of which throve during the late eighteenth and early nineteenth centuries, especially in Edinburgh, is the so-called Luckenbooth brooch. These tiny brooches are heart-shaped, or their design is a variation of the heart. The design betrays the purpose, for the brooches were made as tokens of betrothal and were used widely for this purpose in Scotland. It is impossible to say when they first came into use, but certainly they were in existence well before the middle of the eighteenth century. The heart brooch had been known in England since medieval times, but some Scottish examples show a close resemblance to Scandinavian heart brooches, notably perhaps to Norwegian ones. There is a Norwegian type consisting of a simple heart in outline surmounted by a crown and fixed by a bodkin-like pin swinging across the heart, and a Scottish form closely similar to this is one of the commonest. This seems, indeed, to be the earliest Scottish form. There is a fairly large dated brooch of this kind inscribed *Ruth I Chap. and verse 16th 1736*.

The name Luckenbooth is derived from the Luckenbooths, or Locken (locked) Booths, a group of wooden booths or shops which at one time clustered up against the High Kirk of St. Giles in Edinburgh. Among these were the shops of various jewellers who sold brooches of this kind. There is, however, no question but that the brooches were made and sold in other parts of Scotland. Among the burgh records of Tain for 1787 is a catalogue of a roup referring to 47 heart brooches of silver and one of gold. The marks of several Inverness silversmiths appear on heart brooches and there is a type which, in my view, must especially be associated with Inverness. Its peculiar features are (1) the crown, which is conventionalised into a device rather like a pair of spectacles; (2) the odd, angular projections on the heart itself; (3) a leaf ornament like a fleur-de-lys upside down, at the lower extremity; and (4) a small, chevron-like bar sometimes present within the lower part of the heart.

Many of the brooches consist of twin hearts, overlapping, a modification of obvious significance. The crown spans both. A type which appeared after 1800 portrays the heart with a twist to its tail. This, and other types of the time, were fretted out of sheet metal, and the decoration may be heavy engraving or a setting of garnets or pebbles. Garnets are frequently used and some brooches set with them are very pretty. Most heart brooches are of silver, not always of good quality, but a very few are of gold, though these are generally small and slight. Whitelaw has stated they were cast in moulds and finished by hand.[1] Some are stamped with the maker's hall-mark or his initials, a few with the town mark. Initials are commonly engraved on the backs. They record the

---

[1] *Glasgow Archaeological Society—Transactions*, Vol. VI, p. 128

donor, perhaps also the recipient. The date of presentation may also be present. *My ♡ ye have and thin I creve* is a typical inscription. Biblical quotations are more rare. Witch Brooches is a less common term for these small pieces, and there is a tradition—unsupported by the inscriptions—that they were pinned to childrens' skirts to ward off the evil eye.

Brief mention should be made of wine-labels, a branch of the goldsmith's craft which has become popular with collectors. Considerable numbers of these were produced in Scotland in the late eighteenth and early nineteenth centuries. As a rule, they are plain to the point of severity: shaped, rectangular plates with block lettering. There are delightful exceptions, however. I recall a label engraved *Calcavella*, with floral and shell moulded border, by Robert Keay of Perth, and a shaped label of rococo design with the cryptic inscription *British*, of Edinburgh origin. Both are in the collection of Mr. Alexander Cuthbert, Hon. Auditor of the Wine Label Circle. Perhaps the most interesting aspect of these little pieces is the light they throw on the habits and tastes of the households of the time. They show that Scottish cellars were stocked with quite a variety of unusual wines. In addition to the Calcavella already mentioned, Keay also made a label for Frontiniac, a muscat wine made at Frontignan, for Lisbon, a white wine made in the province of Estremadura, evidently quite popular in this country, and for Paxarette, a very fine though somewhat sweet sherry of the old monastery of Paxarete, in the Jerez district. Claret labels of Scottish origin are numerous, for claret, not whisky, is the traditional drink of Scotland and one of the strongest links in the 'Auld Alliance'.

The national sport, golf, has produced a number of interesting silver trophies. One belonging to the Royal and Ancient Golf Club at St. Andrews seems to date from about the middle of the eighteenth century, although unfortunately neither the silver club nor the balls attached to it carry any hall-mark. The balls, fastened to the shaft by short lengths of silver chain, were presented by successive captains and each bears the donor's name and the year. The earliest is of 1754. These balls faithfully reproduce the ancient leather-covered balls, tightly filled with 'a top-hatful of feathers'; while the club is in the form of a driver of early type, the head engraved with a figure of St. Andrew, the hand-grip gilt. Edinburgh seems the likely source of origin, since a number of such clubs were made, including one for the Royal Burgess Golfing Society of Edinburgh.

Pl.82.i

PLATE 101

Tea Caddy: Edinburgh, 1795-96. Makers: W & P Cunningham

Silver gilt Coffee Pot: Edinburgh, 1782-83. Maker: Robert Bowman

PLATE 102

Goblet: Leith, with Edinburgh marks for 1820–21.
Maker: John Hay

Salver with cast border: Edinburgh, 1814–15. Makers: W & P Cunningham

PLATE 103

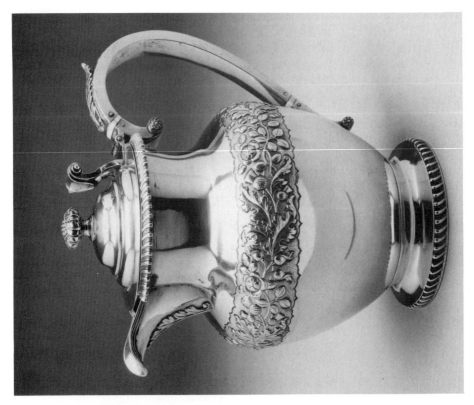

Jug for Hot Water or Mulled Wine: Edinburgh, 1822–23.
Maker: George Fenwick

Egg Cruet: Edinburgh, 1832–33. Maker: George Paton

PLATE 104

The Canongate Bowl: Canongate, early 18th century. Maker: Patrick Inglis
(p.173)

Lemon Squeezer: apparently by David Manson, Dundee, with Edinburgh marks for 1816–17

NOTES TO CHAPTER XIV

THE PATRICK ROBERTSON URN (pp.161-162, last four lines)

This urn has been the subject of an excellent article by Malcolm Baker in 1973. He points out the similarities between this urn and others by Bolton and Fothergil. He demonstrates from their letter-books at Birmingham Assay Office that there was a certain amount of trade in English silver sold by Scottish goldsmiths in Edinburgh during the latter part of the eighteenth century. (See also my own 1972 article: *Scottish Silver: Marks are not Everything* in *Antique Finder*, where a pair of candlesticks is illustrated together with their marks, showing Sheffield marks for 1788-9 overstruck by Edinburgh marks and Patrick Robertson's maker's mark.)

CREAM SCOOP BY ROBERT SWAN (p.161, line 15)

This object has aroused learned controversy and not a little amusement. There is a vociferous body of opinion that maintains that anyone who has ever tried to scoop cream with such an instrument is in for a disappointment. The alternative use suggested is as a crumb scoop. I have tried this idea and can report that while it is not so good on a wooden surface, it works better and more easily than a brush on a table-cloth, especially if one slightly lifts the edge of the cloth towards which one is scooping. Robert Swan is first found mentioned in the trade directories in 1790.

CANONGATE (p.161, line 23)

Further down the same paragraph, reference is made to three men who are said to have worked in Canongate; this information is now out of date. (See the Canongate section of Chapter Fifteen, pp.170-179)

LATER SILVER (p.162, last two lines)

Mr. Finlay states that the period between 1790 and 1820 is not popular with collectors. However true that may have been when he wrote it, it is not so any longer. Good quality silver of this period is keenly sought after by those who either cannot now afford earlier pieces or else prefer the later styles. The period does indeed have merits of its own, as I hope the new illustrations to this chapter show.

NEW ILLUSTRATIONS

Apart from the White Rod of Scotland, I do not intend to say more about the nineteen pieces which are newly illustrated in this edition than is already said about them in their captions. Suffice it to say that they show a wide range of ideas, not all of them native Scottish ones, and a high degree of skill which had not deserted the goldsmiths of Edinburgh, even after the influence of English designs had made itself so obviously felt in Scotland.

THE WHITE ROD OF SCOTLAND (pl.92,ii. and Colour frontispiece)

The illustration shows the Unicorn which forms the upper terminal of the earliest of the three surviving White Rods. It was made in Edinburgh by John Clark and bears the date letter for 1758-9. The rod is of silver with a gilt central knop and another at the lower terminal engraved with the Royal Arms. It is the wand of office of His Majesty's Principal Usher, or Usher of the White Rod. There is a good article about the Ushership by J. H. Stevenson (who was not aware of the existence of this particular rod) in Northern notes and Queries for 1897. The usher to whom this rod pertained was Alexander Coutts of Redfield, one of the banking family of that name. When he acquired the Ushership by purchase in 1758 he lost no time in commissioning a rod and chain of office from John Clark, an Edinburgh goldsmith, and set about rescuing the office of Usher from the dilapidation into which it has fallen. He managed to gain official recognition in some respects as a British Officer of the Crown, somewhat analogous to Black Rod at Westminster. He received a summons to attend the coronation of George III when he walked side by side with Black Rod. Despite having gone to the trouble and expense of entailing the Ushership in 1759, he sold it in 1766 to Sir James Cockburn, the representative of the family to whom it has previously belonged. He retained his insignia, however, which have descended by inheritance to the present owner.

The next rod, made by John Clark for Sir James Cockburn in 1766, is still in existence, as is the rod made in London for Sir Patrick Walker in 1817 which he carried at the coronation of George IV and also on the occasion of that monarch's visit to Edinburgh in 1822. At Walker's death in 1837 the ushership passed by inheritance jointly to his two maiden sisters who left it in turn, with all their other possessions, to a trust, known as the Walker Trust, set up for the benefit of the Scottish Episcopal Church, with whom the Office of Usher now resides.

The gold chain and gold, enamelled and jewelled medallion, signed by Clark, represent the very highest peak of goldsmith work of which any eighteenth-century Edinburgh goldsmith was capable, comparing favourable with anything being made in London at the time. Clark, who was also a maker of scientific instruments including his famous series of silver microscopes (one of which belonged to Alexander Coutts), was a superb silversmith, goldsmith and jeweller and the rod, chain and medal of 1758-9 place him in the very top league in these fields. The jewels and enamelling are of the greatest beauty and the highest order of workmanship. (See colour frontis)

Chapter Fifteen

THE BURGH CRAFTSMEN: EIGHTEENTH AND NINETEENTH CENTURIES

(by Henry Fothringham)

IT should not be thought that Edinburgh was the only town in Scotland where worthwhile silver was made during the eighteenth and nineteenth centuries. The output of the provincial silversmiths was diverse and interesting, and the quality, although variable, sometimes equalled the best Edinburgh workmanship. An added zest, so far as the modern-day collector is concerned, is provided by the extraordinary proliferation of different marks used in the various burghs round the country, and numerous marks not yet satisfactorily ascribed. This diversity was due to the fact that each worker struck his own maker's mark and accompanying marks for himself, since there was no assay office in Scotland except in Edinburgh and, from 1819 to 1964, in Glasgow. A few provincial goldsmiths ordered to do so by the Privy Council and urged to comply by the Edinburgh Goldsmith Incorporation, began adding date letters to their own marks in 1681, concurrent with the Edinburgh cycle, but owing to the lack of central co-ordination the system gradually fell out of use. Random letters of the alphabet, however, are frequently not date letters, but have some other significance, if they mean anything at all.

Locally struck marks after 1784 were technically illegal because they avoided the '*Act for granting to his Majesty . . . certain duties on all Gold and Silver wrought Plate made in Great Britain*',[1] which came into force on 1 December that year. It was this Act, and not the Act of 1836,[2] which required provincial goldsmiths from all over Scotland to send their work to the Edinburgh Assay Office to be assayed and marked. The measure

[1] 24 Geo. III, c.53.   [2] 6 and 7 Wm. IV, c.69.

succeeded completely in Canongate and Glasgow, as far as one can tell, but met with little or no success elsewhere, so that it had to be restated in the 1836 Act as if it were not already the law of the land. The minute books of the Edinburgh Goldsmiths Incorporation often refer to abuses by silversmiths in Aberdeen, Dundee and elsewhere, who were continuing to mark their own work, often substandard, without the benefit of assay, until many years after the second of those Acts of Parliament. In any case, the 1836 Statute was, as Mr. Finlay said in the first edition, an unfortunate one.

> "No doubt it was inevitable; a stage in one of those rational processes for the promotion of administrative convenience which are now of such constant occurrence that they happen unnoticed. It may be argued, however, that rationalisation is an unnatural process which, oftener than not, in the end weakens the social system and renders it more easily subject to decay; and the decay of the silversmiths' craft in Scotland after 1836 in turn helped to weaken, if only in a minor degree, the self-sufficiency of many of the burghs. In the seventeenth and eighteenth centuries craftsmen even of some of the smaller burghs were well able to supply the needs of the Communion table and of the laird's lady, and as late as the second quarter of the nineteenth they were well able to supply table silver for minister and laird. The nucleus of the late Major J. Milne-Davidson's fine collection of provincial silver was inherited from generations of ancestors who had occupied manses in Banffshire and ordered their table silver locally or, at furthest, from Aberdeen; and there must still be many houses, especially in the north-east of the country, where interesting small domestic pieces of local origin still lurk, perhaps un-recognized, in cupboards and attics."[1]

CANONGATE

Even before Glasgow and Aberdeen, Canongate takes pride of place after Edinburgh, as far as silver is concerned. The first goldsmiths to work in the Burgh appear at the very beginning of the sixteenth century when James IV began to build a palace at Holyrood and established his mint there. It appears that coins may have been minted as early as 1501. By 1504, a goldsmith named Matthew Auchinleck was in charge of the mint. His son, another Matthew, took over in 1507 and was in turn succeeded in 1527 by Joachim

---

[1] First Edition, p. 152.

Hochstetter, an enterprising German, who was the first of a number of tolerated foreigners to work in the burgh as moneyer or goldsmith during the sixteenth and seventeenth centuries.

At least two goldsmiths, Patrick Gray and John Achesoun, were numbered among the thirty-two hammermen who received a Seal of Cause on 8 March 1535/6,[1] and two of the other men named in the document may also have been goldsmiths. Though never as numerous as the goldsmiths of Edinburgh, those of Canongate were just as skilful and imaginative in their work. Indeed, the Tulloch and Galloway Mazers made by James Gray[2] in 1557 and 1569 respectively are perhaps the finest example of silver work ever produced in Scotland. The presence of the court at Holyrood resulted in many of the nobility and gentry having town houses in the burgh, and this generated a thriving business for the goldsmiths and jewellers until the Union of the Crowns in 1603. Throughout the seventeenth century there are some twenty-nine goldsmiths' names recorded, though very few have surviving work ascribed to them. Before moving on to the eighteenth century, which is the proper subject of this section, I mention here some of the items of Canongate silver made before that period.

The Royal Museum of Scotland possesses a disc-end spoon by George Cunningham, elder, dated 1589.[3] The same goldsmith made the spectacular seal box for John Grahame, 3rd Earl of Montrose, to protect the Great Seal appended to the splendid and beautifully illuminated commission granted to him by James VI as his Commissioner-General in Scotland in 1604.[4] The box is engraved with the Royal Arms on one side and those of the Earl on the other and carries the inscription:

> *'John Eril of Montrois Lord Grahame & Mugdok, Heigh Chanceller of Scotland Anno Do. 1604.'*

Cunningham's spoon and seal box are both marked with a standard mark, X1D, indicating eleven pennyweights fine, in addition to the marks of town and maker, as is another disc-end spoon, in private hands, known as the Oliphant spoon, made by Robert Kerr (admitted in 1620) in about 1625.

---

[1] *Book of the Records of the Ancient Privileges of the Canongate* p. 36, Nos. 85 and 86.
[2] See pp. 71–2 and plate 23.
[3] See pp. 71 and 98, and plate 36 and *P.S.A.S.*
[4] Sir J. Balfour-Paul: *The Scots Peerage*, Vol. VI, p. 236 and footnote.

Nicholas Jorgenson, who was admitted in 1638, and who died in 1644, is the maker of the communion basin at Forgue, Aberdeenshire, which The Rev. Thomas Burns dismissed as being 'of foreign manufacture'.[1] It measures thirteen inches in diameter and the central boss is engraved with the arms of the donor. The rim is engraved:

> 'Giftit to God and His Church of Forgue by James Viscount of Frendrought Lord Crichtone'.

The Turriff presbytery records note that it was presented in 1643.[2] Robert Banks was admitted in 1652 and appears to be the maker of the Tulloch coconut cup, c.1655. Michael Ziegler, admitted in 1683, made the pair of communion cups for Flisk, in Fife, in c.1685, while George Ziegler made two pairs of cups, one for Bolton, East Lothian, in 1696 and the other for West Linton, Peeblesshire, in 1702. Walter Grahame is the first maker known to have used date letters in Canongate. A thistle cup by him in a private collection bears the gothic O for 1694–5.

When considering the eighteenth century, a word of warning is necessary. By this date a number of clock and watchmakers belonged to the Hammermen, were not, by any stretch of the imagination, goldsmiths and jewellers as well. However, the lists of masters elected annually to oversee each branch of the trade's activities often include the names of clock and watchmakers as masters of the goldsmiths' craft, even when a goldsmith was available to fill the post. This should not be taken to indicate that they were goldsmiths, rather that their particular craft was administered together with that of the goldsmiths and jewellers, as far as internal inspection by the Incorporation was concerned. Only one such man, John Champion, has any claim to a foot in both camps and even that is doubtful. He was actually a clockmaker but is once referred to as 'jeweller' in an assessment roll of 1715. I know of no work by him and there is no evidence that he ever practised as a goldsmith; accordingly I have left him out of the present discussions. The goldsmiths given below include all those who were admitted to the Incorporation during the eighteenth century, as far as their own records show. Certain men such as James Kerr, an Edinburgh goldsmith who was made a burgess of Canongate in 1732 but who was never a member of the

[1] Burns: *Old Scottish Plate*, p. 207.   [2] Ibid.

Canongate Hammermen's Incorporation, are omitted as it seems certain that they never practised in Canongate or used distinctive Canongate marks.

David Dunlop was admitted in 1701 and was a master by 1707. His will was registered in 1710. Marks ascribed to him are found on dog-nose spoons.

James Aytoun was admitted in 1706, having served his apprenticeship with Walter Grahame. I know of no work by him at present.

Peter (sometimes Patrick) Inglis was admitted on 2 August, 1716 and is last referred to in 1727. He is the maker of the famous Canongate Bowl, a small punch bowl of superb quality in a breathtakingly beautiful and simple octofoil design.[1]

Colin Mitchell, having been apprenticed to Peter Inglis on 10 June 1717, was admitted on 22 July 1727. His workmanship is excellent and he dominated the scene until his death in 1753. He was a very colourful and interesting character, as is revealed by his private papers. A Jacobite sympathiser, Mitchell supplied a silver sword hilt to Cameron of Lochiel, but that did not prevent him from giving evidence against other Jacobites in order to protect himself from suspicion.[2] He took Peter Cuthbertson as an apprentice on 14 August 1734.

John Smith was admitted on the same day as Colin Mitchell. No work of his is known for certain. He took an apprentice named James Hamilton on 9 April 1730 for six years, but is not mentioned again in the Incorporation's records.

Peter Mitchell was admitted on 1 February 1728. His essay was 'ane stone ring with ane silver spoon and fork'. (The usual essay at this time included a plain gold ring rather than one with a stone set in it). He took an apprentice, William Buchanan, for the unusually short period of five years, instead of the normal six or seven, from 5 February 1731. He was a master for the fourth time in 1732 and is not mentioned again in the records.

Before the admission of the next goldsmith, James Hill in 1732, the Canongate Hammermen, evidently worried that the goldsmiths' art was in decline and disrepute in the burgh, defined the rules under which its goldsmiths and jewellers should operate. It is most unusual for any Hammermen's Incorporation to be in the least bit concerned about its

---

[1] See Plate 25.
[2] *A List of persons Concerned in the Rebellion* (1745) S.H.S. 1st Series, Vol. 8, p. 339.

PLATE 105

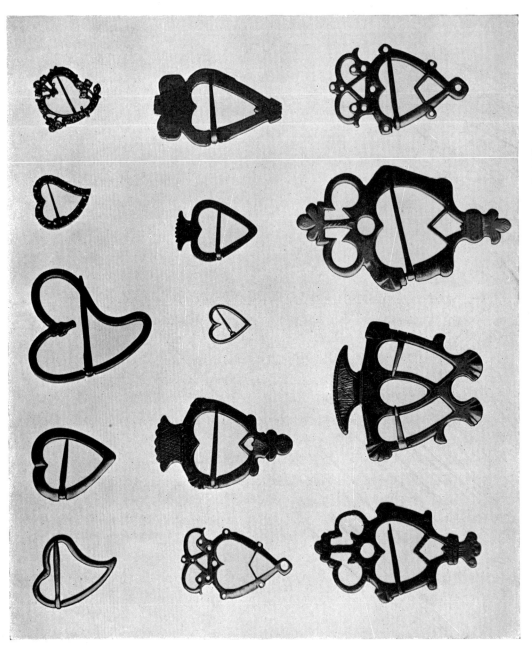

Luckenbooth Brooches: late 18th and early 19th centuries *(p. 164)*

PLATE 106

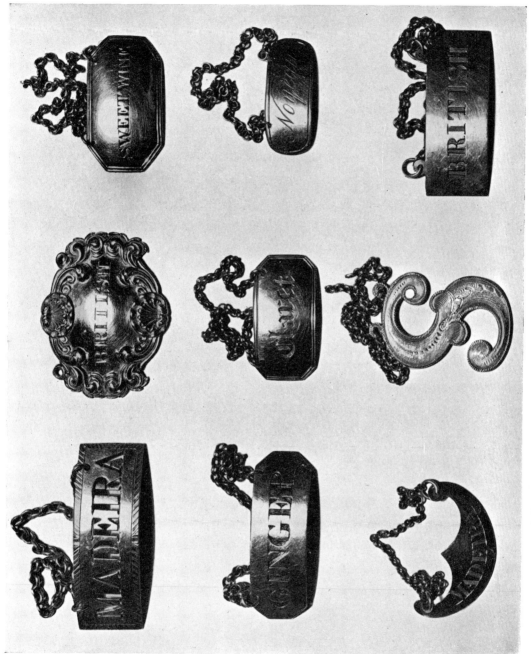

Wine Labels: Edinburgh, Aberdeen and Dundee, late 18th and early 19th centuries (p.165)

PLATE 107

Tea Caddy: Glasgow, c.1735. Maker: Robert Luke;
Cream Boat: Glasgow, c.1740. Maker: James Glen *(p.182)*

Basting or Hash Spoons: Glasgow, early 18th century. Maker: John Luke

PLATE 108

Pair of Mugs: Aberdeen, c.1735. Maker: George Cooper

Tea Service: Aberdeen, c.1730. Maker: George Cooper
(p.188)

goldsmiths' marks, or the standard to which their work was to be assayed, and I therefore quote the greater part of the entry, dated 21 July 1731, because of the number of interesting points it raises. (The only parallel I have noted is mentioned in the Glasgow section of this chapter, but the Glasgow case is somewhat different.) The measure was probably prompted by the Incorporation having received a letter from the Goldsmiths Incorporation of Edinburgh, in July 1729, reminding them of their obligations. The entry is entitled:

ACT ANENT GOLDSMITHS AND JEWELLERS

'The which day the Deacon, Boxmaster and remanen masters and members of the Incorporation of Hammermen in Canongate being met . . . with respect to the art of Goldsmiths Craft, and taking to their serious consideration, as they are entitled to do, and have right by their ancient Seal of Cause long before the Reformation from popery, and by Charters and Acts of Parliament ratifying and confirming their Seal of Cause, to admit and receive freemen goldsmiths within the burgh of Canongate and other parts of the Priviledge thereof; so far maintaining the said trade they . . . Inact, statue and ordain that no freeman goldsmith within the said burgh or other parts of the their Priviledge make in work or cause work in Silver under the just fineness of Eleven pennie fyne, under the certification contained in the fifty-sext act, sext par. of Mary, 1555 years.[1] And that every said goldsmith mark the silver work that he makes with his own mark and with the Burgh's mark; and if he makes any silver above the said fineness, that he with his mark make ane prent of the just poynt of the fineness that it is of, that it may be known to all what fineness it is of. And that no goldsmith or jeueller make in work or set furth of his own Gold, or other men's Gold, under the just fineness of 22 carrat fyne, under the pain contained in the said Act of Parliament. And in obedience to and in compliance with the said Act of Privy Council,[2] the said trade of Hammermen discharge all goldsmiths and jeuellers within the burgh of Canongate and other parts of their Priviledge to work in gold and silver except of the fineness foresaid; And appoints and ordains the said goldsmiths and jeuellers in Canongate to keep an Essay Box of all plate made by them, which box

---

[1] Mary c.34, 20 June 1555. (A.P.S. Vol. II, p. 499).
[2] *Register of the Privy Council of Scotland, 1681–2.* Folio 256a. Printed Volume: 3rd series, Vol. VII, p. 104 etc.

is to be sent to his Majesty's Goldsmith once in the year to be tryed by him, and thereafter by the Essay Master of his Majesty's Mint. And the goldsmith or goldsmiths in the said burgh of Canongate shall set his name upon his work, marked with the A.B.C., and any other work otherways made or marked by him, or which he shall have in his shop or possession, after the day and date hereof, shall fall under the certification in the said Acts. And further, the said Trade of Hammermen, to show furth their ready compliance with the said Acts, and for the well and benefite of his Majesty's leidges, and to the discouraging of evill practices in the art of Goldsmith or Jeueller Craft, Inact and appoint and Ordain all freeman goldsmiths and jeuellers already received within the burgh of Canongate and other parts of their freedome forthwith to grant Bond and sufficient caution to the said Hammermen that in case it shall be found that the said goldsmiths or jeuellers have transgressed or shall trangress the said Acts, that the transgressor shall not only make up what damage any of the leidges hath sustained or may sustain through the insufficiency of his work, but after he is found capable and convicted of his trangression, he shall never be found thereafter to work within the said burgh of Canongate or any other part of its Priviledge under the penalty of £5 Sterling money to be paid to the said Hammermen for the use of their poor by and at our performance, and ordains all goldsmiths and jeuellers to be received freemen within the said burgh of Canongate to grant bond and sufficient caution to the said trade of Hammermen in their above terms and under the penalty and certification demanded at their entry in all time coming.

[Signed] Peter Mitchell. Colin Mitchell.'

A number of interesting points arise from the above extract, but there is room to draw attention to only a few of them here: i) The Incorporation laboured under the delusion that the legal standard for silver was still the old Scots standard of eleven pennyweights fine, as prescribed by the 1555 Act, and were genuinely unaware (as indeed were all other Scottish goldsmiths at that time, except those of Edinburgh who pretended to be) that the 1720 Act[1] had established Sterling as the legal minimum.   ii) The goldsmith is to mark his work himself, not only with his initials but also with his own town mark and an annually changed date letter. (The date letter system had been insisted upon by the Privy Council in 1681 and was intended to apply to the

---

[1] Act 6 Geo. I, *c.*11, 1 June 1720.

whole country and not just to Edinburgh. In practice, however, it was little used in Canongate.)   iii) Each goldsmith was to keep his own 'Essay Box' i.e., a box to contain scrapings from all his work, which was then sent to be assayed independently. How far this regulation was ever complied with is impossible to say, but my estimate would be 'not at all'.   iv) Lastly, there were only two goldsmiths active in the burgh in 1731 to sign the Act, Peter and Colin Mitchell.

The first goldsmith to be admitted after the passing of this Act was James Hill, on 14 October 1732. He continued to be an active member of the craft for 38 years, being elected a master for the nineteenth and last time in 1770. He was Deacon in 1764–6. During all that time only two apprentices were registered by him in Canongate: James Halliday in 1743 and Alexander Mason in 1762, but there may well have been others.

As early as June 1731, more than a year before his admission, he was already in trouble with the Goldsmiths Incorporation in Edinburgh. After much argument they permitted him to become bound apprentice to the elder Charles Dickson, goldsmith in Edinburgh, in 1736. This was a cunning device to gain eventual admission to the Goldsmiths Incorporation there, which eventually happened in 1746 when his essay was "a canister snuff box and a plain gold ring". As an Edinburgh craftsman, he took several further apprentices, one of whom, Alexander Mason, had already been bound to him in Canongate but had to be re-bound six months later in Edinburgh in order to keep within the Goldsmiths Incoporation's rules.

Peter Spalding was admitted on 6 September 1745, having 'made faith for professing the true protestant religeon', showing that in those troubled times of the Jacobite rising the Incorporation wished to prevent the entry of Espicopalians and Catholics to their number. His essay was 'a silver spoon and a fork and a cross-set five stone ring'. He is last mentioned in Canongate when he was chosen as a master for the eleventh time in 1763. His mark is found on some pieces of flatware of elegant design. Meanwhile he became a freeman of the Edinburgh Goldsmiths Incorporation in 1753.

Thomas Robertson was admitted on 30 August 1748, having presented for his essay 'a pocket spoon, knife and fork, with a plain gold ring'. There is no further mention of him in the Incorporation's records.

Peter Cuthbertson was admitted on 24 February 1755, having been apprenticed to Colin Mitchell as far back as 1734. His essay was 'a cannister snuff box and a plain gold ring'. He was elected to serve as a master at the annual elections in May the same year, but is not mentioned again in the Incorporation's records. His will was registered on 21 December 1756. He is presumed to have worked as journeyman to Colin Mitchell until his late master's death in 1753. He may thereafter have marked some work with his own initials before his admission as a freeman. His work is very rare and is much sought after by collectors.

Alexander Drummond was admitted on 15 August 1760. Five days later he took Henry Roxburgh as an apprentice for seven years, but is not mentioned again in the records. His marks have been recorded on flatware, although his essay, 'a seal and a plain gold ring' suggests that he may have confined his brief activities mainly to jewellery and goldwork.

William Craw, the son of a freeman hookmaker of the same name, was admitted on 22 November 1760. His essay was 'a cross ring and a pair of buckles'. He registered two apprentices, John Robertson in 1761 and John Hamilton in 1765. He was a master seven times during his active decade with the Incorporation. He does not figure in their proceedings after 1770, but was still alive in 1781, when he is stated to be working outside the burgh. From this it appears that he is identical with the William Craw, goldsmith, who became a burgess of Dumfries by purchase as a stranger on 18 December 1769. While still in Canongate he made the pair of Communion Cups for Auchtertool in Fife in 1763, and several pieces of a domestic nature, such as salts and salvers. Perhaps his most spectacular surviving work is the Trotter Tankard, standing 8½ ins. high and weighing 43 oz., and engraved with the arms of Trotter of Mortounhall (on the southern outskirts of modern Edinburgh) and of Charterhall in Berwickshire. This man's father, John Trotter, Maitland tells us,[1] built a family enclosure in Greyfriars Churchyard 'erected for his Great Grandfather, but now renewed to be the Resting place of him and his, whether they deserve it or not'! The Trotter tankard passed in 1984 from the Morris Collection into that of the City of Edinburgh, housed in Huntly House, Canongate, close to where it was made in the 1760s.

William Tibbetts, the son of a freeman blacksmith, was admitted on 1 May 1762. His essay was 'a three stone ring and a plain gold ring', from which one may perhaps infer that he was principally a jeweller. No

[1] William Maitland: *The History of Edinburgh* (1753) p. 202, i.

silverwork has yet been ascribed to him. He was a master in 1764 and 1765 and is not mentioned thereafter in the records.

Michael Forrest, having been booked journeyman with James McEwan in Glasgow in 1763, was admitted on 16 August 1770 when his essay was 'a punch spoon and a plain gold ring'. He registered one apprentice, Burnett Mills, on 18 May 1771. He was a master for five consecutive years until 1775, after which the records do not mention him again. As well as some very elegant Old English pattern flatware, his marks are found on a beautiful pair of hexafoil candlesticks (in a private collection) which, from their style, must have been made soon after his admission.

John Robertson, having been apprenticed to William Craw on 28 February 1761 for six years, was admitted on 23 November 1773. He probably worked as a journeyman for his former master before his own admission. He was elected a master four times and was still working in 1784. He is the maker of a lovely and unusual swing-handled oval sugar basket, the inverted pear-shaped body of which is chassed with flowers and foliage. The basket is now in the Edinburgh City Museum, Huntly House. The Museum has an excellent collection of Canongate and Edinburgh silver which has been built up over the last twenty years or so, and which repays careful study.

Andrew Milligan was admitted as a freeman goldsmith on 20 October 1775, having made a silver watchcase as his essay. He quickly became Deacon of the Incorporation and is still being mentioned in its proceedings a decade later. He took an apprentice, Alexander Scott, on 27 March 1777 when he is described as 'goldsmith and watchcase maker in Canongate'. By 1788 he had moved out of Canongate and had premises in Parliament Close, and remained in business at various addresses in Edinburgh until 1823, a working span of almost half a century. Despite being principally a watchcase maker, his marks have been seen on flatware of about 1780.

Lastly comes Robert Clelland, who was admitted on 5 November 1776. He took an apprentice, James Robertson, on 3 December the same year, and discharged those indentures on 26 July 1783.

The Canongate goldsmiths were unable to avoid their legal obligation to send all their work up the hill to the Edinburgh Assay Office at Goldsmiths' Hall in Parliament Close from 1784 onwards, in compliance with the Plate Duty Act passed that year, and, consequently, locally marked Canongate silver ceased abruptly and forever at that date. The maker's marks of those who continued working in the burgh after 1784 are therefore found with ordinary Edinburgh Assay Office marks.

The earliest town mark of Canongate was a *stag lodged*, with a cross between its antlers. This probably persisted until 1681 when its place was taken by a *stag's head erased*, some makers using a cross between the antlers and some not. However, not all stag's heads come from Canongate, thinking that they do so is an error that has misled many people until comparatively recently. Those perched on top of the letters F, R or M are Maltese, as demonstrated by Victor Denaro,[1] while those accompanied by an anchor are usually Dumfries or else remain unascribed for the time being.

Although a system of date letters was supposed to have been in use throughout Scotland from 1681 by order of the Privy Council, it was consistently practised only in Edinburgh, and, despite the repetition of this requirement by the Hammermen's own resolution of 1731, was hardly used at all in Canongate. Some letters used as marks are not date letters. There are in addition some anomalous marks, particularly two associated with William Craw. One of them is an animal usually described as a cat, which may be meant to mimic the English lion passant mark. The other is a crowned thistle, which Jackson illustrated upside-down in his table of unascribed Scottish marks. The significance of these two marks, if there is any, has not yet come to light. It must be remembered that Craw moved to Dumfries and the crowned thistle mark may therefore relate to his work there, rather than in Canongate.

GLASGOW

Glasgow silverwork might be assessed as lying somewhere between Edinburgh silver on the one hand and provincial work on the other. Until 1819 Glasgow was much like any other large provincial town, and her goldsmiths belonged to the Hammermen's Incorporation. In 1819, after much lobbying of their M.P., they persuaded Parliament[2] to set up a Glasgow Goldsmith's Company with its own assay office, to serve the City of Glasgow and an area forty miles to the west and south thereof. Dissatisfaction with the existing system had been building up during the previous thirty-five years; the political lobbying which brought about the

[1] *P.S.A.S.*, Vol. 102, pp. 237–240.   [2] Geo. III, *c.*28.

opening of the Glasgow Assay Office was a direct result of the inconvenience, delay, annoyance and extra expense caused by having to send all work cross-country to Edinburgh for assay, in compliance with the 1784 Act mentioned above. Many goldsmiths and jewellers continued to become members of the Hammermen as well as of the newly-constituted Company, and over seventy of them are recorded in the Hammermen's records between 1819 and the close of the nineteenth century.

Glasgow silver marks until 1819 follow the usual pattern: the town mark, based on the Arms of the City, is usually flanked by two strikes of the maker's mark, each goldsmith having his own particular version of the town mark. William Clark (admitted 1693) carried this personalisation to the extent of adding his own surname to the already complicated tree, bird, bell and fish motif. A cycle of date-letters was introduced in 1681, but during the first decade of the eighteenth century it disappeared from use, just as it happened in other provincial centres. In the middle years of the century some makers added the letter S to their other marks, and Messrs. Milne and Campbell often used the letter O. Whatever these may be, they are not date letters. The suggestion that the S may stand for 'silver' or 'standard' is a possibility but remains unproven. It can hardly indicate 'sterling' since it appears that the old Scots standard, contrary to what the law required, was still in use. In 1784 the locally-struck Glasgow marks suffered the same fate as those of Canongate and vanished forever; virtually all work was sent to Edinburgh for assay and marking, the exceptions being very few indeed.

The 1819 Statute which set up the Assay Office also prescribed a set of hallmarks differing from those of Edinburgh. Besides the maker's initials there were to be: 1) a Lion Rampant signifying Sterling Standard (an innovation for Glasgow). 2) A Town Mark based on the Arms of the Burgh, similar to what had been in use previously. 3) A Date-letter letter cycle of twenty-six letters which began with "A" for 1819 and was therefore out of phase with the current Edinburgh cycle. The Sovereign's Head for a duty mark as used in all other assay offices. If the Assayer suspected that a fraud was being perpetuated, he was required to weigh the offending object in water (to ascertain its specific gravity) and to try the effect of magnetism (to detect an iron core in an object such as a candlestick).

The argument that the lack of early Glasgow plate was due to the ravages of the Civil War, when domestic plate was called in to be melted down, is partly true, so far as it goes, but of course it applied to the whole country and not just to Glasgow. It should also be remembered that until about the time of the Union of the Parliaments in 1707, Glasgow was a town of only about 12,000 inhabitants and certainly not the great city she was soon to become. The amount of silver produced up to that time must have been relatively small, probably less than Aberdeen. Mr. Finlay wrote in the first edition:

'She owed her swift expansion and prosperity directly to the Union, which opened foreign and American ports to Scottish traders. Her merchants were quick to see the possibilities of tobacco, and by 1724 Glasgow was importing four million pound, annually. Within a few years she rivalled Bristol in the tobacco trade and a bitter feud arose. The American war was to destroy this trade; but it had helped create the great Clyde shipbuilding industry, the Clyde itself had been dredged and made into a first-class port, enterprise had been fostered and the machinery of industry and trade set up. Cotton succeeded tobacco, and by the end of the century Glasgow had grown to be a thriving city of some 50,000 inhabitants. The amount of surviving Glasgow plate of date from 1707 onwards shows a marked and significant increase. When in 1781 the English engineer Golbourne was successful beyond all expectation in his scheme for deepening Glasgow's river, the city fathers spontaneously added to his contract fee of £2,300 a free gift of £1,500 and presented him with a piece of plate. Whether it was Glasgow plate is not recorded, but the incident indicates that the city had attained the status of a munificent mercantile capital.

I know of no example of presentation plate made in Glasgow in the eighteenth century.[1] Those pieces made for public view, if they may be classed, are confined to a group of Communion cups, and it is not a large group. The finest are probably the pair at Strathblane, by Robert Brock, but those are as early as 1699. Most of the Glasgow cups were made for churches in the city or its vicinity: Barony, Rutherglen, Greenock,

[1] An example of such a presentation piece came to light in 1958 in a dealer's advertisement. There seems to be a slight discrepancy as to date, but it was nevertheless an interesting item, and probably important. Sadly, the dealer in question has since died and all trace of the tray has been lost. The advertisement read as follows: 'A magnificent George II Scottish silver tray made by James Glen in Glasgow *circa* 1750. It was originally presented by the City of Glasgow, whose arms it bears, and it was given to Richard Oswald, who was principal negociator with Benjamin Franklin of the treaty between England and the United States of America after the War of Independence. Diameter 22 ins. Wt 145 oz.'

Kilmarnock and Douglas. The High Kirk, the Tron and Blackfriar Churches have cups without hall-marks, but they bear the city arms and are probably of local manufacture. They are not distinguished in form — perhaps they are of date too late for this — and they are without engraved decoration except for arms and inscriptions. The Lukes, the versatile family of goldsmiths mentioned in Chapter X, were responsible for several of those dating from early in the century: The Barony, Greenock, Kilmarnock, New Kilpatrick, Bonhill and Dumbarton have cups made by Johan-got-hilf-Bilsings, an incomer, who obtained admission to the Incorporation in 1717.

A considerable quantity of post-Union domestic pieces of Glasgow manufacture survives. Scottish types, in spite of the late date are well represented. A thistle-cup of about the middle of the century, by Samuel Telfer (admitted 1747) is in Sir J. Stirling-Maxwell's collection. It is by far the latest example of this type of cup that I have seen. Jackson records a quaich by Adam Graham, which might have been made as lately as 1770. From the Luke family come two superb pieces in a private collection, proving that as craftsmen they were second to none in Scotland: a tankard of about 1709 by John, and an exceptionally beautiful teapot with stand by Robert, which might be dated as 1725.'[1]

The collection of the late Mr. John Noble of Ardkinglas has now been dispersed, but it contained an impressive tea-kettle and stand by James Glen, about 1745 (which has recently been acquired by Glasgow City Art Gallery and Museum), and a tea caddy by Robert Luke, now is the same museum. The city possesses a large collection of Scottish silver, Edinburgh, Glasgow and provincial, including much of the Victor J. Cumming and Milne-Davidson collections; Glasgow pieces span the seventeenth to twentieth centuries. These include communion cups from Strathblane by Robert Brock, from Cardross and Fintry by John Luke, and from Lochwinnoch by James Glen. The Cardross Cup is one of a pair which left the parish long ago and was for a time in the collection at Sudely Castle. John Luke is also represented by three thistle cups (two large and one tot-sized) and a quaich, while Robert Luke is the author of two half-pint beer mugs, one slightly shaped, the other straight-sided. In the second half of the eighteenth century we find a cup and cover, a coffee pot and a cake basket, all by Milne and Campbell. This last is a curious and rather unsatisfactory piece of wire work

[1] First Edition pp. 153–5.

to which the wheat decoration has been inartistically applied. One cannot help feeling that the makers could have done better both as to quality of work and basic design. It contrasts most unfavourably with the superb cake basket by William Scott of Dundee (in Dundee City Museum), which has led some people to think that the latter basket was only retailed by Scott who must have bought it from a goldsmith in Edinburgh or London, despite its marks. Adam Graham made a fine coffee pot, and is also responsible for one of the two silver-gilt two-handled cups without covers. The other is by James McEwen and they must date to about 1775–80. One strange item in the museum's collection is a classical goblet by Adam Graham; its curious colour may be partly due to its being made of silver from the Isle of Islay. The late Mr. John Noble told me that this piece was his favourite item of Glasgow silver.

Nineteenth-century Glasgow silver tends to be robust and heavy, and whatever we may think about its taste and design, its high quality is undeniable. To mention just one group by way of example, the city has a very fine punch bowl, lemon strainer and punch ladle, all by Marshall and Son, dating back from different years in the 1820's. The heavy style and quality of the bowl is very distinctly Glaswegian, and typifies the prosperity and convivality of the city and her citizens at that period.

Perhaps the most exceptional and remarkable piece of nineteenth-century Glasgow silver in the city's collection is the prosperous-looking two-handled cup and cover by Robert Gray and Son which the Glasgow Goldsmiths' Company presented to Kirkman Finlay, their MP, in gratitude for his help in the House of Commons over the establishment of the Glasgow Assay Office. Kirkman Finlay, Lord Provost of Glasgow, was the Member of Parliament for Glasgow Burghs from 1812 to 1818, and was Rector of Glasgow University in 1819.[1] The Minute book of the Glasgow Goldsmiths' Company records on 1 July 1822 that the members voted unanimously for a piece of plate *'not exceeding the value of eighty pounds'* to be presented to Kirkman Finlay, the expense to be defrayed from the Company's funds; and on 27th December following:

> 'Messrs. Robert Gray & Son produced the cup intended for Mr. Finlay, as ordered at the last general meeting in July, with an account for the same'.

[1] *Joseph Foster: Members of Parliament, Scotland*, p. 136.

PLATE 109

Tea Pot: Aberdeen, c.1796. Maker: James Erskine

Table Candlesticks: Aberdeen, c.1750. Maker: Coline Allan
(p.189)

PLATE 110

Coffee Pot: Aberdeen, c.1775-80. Maker: James Wildgoose

Coffee Pot: Aberdeen, c.1755-60. Maker: Colin Allan

PLATE 111

Octagonal Tea Pot and Stand: Dundee, c.1795. Maker: Edward Livingston
(pp.193-194)

Three Piece Teaset: Dundee, c.1820. Maker: Edward Livingston
(p.194)

PLATE 112

Oval Cake Basket: Dundee, c.1785. Maker: William Scott
(p.183)

Pair of Candlesticks: Dundee, c.1825. Maker: Alexander Cameron
(p.194)

PLATE 113

Pair of Small Covered Cups: Perth, c.1800. Maker: Robert Keay, Elder
(p.196)

Beaker with "Murray Gate Society" inscription: Dundee, c.1800. Maker: James Douglas
(p.194)

PLATE 114

Pair of Goblets: Aberdeen, c.1810. Maker: William Jamieson
(p.190)

Set of four Salt Shakers: Perth. Maker: Robert Keay, Younger, with Edinburgh marks for 1853-54

PLATE 115

Coconut Cup: origin unknown, 18th century; Coconut Cup: Inverness, c.1720. Maker: William Maclean
(pp.204-205)

PLATE 116

The Forres Communion Cups: Inverness, 1724–25. Maker: Simon McKenzie
(p.205)

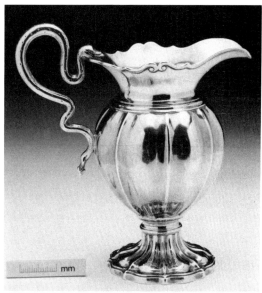

Cream Jug: Glasgow, c.1780. Maker: John McEwan   Cream Jug with Snake Handle: Inverness, c.1785.
Maker: Robert Anderson

PLATE 117

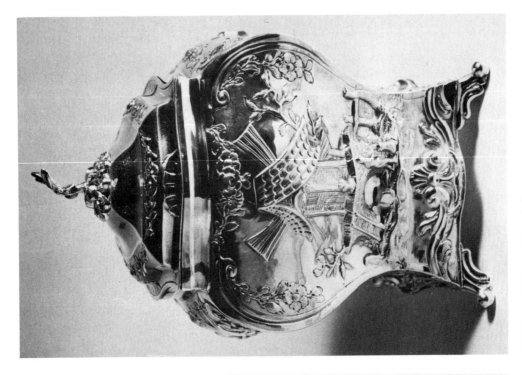

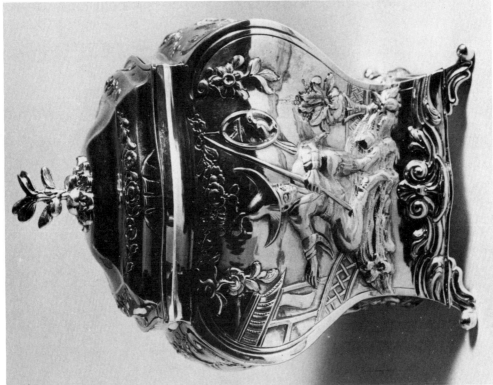

Two views of a Tea Caddy: Glasgow, c.1765. Makers: Milne & Campbell

PLATE 118

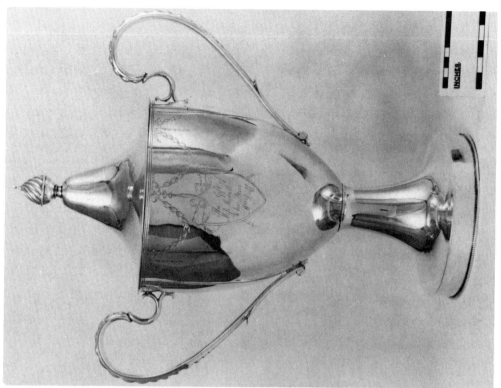

Cup and Cover: Banff, c.1790. Maker: William Byres
(p.213)

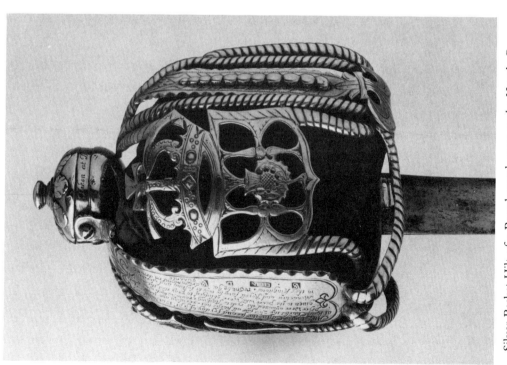

Silver Basket Hilt of a Broadsword, won at the Huntly Race
in 1701. Maker: William Scott

PLATE 119

Coffee Pot and Stand: Elgin, about 1760. Maker: John P. Cruikshank
(p.209)

PLATE 120

Sugar Bowl and Cream Jug: Banff, c.1735. Maker: Patrick Gordon
(pp.212-213)

Oval Sugar Basket with Swing Handle: Canongate, c.1780–84. Maker: John Robertson
(p.178)

It is not possible in the available space to do more than touch upon a few of the less well-known aspects of Glasgow's goldsmiths and their activities. Although a great deal is now known about them, this is not the place to attempt to cover the whole subject. I will merely content myself with exploring a few of the little-known facets of Glasgow goldsmiths and their work.

A certain amount of cross-fertilisation of ideas and skills took place because of men being apprenticed in one town and going on to further their careers in another. We find Glasgow involved in this interaction on several occasions. Johan Gothelff-Bildtzing was booked journeyman with Alexander Kincaid, Edinburgh, in 1709, before being admitted to the Glasgow Hammermen in 1717. Orlando Jackson was apprenticed in Edinburgh to John Welsh in 1750, and booked journeyman with David Warnock in Glasgow in 1757, before settling himself in London by 1760. Michael Forrest was the first journeyman to be taken by James McEwan, Glasgow, in 1763, and was afterwards admitted to the Hammermen of Canongate in 1770. Nearer home, William Hannay, who worked in Paisley from 1794, was booked journeyman with James Wyllie in Glasgow in 1791.

A rather curious feature which emerges from the Glasgow City Accounts is the fact that the city fathers would sometimes place commissions for silverwork with Edinburgh goldsmiths, even though there were goldsmiths in their own bounds who would have been equal to the tasks involved. There is nothing to suggest that Glasgow goldsmiths were too incompetent to make freedom boxes and the like, so there remains a mystery to be solved. In 1746 the City treasurer paid James Mitchellson, jeweller in Edinburgh, £56. 2s. Stg.

> "for a gold box for holding the Duke of Cumberland's burgess ticket, chasing the Duke's arms thereon and engraving the touns arms thereon".

In 1747, William Aytoun, goldsmith in Edinburgh, was paid £6. -s. 3d. Stg. for

> "a square silver box, and engraving two coats of arms thereon, for holding a burgess ticket sent to London to Sir Everard Falconer, secretary to his Royal Highness the Duke of Cumberland, for services".

Later the same year James Glen, Glasgow, was paid for a similar box sent

"to John Payne Esquire, for services to the town".

In 1752, Ebenezer Oliphant, Edinburgh, was paid £24. 4s. 4d. for

"a silver tea kettle and lamp, weighing 66¼ oz., at 8s. the ounce, with the chaseing and ingraving the toun's arms being £1. 15s. Stg."

This kettle was

"given in compliment to Mr. James Stirling for his services, pains and trouble in surveying Clyde towards the deepening thereof by locks".

There is an unusual entry in the bill rendered by Johan Gotlieff Bilzinds to the Kirk Session of Dunbarton for their Communion Cups in 1731; their books record it as follows:

"To Baldzing, goldsmith, Glasgow, for two Communion Cups weighing thirty-three ounces, one drop and a half, at five shillings four

pence per ounce,	£ 8. 16s. 4d.
To workmanship . . .	£ 1. 13s.
To duty at six pence per ounce,	£ -. 16s. 6d.
To engraving,	£ -. 2s.
TOTAL:	£11. 8s. 6½d."

We are left wondering which side of the transaction was responsible for adding up the total! The oddity of the entry lies, however, not with the rather curious effort at addition but in the inclusion of "duty at six pence per ounce". To find this in the account of a goldsmith working anywhere in Scotland outside Edinburgh is unexpected and very unusual, to say the least, and raises all sorts of questions as to the extent to which duty was collected in Glasgow and possibly elsewhere.

There is an interesting item in the City's archives which reminds one a little of the long Act in the Canongate Hammermen's records of 1731; On 12 May 1737, the Hammermen of Glasgow handed in a petition, craving the council to authorise the Deacon and masters of their craft to elect "a skilled person for searching, trying and stamping the silver work made within the city, and to give what yearly gratification to the stamper the council shall think fit".

What became of this idea is unrecorded, but all the evidence of the surviving silver would suggest that it came to nothing. The letters S and O, as stated above, always appear to be peculiar to the individual workers who used them, and are therefore highly unlikely to have been applied to an individual's work by a third party. It is also noteworthy that the Incorporation did not simply appoint one of their number to the position of assayer and stamper as a purely internal matter, since they usually resented and resisted all interference from any outsiders.

The Glasgow Assay Office operated from 1st July 1819 until its closure on 31st March, 1964. Its fortunes fluctuated over those one hundred and forty-five years, beginning with a steady and maintained increase in the volume of work being sent for assay. Had the company been allowed to accumulate its profits from the hall dues, it would rapidly have become extremely rich, a factor which could have helped it over the leaner patches in its history. After the first world war the amount of silver sent for assay had declined and never fully recovered, resulting in the office operating at a loss; this led to its inevitable closure in 1964, as recommended by the Report of the Departmental Committee on Hallmarking[1] after a meeting in Glasgow in 1957.

ABERDEEN

'As a producer of interesting silverware Aberdeen is in many ways chief among the provincial towns. Until the nineteenth century she rivals Glasgow. Glasgow had outstripped Aberdeen in population and in industry before the end of the nineteenth century, but it is often forgotten that Aberdeen remained the chief port and shipbuilding centre in Scotland until steel ships replaced wooden ones, and that even in the middle of the nineteenth century her clipper ships were first of their kind in the East India trade. Culturally, the northern city had always been notable, and in the eighteenth century she contributed her quota to the

[1] Report of the Departmental Committee on Hallmarking. H.M.S.O. 1959, p. 133.

group of eminent Scots scholars so extravagantly praised by Buckle. It is not surprising that her goldsmiths were able and doubtless prosperous throughout this time.'[1]

Approximately fifty goldsmiths have so far been identified as working in Aberdeen between 1280 and 1700. Surprisingly, there seem to have been only about twenty masters during the whole of the eighteenth century, and at least seventy-five during the nineteenth. The eighteenth century scene is notable for the quantity and quality of beautiful table-silver such as tea-pots, coffee pots, mugs and salvers, as well as a number of more unusual objects.

William Scott the younger, one of the family of Scotts discussed in Chapter X, is the author of a set of wavy-end tablespoons in a private collection, marked with the monogram VS, ABD and the letter D, which could perhaps be the date letter for 1708–9, though this is far from certain. Scott's maker's mark is also found with Banff and Elgin town marks.

Robert Cruickshank, a burgess of Old Aberdeen, made a small quaich now in the City's collection and which may be dated to around the reign of Queen Anne. Not much later in date is a large lidded tankard by him belonging to Kings College, Aberdeen. He also made a remarkable racing trophy in a private collection dating from 1725. It is marked with the maker's own initials, a town mark O ÆB D, for Old Aberdeen, and the letter C which appears on most of his work and is therefore not a date letter. Similarly marked is a pair of three-pronged forks in the same collection, and other forks from the same set have appeared on the market in recent years.

> 'His punch is on the silver basket-hilt of a broadsword in the collection of H.M. the Queen. This is yet another Scottish racing trophy. On the knuckle-bow is inscribed: *Given by the Duke of Gordon and Winn at Huntly Castle the second Thursday of Sept 1727 year All horses not exceeding 13 hands and 2 inches high are admitted to runn and the winning Horse to be sold for ane Hundred merks if required by the Judge of the Race. The riders staiking Crouns a piece which are given to the Poor to pray that the Monarchy and Royall Family may be lasting and Glorious in these Kingdoms.*'[2]

George Roberton, 1708-27, is the author of a very fine set of six wavy-end tablespoons of about 1710. Robertson seems never to have used a date-

---

[1] First Edition, p. 155.   [2] Ibid.

letter sequence, and from about this time date letters cease in Aberdeen. In the city's collection are two teapots, a sugar caster, a pair of beer mugs and a salver on central spreading foot (the type commonly called a tazza), while the Royal Museum of Scotland (Chambers Street) has two salvers in different sizes.

One of Robertson's apprentices, George Cooper, 1728–1748 served four years with his master from 29th March 1723 and stepped into his master's shoes in 1728. Although he lived on until 1765, I have no sure evidence of his practising as a goldsmith after 1748, in which year his apprentice, the great Coline Allan, appears to have taken over his business. Cooper's work is almost always exceptionally well made and very pleasing. A teapot by him in a private collection is worthy of Colin McKenzie, perhaps even of James Kerr himself.

> 'In the Royal Academy exhibition was a teaset by Cooper, lent by the Countess of Southesk. It is one of the most rare things of its kind in Scotland and came into the family of the Burnetts of Kirkhill, near Dyce, by the marriage of a daughter to Alexander Bannerman in 1737. Its most remarkable features are the pair of octagonal tea-caddies and the sugar bowl with a domed cover which can be used as a stand for the teapot.'[1]

Cooper is represented in the City of Aberdeen's collection by several items of hollow ware including the above-mentioned tea-service. There is also a teapot, tea caddy, sugar bowl, lemon strainer and a snuff mull; but most spectacular of all is a large tea tray supported by six shell feet. It has a pie-crust rim and is engraved with the arms of Duff. It was formerly in the collection of the late Mr. W. S. Bell and was one of the items he used to keep at home, instead of in a cabinet in his office, and it was the most highly-prized item of his Aberdeen collection. It is worth a visit to the Aberdeen Art Gallery and Museum just to gaze upon it.

Equally worthy of praise is Coline Allan, Cooper's apprentice and eventual successor to the business. Apprenticed in 1736, he was admitted to the Hammermen in 1748 and appears to have taken over his master's business almost at once. He took at least eight apprentices of his own between 1749 and 1762, and others may remain unrecorded. Four of them

---

[1] First Edition, p. 156.

went on to become freemen of the Hammermen themselves: James Wildgoose (1762–95), James Gordon (1766–81), Alexander Thomson (1770–79) and James Smith (1778–1828). Allan died in December 1774. His will is an intriguing document, not registered until July 1777. In the inventory attached to it are mentioned his tools, which were rouped for £57.2.10d. (Scots money), but it is not stated who bought them.

In a private collection is a fascinating small baluster hot milk jug by Allan with a domed lid, standing 6½ inches high. A pair of curious travelling candlesticks, in which the stems unscrew form the bases, was marked by him but perhaps only as the retailer of someone else's work, so untypical of him are they. The pair was sold from the Noble collection and, having passed through the Morris Collection, is now back in the City of Aberdeen. The City Museum also has a superb coffee pot, a teapot, a salver and a pair of circular salts with wavy rims. In addition there are recorded several salvers, teapots and stands, a dish cross (very rare in Scottish terms) and a considerable amount of flatware, all from his hand.

Coline Allan's first apprentice, with the intriguing name of James Wildgoose, became a burgess in 1763, but was already a freeman of the Hammermen by 1762. His output was smaller than his master's, but he was scarcely any less proficient as a craftsman. He took two apprentices who later became masters: John Leslie, apprenticed 5 July 1763 and William Byres, apprenticed 3 August 1768, both for an apprenticeship of seven years. Among his finer work are two teapots of almost identical inverted pear form, one plain and the other exuberantly decorated with contemporary repoussé flowers and foliage; and there is a magnificent baluster coffee pot in the City of Glasgow's collection, similarly decorated.

Next in line after Wildgoose comes James Gordon, who was apprenticed to Coline Allan on 27 May 1755 and became a freeman in 1766. George Roger was apprenticed to Gordon in that year and qualified in 1781. By the following year the two men had entered into partnership as James Gordon and Co., which explains the absence of personal marks for Roger. In about 1795 Gordon appears to have retired from the business, which nevertheless continued to bear his name although Roger operated it alone. The firm was among the very first to send work to Edinburgh for assay and marking in compliance with the Plate Duty Act of 1784, and they were followed in their law-abiding behaviour by John Leslie and James Erskine, but most of the work of these three firms, who dominated the last years of the century, continued to be marked and sold locally, thus illegally avoiding the payment of the King's duty in order to keep their costs down. Although the firm continued to produce the usual range of hollow ware, it was during this period that flatware came to predominate in Aberdeen's output, as it did in all the other provincial burghs of the kingdom. There is evidence that if candlesticks, cake-baskets and the like were required, it was quicker, easier and cheaper for a small provincial firm to buy them from Edinburgh, Sheffield, or even London, and, having carefully marked them, to sell them to the unsuspecting local laird, rather than actually make them on the premises.

The only other notable maker of the late eighteenth century is Nathaniel Gillet, whose work is represented in the local museum by two teapots, one decorated and the other plain, and also by a sugar or biscuit box of bulbous form and repoussé decoration. The plain tea-pot, along with many other items from the silver collection, was stolen from the museum recently and has not so far been recovered.

I intend to deal in rather less detail with the nineteenth century, and to notice some of the hollow-ware produced. Besides snuff boxes, wine labels, vinaigrettes and the like, William Jamieson (1806–1841) the most prolific and ambitious Aberdeen goldsmith of the early years of the century, produced a coconut cup with silver mounts, and a most unusual cylindrical spice canister, its three compartments unscrewing from one another and engraved with the words of 'GINGER', 'NUTMEG' and 'CINNAMON'. Both of these are now in the Museum in Aberdeen, together with a rather less distinguished nutmeg grater. At various times I have also seen sets and pairs of salts, a wax-jack, a pap-boat, a baluster beer mug, wine funnels and stands and several teapots. One rather weird teapot is especially remarkable; it is completely spherical, about the size of a tennis ball, standing on three paw feet and having an un-insulated silver handle. Lastly I should mention a superb pair of goblets about 7 inches high, with gilded interiors, dating from about 1810. The rims are decorated with a running motif of grapes and vine leaves.

George Booth, Jamieson's contemporary, also made a pair of goblets, the lower halves of the bodies being fluted and the same decoration repeated on the feet. I have also seen salts, mustard pots, several teapots, a milk jug and a beer mug, besides the usual snuff boxes and bottle tickets.

James Pirrie, one of Jamieson's apprentices, made a small salver with gadrooned edge, on three herring-bone bracket feet. As the century advanced medals became increasingly popular for scholastic and other purposes, and many makers, including James Pirrie, Emslie and Sutherland and James Walker, turned them out as occasion demanded.

Aberdeen marks, despite their great diversity, are mostly quite straight-forward to recognise. The normal mark, beside that of the maker, is a contraction of the town's name, ABD, or a shield with three castles, based on the arms of the burgh. From the 1770s onwards, various less obvious marks made their appearance, including several Zodiac symbols, the reasons for which can only be guessed at. By the nineteenth century certain makers used a thistle, while Alexander Grant and Charles Torchetti (both 1825) used a fleur-de-lis. From 1784 onwards, a number of goldsmiths sent their work to Edinburgh for assay, and consequently Edinburgh marks are sometimes found along-side those of Aberdeen. George Sangster (1839) often retailed the fully marked work of Hayne and Cater of London, adding GS, ABD, to the existing London marks.

In the past a number of mid-eighteenth century marks, often including an alligator's head, have been claimed for Old Aberdeen, due to the likeness between one of the maker's marks and one of Coline Allan's punches. Mr. Robert Barker has now shown that this whole family of marks originates from Jamaica.[1] In 1747, he tells us, the Jamaican legislature passed an Act which led to the appointment of an assayer who was to 'mark the said gold and silver wares with the stamp or mark of an alligator's head and the initial letters of his own name',[2] in addition to the maker's initials already there. The usual initials found in this entertaining group of marks are AD and CW for Anthony Danvers and Charles Wood, assayers, and the initials of five goldsmiths: Charles Allan, William Duncan, George Hetherington, Abraham Kipp and Gerardus Stoutenburg. This last man used the initials GSB.

Another joker in the pack, is the mark "J. Douglas", formerly guessed by Jackson and others to come from Aberdeen. It is in fact the mark of James Douglas working in Dundee.

---

[1] *Proceedings of the Silver Society*, Vol. III, No. 5, pp. 133–7 (1986).
[2] Ibid. p. 135, i.

DUNDEE

Although the goldsmith's art in Dundee is certainly older than the sixteenth century, there are at present no goldsmiths' names known before that of Ranald McGreig, who became a burgess in 1517. There were seven more before 1600, twelve in the seventeenth century and a further twelve in the eighteenth, while over fifty are recorded in the nineteenth century. It would appear that many of the latter were merely retailers. Surviving examples of eighteenth-century work other than flatware are not all that common, but Dundee City Museum has acquired a fine representative collection over the last fifteen years or so.

Taking church plate first of all, besides the lovely cups by Robert Gairdyne and others, mentioned in Chapter X, there is a plain communion cup by Alexander Smith, *c.*1726–30, the only piece of his work so far recorded. Smith had difficulty making up his mind as to which profession he was best suited to. He was first entered with the Hammermen in 1718 as a clockmaker and gunmaker, and then as a goldsmith in 1726. By about 1731 he had returned to being a clockmaker, so his silver-producing career only lasted about four or five years. Dundee also possesses cups dated 1733 by Charles Dickson the younger, who, like his father, was a member of the Edinburgh Goldsmiths' Incorporation as well as of the Dundee Hammermen. Neither man spent more than a few years in Dundee, but they brought with them the use of a date-letter cycle, synchronous with that of Edinburgh. The parish of Oathlaw (Finhaven) has a baptismal basin by Alexander Johnstone, inscribed

> "*Ex dono Johannis Dick de Pitkerro in Usum Parochise Suae Nativitatis de Othlaw A.D. 1742.*

The same parish also possesses a pair of cups by William Scott; these are referred to in the Kirk Session records for 14 June 1789, to the effect that the old cups were unfit for their purpose and that they should be replaced by a new pair, costing £10:

> 'Accordingly two silver cups are now procured, and the value given to the minister to be transmitted to Dundee to the maker, and his receipt demanded for the same.'

Turning to secular silver of the eighteenth century, besides the usual spoons and ladles, Alexander Johnstone, who was apprenticed to the younger Charles Dickson, made an excellent teapot and stand dating to about 1745, now in a private collection. It is of the very finest quality, and demonstrates the advantage of having learned the trade from an Edinburgh master. Dundee Museum has a similiar pot by him, and he also made a small waiter in a private collection. Johnstone was an active Jacobite and joined Prince Charles Edward Stewart's Life Guards after their victory at the battle of Prestonpans in September 1745, and took part in the battle of Falkirk, 17 January 1746. He was probably also at the fateful battle of Culloden, and was afterwards taken prisoner by the Hanoverians. It is thought that this effectively ended his career.

The museum has some work by John Steven, including a Communion Cup, a pair of salts and an item extremely unusual in Scottish terms, a table bell, bought with the assistance of the National Art-Collections Fund. Steven, the son of an Edinburgh merchant, was admitted in 1746 and died in 1775 at the age of 51. In his twenty-nine years as a master he took at least ten apprentices, and his output was considerable in quantity and excellent in quality.

William Scott, maker of the Oathlaw Cups mentioned above, was already in business as early as 1776 when the Deacon Convenor of the Nine Trades commissioned from him a gold medal and chain costing £27.13s. He took several apprentices, of whom Edward Livingstone became the most prominent master. Scott is represented in the City's collection by a pair of compressed circular salts which are undoubtedly his work, and by a superb cake basket of about 1785 which, though undoubtedly marked by him, may perhaps be too good to have come from his own hand. It is possible that he may have retailed the basket, having bought it from a goldsmith in Edinburgh, London or elsewhere. It must be said that there is no actual evidence that the basket is not by him, but its quality and beauty introduce an element of doubt, especially if one compares it with the Glasgow cake basket in that City's collection. He made many smaller items of fine quality, including an elegant pair of shoe buckles in private ownership.

Edward Livingstone, his prize apprentice, was perhaps a shade less gifted, yet his work is competent and occasionally surprising. Perhaps his finest surviving item is a beautiful octagonal teapot and stand with ivory handle and ivory pineapple finial, in private hands. It must date from very early in his working life, which began in 1790. He worked for thirty-four years and produced a range of domestic items, including wine funnels, bottle tickets, jugs and mugs. Dundee museum has a three-piece teaset by him, which, judged on style, must have been among the output of his last years. The museum also has two wine funnels and a pair of shoe buckles: At William Scott's death in 1799, Livingstone bought his late master's tools and punches and three books from his library: *Incas of Peru, Merchant's Companion* and *Tristram Shandy*.

James Douglas, admitted in 1795, made a small engraved salver in about 1800, in a private collection, and Dundee Museum has a good quality beaker by him inscribed:

From The Dundee Murrygate Society to William Fairweather, 1800.

His marks, some of which he shares with Edward Livingstone, were mistakenly ascribed by Jackson to Aberdeen.

The nineteenth century is rather less interesting but nevertheless contributes some surprises when it comes to accompanying marks. The only goldsmith of that century I shall mention briefly here is Alexander Cameron, Dundee's most prolific maker of flatware. Already in business by 1818, he was stilll working in the late 1840s. He occasionally sent his work to Edinburgh, and even Newcastle, for assay, but he marked the bulk of his work himself, and is one of the people complained about for doing so by the Edinburgh Goldsmiths Incorporation. Tea-sets and other such ambitious works by him are on record, and Dundee Museum has a splendid pair of candlesticks, for years the only Dundee silver in its possession.

Since the sixteenth century, the ordinary town mark of Dundee has been a "Pot of Lilies", taken from the Arms of the City. It normally assumes the form of a two-handled vase containing three daffodils, and the maker's mark is usually struck either side of it. The Dicksons, as mentioned above, introduced date letters, but this did not catch on. Alexander Johnstone used a few letters which, judging from their distribution, may have had the intention of continuing the cycle, but the letters were not changed annually and are not a reliable guide as to date. William Scott and Edward Livingstone used random letters, usually an m, in the same meaningless way. Livingstone is the earliest maker to introduce a range of quite different marks, the meaning of which is not clear, including a crowned heart (also used by Douglas). The trend continued into the nineteenth century: Cameron and others used the town's name in full in two lines, $\frac{DUN}{DEE}$, and thistles, crowns, starts and other irrelevant marks continued throughout the century.

PERTH

Perth has a very ancient history going back to Roman times, and lays claim to having been the effective capital of Scotland from the mid-twelfth to early fifteenth centuries, and the history of goldsmiths there is a lengthy one. About eighteen goldsmiths are known to have worked in the city before 1600 and there are certainly others as yet undiscovered. Henry the Bald was Royal goldsmith to William I, the Lion, from 1195 until the King's death in 1214, and continues to be mentioned until 1220. Andrew Lufe, goldsmith, founded in St John's Kirk, the Altar of St. Eloy, patron saint of goldsmiths (and of all Hammermen), in 1431, by which time the Hammermen appear to have had a corporate identity of their own, ranking among the very first incorporated trades in the kingdom.

There is certainly a falling off of numbers in the seventeenth century but this is made up for by some surviving silver, including two items by Thomas Ramsay (1597–1612) and several pieces of church and domestic plate by Robert Gairdyne (1659–1708). These include the Innerpeffray and Kinnoul Communion Cups, and another which had been converted to the use of the Scottish Episcopal Church.

Only ten goldsmiths have so far come to light in the eighteenth century. Of these, James Ferguson and Alexander Cruickshanks have no marks ascribed to them, and it appears that not all were members of the Hammermen's Incorporation. Cruickshanks had been apprenticed to Coline Allan of Aberdeen and was in turn the master to whom James Cornfute of Perth was apprenticed, thus giving us an unexpected link between two well known goldsmiths in different burghs. James Cornfute is represented in Perth City Art Gallery and Museum by a cowrie-shell snuff box and a wine funnel, among other items; his work includes a lemon strainer, a set of salts and a pair of shoe buckles in a private collection. Incidentally, the original quaich with curved turn-down lugs which has been so much copied and reproduced over the last half century or so under the name of "the Cornfute Quaich" cannot have been made by Cornfute at all. The shape is manifestly a nineteenth-century one and the quaich must therefore have been made by a later goldsmith of the same initials.

Robert Dickson, 1779–96, is represented in the museum by a teapot stand and a pair of shoe buckles.

Robert Keay the elder, worked from 1791 until 1825, then entered into partnership with his nephew and namesake until 1839, and then the younger man continued alone until 1856. Between them, they were the most prolific Perth makers on record. Their work included not only the usual flatware and serving pieces but the full range of small domestic hollow ware as well, fourteen pieces of which can be seen in Perth Museum. The elder made an attractive pair of two-handled covered porringers in the national collection, while the younger is represented by a splendid teapot-cum-kettle of generous proportions, marked with his maker's mark and Edinburgh hallmarks.

William Ritchie (1796–1814) made mostly flatware but the list of his other output includes wine labels, salts, pepper and mustard pots, snuff mulls and boxes and two items in Perth Museum, —a silver-gilt paten and a moustache brush! A peculiarity of his marks is that he sometimes used a set of small punches for striking the numbers 1 to 12 on a set of spoons. This is a curious practice not noted to be used by any other goldsmith, and I have never seen a complete set with all twelve marks. He occasionally sent work to be assayed in Edinburgh; as a result, his maker's mark can be confused with that of the Edinburgh goldsmith, William Robertson.

Over fifty makers and retailers are in the nineteenth century list but nearly all of them left only flatware, snuff boxes, medals and small odds and ends, or else have no known work ascribed to them.

Mr. Finlay said in the first edition of this book:

> "The Hammermen Incorporation of Perth was still a very active body in the eighteenth century. The records[1] show many instances of the maintenance of the widows and children of freemen. Towards the end of the century the Hammermen were acquiring the functions of an

---

[1] The Perth Hammermen Book (Ed. 1889).

insurance company and were even entering into contracts of the nature of bonds of annuity. The pre-Reformation link with the Church continued and, as late as 1825, there remained careful regulation of the seating in the Hammermen Gallery in the Middle Church. Perth Hammermen were actively interested, as a body, in all public affairs. Several members were 'out' in the 'Fifteen rising. Evidently the Incorporation learned a lesson by the result of the rising, and their loyalty to the reigning sovereign is embodied in a condemnation of the 'American Rebellion', recorded in January, 1778. To their honour, the Hammermen sent an address of sympathy to George IV's Queen when the King stripped her of royal dignities. When she died, they draped their church pews in black and wore full mourning for her, although the magistrates of the town accorded her only 'maimed rites'. In all these proceedings there is no indication that any goldsmith took a leading part. This was remedied, however, as late as 1832, when Robert Greig, then Deacon of the Craft, proposed a motion fully in keeping with the spirit of reform, to the effect that the Incorporation should itself undergo reform by relinquishing certain rights and privileges 'highly injurious to the free trade and intercourse of the burgh'."[1]

As a note to the preceding paragraph, David Greig, goldsmith, 1810–1855, became Lord Provost of Perth and was M.P. for Perth, 1839–41. According to Hansard he never spoke in the House of Commons during all the time that he held the seat.

The earliest known mark used by Perth goldsmiths is the familiar Lamb and Flag motif. This was replaced in the eighteenth century by an Eagle, usually with two heads but occasionally with one, which continued in many forms to be the norm until locally-marked work comes to an end. Having said that, there are twin pitfalls to avoid: 1) Marks that do not look like Perth, but are; and 2) Marks which do look like Perth but are not. As to the first, in the early nineteenth century one occasionally finds a punch containing a thistle and a pot of lilies side by side, looking for all the world like an odd Dundee mark, accompanied by a letter S in a shaped punch. These are found with the maker's marks of Daniel Dewar and also John Scott. Scott also uses, in separate punches, a thistle, a four-legged beastie and a lower case q. As to marks which are not Perth but which might appear to be, there is a series of marks including both an eagle punch and a tree

[1] First Edition, p. 160.

punch, now tentatively ascribed to Dumfries. The mark formerly illustrated by Jackson (2nd Edition, p.554, line 4) is not Perth either, the animal being a Unicorn and not a lamb. The marks ascribed by Jackson to John Sid (*ibid.*, line 12) are probably not Perth at all, and the maker's initials are actually S I, not I S.

DUMFRIES

Dumfries has been, from an early date, the most important town in the south-west of Scotland. It is therefore a matter of some surprise that her goldsmiths remained unknown until very recently. Their disinterment from obscurity is due to the perseverance of Mr. Kirkpatrick Dobie who set about the self-appointed task very thoroughly and has kindly allowed me to make full use of his notes.[1] The two main reasons for the failure of Jackson and the other early investigators to ascribe marks to Dumfries goldsmiths appear to be firstly; that in most instances, the marks are so different from maker to maker that it is often not at all obvious that there is any connection between them; secondly: the goldsmiths were not members of the Hammermen or any other craft and had no Minute book or other records of their own. In 1792 the Statistical Account of Scotland listed 40 freemen of the Hammermen's Incorporation, with 16 journeymen and 14 apprentices, totalling 70 members in all, but 'silversmiths' are lumped together with other professions as not being incorporated in any of the trades of the burgh.[2]

Dumfries became a royal burgh in the reign of David I. Standing on the River Nith, it was an independent seaport, which accounts for the frequent use of an anchor as a silvermark. Her importance as a port increased considerably in 1834 when the river passage to the open sea was cleared of obstructions and allowed much larger vessels to get through, only to wane dramatically with the coming of the railway in 1850. *Jacks Gazetteer* of Scotland (in 1901) says that Dumfries had '*an unusually large proportion of educated and wealthy inhabitants*' and that it was '*a place of opulence, taste and pretention*'.[3] Robert Burns was a honorary burgess of the burgh and lived

[1] See K. H. Dobie: *Dumfries Silversmiths.*
[2] *The Statistical Account of Scotland.* 1st Edn. Vol. 5, p. 136; Reprint. Vol. IV, p. 136.
[3] *Jack's Ordnance Gazetteer of Scotland, 1901*, p. 390, ii.

there for the last five years of his life, dying on 21st July, 1796.

The earliest goldsmith who has so far come to light is Michael Goldsmith in 1453, only five years after the town was sacked by the unfriendly English, a fate it suffered many times both before and since. During one of the visits of James IV to the town in 1504 we find in the Lord Treasurer's Accounts: *'Item to the goldsmyth of Dumfreis for castis of silver for halkis xiiijs'*. Unfortunately he is not named in the accounts; there would be no need, since he was probably the only goldsmith in the burgh at the time. David Wallace (1625) and James Ferguson (1691) are the only others so far noticed before 1700.

The eighteenth century produced a crop of about a dozen goldsmiths of whom only David Coutts and Joseph Pearson have marks ascribed to them at present. The maker's mark (only) of David Coutts is on the pair of communion cups of St. Michael's, Dumfries. In 1753, the town treasurer recorded payment of £3.6s.5d. to David Coutts for repairing the old Cups, which had been described two years earlier by the Kirk Session as *'rent and much decayed'*. These cups must in fact have been remade, not just repaired. Joseph Pearson (1794–1816) is probably the author of a large variety of marks, mostly found on Old English pattern flatware, including, in various unlikely combinations, the initials I P, a wreathed anchor, a stag's head erased, a two-headed eagle, an ordinary anchor, a lower case e and an engrailed punch with the letter S. Various attributions have been suggested for some of these marks, including Canongate, Perth and Paisley, but when one realises that all the sets of marks are interlinked and that all pertain to one man, it is clear that none of these suggestions is correct. Because of links with other suggested Dumfries marks, it looks as if Joseph Pearson originated them all. In an advertisement in the *Dumfries Weekly Journal* of 7 July 1810 he asserts that: *'Every article in the gold and silversmith business is now manufactured in his own premises nigh the midsteeple'*. Four years later another advertisement in the same paper informs us that his stock in trade included, besides flatware, complete tea-sets, bread and fruit baskets, wine funnels, watches and spectacles. In 1816 he gave up business, selling out to Mr. E. McKenzie, whose advertisement claimed that he was *'able to manufacture all kinds of silver and gold work'*.

No less than twenty-nine names are known for the nineteenth century, only about a dozen of whom have marks suspected or definitely ascribed.

The three most prolific of these, all of whose marks are definitely ascribed to them and not just tentatively hazarded, are David Gray, Mark Hinchsliffe and Adam Burgess. David Gray, 1814–41, asserted in 1815 that all his plate was stamped at Goldsmiths' Hall, Edinburgh; the Duty Book at the Assay Office bears out the fact that he sent parcels of flatware for assay between 1814 and 1819 and again in 1839. Dumfries Burgh Museum has a child's mug by him, and his mark is also found as repairer on the butt of the famous "Siller Gun", presented by James VI in 1617 and badly damaged 1808. Gray's marks, like those of Mark Hinchsliffe, were previously misascribed to Canongate, despite the fact that the animal's head he used for a mark is clearly that of a Unicorn and not a stag. It is usually accompanied by a wreathed anchor and one of the letters G or K.

Mark Hinchsliffe, 1821–41, had a journeyman from Edinburgh named Thomas Alexander working for him for the whole twenty years that he engaged in goldsmith work. He ignored the existence of the Assay Office except on one occasion, on 12 November, 1830, when he sent a fish slice and two butter knives weighing a total of eight ounces to Edinburgh for assay. His usual marks are a stag's head, a wreathed anchor and the letter K, accompanied by his name in a circle with M in the centre, incuse, in the way a cutler might mark a knife-blade. He had two other maker's punches, a normal one and another in which his initials appear incuse. His two incused maker's marks are also sometimes found with three other punches, an anchor, a cross and a crown.

Adam Burgess, 1834–49, began work in Castle Douglas, some eighteen miles to the south-west of Dumfries, in August 1834, in which year he began sending work the 90 miles or so to Edinburgh for assay. The last consignment from Castle Douglas was sent on 16 November, 1835, and comprised 48 tablespoons, 18 dessert-spoons and a pair of sugar tongs, all weighing in at 135 ounces. This and other parcels of silver at about the same time were entered in the King's Duty Book as being brought to the office by J. B. Caw, a member of the Edinburgh Goldsmiths' Incorporation, who appears to have been Burgess's acting agent in Edinburgh. His next consignment, weighing 30 ounces, was sent from Dumfries on 17 October, 1836 and consisted of '*24 tea, 6 dessert, 6 salt, 1 mustard, 2 gravy spoons*'.[1] His first trade advertisement in the *Dumfries Courier* states that he was able and

[1] King's Duty Book (Edinburgh Assay Office).

willing to 'manufacture silver forks, spoons and every description of tea service, cups, child's cans and all kinds of gold and silver work'. In 1837 it was advertised that all his dies and punches had been newly made and cut under personal superintendence; we may therefore expect to see a change in his marks at this date, but which of the changes among his many marks is indicated is not clear. The *Dumfries Times* reported on 28 February, 1838, that his journeyman Mr. Holloway, had absconded with the tools of the trade and other articles, but was apprehended at Carlisle and brought back to gaol. Burgess appears to have become bankrupt in 1843 but was in business again by 27 May 1844 when the *Dumfries Courier* advertised that '*Adam Burgess, Watchmaker, Clockmaker and Silversmith had opened a brass foundry business*'. He probably went broke again and by 1849 is described as a watchmaker, back in Castle Douglas.

Perhaps we see in Adam Burgess something of the difficulties which must have been experienced by nearly all provincial goldsmiths at that time, in all but the very largest places; his advertisements make it clear that he is longing to make tea-services, cake baskets and the like, and was no doubt able to do so as his advertisements claim, but the surviving records do not mention any such work being sent up for assay.

His items other than flatware are all small and are few and far between. It was clearly a struggle for him to get any good commissions and he must have felt considerable frustration at being condemned to turning out nothing but a monotonous flow of spoons and ladles, varied with the occasional fork.

The silvermarks of Adam Burgess may be grouped into three categories, all linked by maker's marks in common: first, his initials accompanied by genuine Edinburgh Assay Office marks; second, a set of punches which is quite blatantly a forgery, or at least a close imitation, of the Assay Office marks for 1835–6, consisting of a two-towered ruined castle, a thistle, and the gothic letter D, together with a tree mark in an oval punch, intended to look at a quick glance like the Monarch's Head duty mark. The punches are never exact copies of genuine marks, however, presumably because Burgess could then claim that they were not forgeries but merely happened to possess a passing likeness to the real thing. Three such sets of punches have been discovered, and there may be others also, each slightly different as to shape of punch and other small details. It was this set of Edinburgh-like marks which was once upon a time misascribed to Andrew Black of Alloa, a clockmaker who never made any silver at all. The third group of marks consists of the maker's initials, a different type of ruined castle, a Roman letter D and a wreathed anchor. In rare instances his maker's punch is just the letter B.

Because individual makers tended to use marks which were quite different in character from those of other goldsmiths in the same burgh, there is little point in trying to discuss Dumfries marks in general. The collector should avoid falling into the error of ascribing all sorts of marks to Dumfries which perhaps comes from elsewhere. (I have tried to provide an accurate guide to the present incomplete state of knowledge about Dumfries marks in the new "Jackson" which was published in 1989 and to which the reader is referred for further clarification.) As an example of the traps to be avoided, beware of the maker's punch J W H, which is often found with Edinburgh marks between 1809 and 1823, and usually with the maker's (or retailer's) mark of either Alexander or William Henderson. This J W H turns out not to be James Walker Hinchliffe of Dumfries, but is in fact the mark of J. & W. Howden, an Edinburgh firm operating at various addresses in the city between the dates stated aboved.

INVERNESS

The capital of the Highlands, Inverness became a royal burgh at a very early period. Sadly, most of her ancient history is forever lost to us because the town's records were destroyed by fire in 1556. The late Miss Margaret MacDougall, curator of Inverness Museum until her death in 1960, knew every nook and cranny of the surviving archives and was the first to compile useful information about the goldsmiths of that burgh, and much of what follows is based upon her notes.[1]

During the second half of the seventeenth century, the number of tradesmen in the town grew rapidly and they petitioned the Town Council for permission to form themselves into Incorporations. The Merchants' Guild resisted this idea vigorously . In 1676, however, differences arose over the method of electing the Town Council, and a committee from the

[1] Now published as Margaret O. MacDougall: *Inverness Silversmiths*. n.d.

Convention of Royal Burghs visited Inverness to investigate the complaints. As a result, the town received a Sett, or rules for the management of its affairs. There were to be six incorporated trades, one of which was to be the Hammermen's Incorporation, which included those trades such as blacksmiths, lorimers and coppersmiths as was usual in other burghs. However, at the time of the committee's visit to the town, there was no goldsmith, silversmith or jeweller working there and these categories were consequently omitted from the Hammermen's remit. Thereafter goldsmiths continued to be admitted burgesses as merchants, as before, an oversight which was to lead to dispute some thirty years later.

In 1708 George Leith, goldsmith, decided to work at his trade without first renouncing his status as a merchant burgess. Miss McDougall takes up the tale:

'A customer ordered half a dozen silver spoons and he proceeded to make these in his own workshop. The craftsmen heard of this and two silversmiths, Simon MacKenzie and William MacLean, accompanied by the Trade's Deacon and officer, went to Leith's workshop and confiscated the spoons which he was making. Thereafter, the whole affair was brought before the Town Council, who fined MacKenzie and MacLean and deprived them of their burgess-ship. The problem was two-fold: was Leith a craftsman or a merchant, and were MacKenzie and MacLean, who had also been admitted as guild brothers, within their rights in acting as craftsmen? Clarification was necessary, and in 1709 another committee of the Convention of Royal Burghs came to Inverness to settle the dispute. As a result, some alterations were made to the Sett of 1676: silversmiths were declared to be craftsmen and provision was made for them in the Hammermen's Incorporation, it being agreed that not less than two were necessary to carry on the trade in Inverness. From this time onward, however, this minimum number was rarely exceeded until into the nineteenth century.

'Although MacKenzie and MacLean had been severely fined and deprived of their burgess tickets by the Council, their interpretation of the original Sett would seem to have been upheld by the Convention's Commissioners. At any event, they resumed their status of craft freemen, whilst George Leith is never mentioned again [in Inverness]. By the terms of the new Sett, the Town Council were empowered to admit members to any craft if the number of members fell below the number specified. The craftsmen did not take kindly to this provision, which they considered to be an interference in their affairs, and members admitted in this way are occasionally known to have been omitted from craft membership records, as was the case with Thomas Borthwick. Another provision of the Sett laid down that any man leaving his craft or trade could become a guild brother upon paying whatever fee was due to the guildry. At least two silversmiths severed their connection with the craft. Robert Innes gave up his craft membership and joined the merchant's guild in 1716 and later became a town councillor. And Robert Naughton severed his connection after ten years, becoming a merchant in about 1824, whilst his partner Charles Jamieson continued to associate with the Hammermen. By this time, however, the old distinctions between merchants and craftsmen and "unfreemen" were more and more disregarded in the burghs of Scotland. The Act of 1846 which abolished trading privileges to a very large extent acknowledged what had already happened and hastened the decay of the craft guilds which no longer controlled their members, as in the past'.[1]

It is often surprising how much was required of an aspiring goldsmith when making his essay in order to be admitted to the Hammermen. While in Edinburgh the usual essay was, say, a teapot and a wedding ring, in Inverness we find Colin MacKenzie in 1727 being required to produce: '*a sword hilt in silver . . . and he is also obliged to make as another part of his essay a raised decanter in silver and a chiny fashioned teapott also in silver*'. The goldsmith capable of such work was certainly no itinerant tinker but an excellent craftsman. Silver being a precious metal, MacKenzie would doubtless be asked to make these items for his essay because they were already on order and about to be made anyway in his master's workshop. The only special circumstances about making an essay were that it should be done under the supervision of an independent goldsmith, not his master (to prevent cheating) and that it should be made within a specified time. The time allowance was occasionally extended during the winter months because of the short hours of daylight in so northerly a latitude.

A considerable quantity of flatware was produced during the eighteenth century but quite a number of pieces of hollow ware survives also. William MacLean, 1702, made a rather unassuming coconut cup which is now in

[1] Margaret O. MacDougall: *Inverness Silversmiths.*

the Royal Museum of Scotland. It bears a presentation inscription from Provost Duff and it probably dates from around 1705. The letter A in a punch accompanying the marks of maker and town is the date letter 1705–6. The cup is unsophisticated but competently made. The nut is left unpolished and the silver rim, straps and foot are plain but functional. Of rather better quality is a small quaich in a private collection also by McLean, with the letter E, the date letter for 1709–10. Staying with date letters for a moment, a cycle was introduced in 1681, just as it was in other centres, and certain makers continued to use it for the next forty years or so. Simon MacKenzie marked one of his thistle cups with the letter B, which appears to be the date letter for 1706–7 and another with the letter C for the following year, while the T on the Forres communion cups (now in private hands) is the date letter for 1723–4, a date corroborated by the inscriptions on the cups themselves.

John Baillie, who in 1735 submitted the same daunting triple essay as Colin MacKenzie had done eight years earlier, was at least his equal as a goldsmith. In a private collection there is a superb pair of beer mugs by him, every bit as good as the best which Edinburgh could produce.

The middle and later years of the century saw an emphasis on quaichs of a small or individual size, more than in any other town in Scotland.[1] This has sometimes led to the erroneous idea that the quaich was originally a uniquely Highland vessel, whereas in fact it appears just as early in Edinburgh and Glasgow, if not earlier; Inverness appears to be the town of its adoption rather than of its origin. John Baillie and Thomas Borthwick, 1772, were the chief quaich makers during the eighteenth century, while Alexander Stewart and Charles Jamieson dominated the first quarter or so of the nineteenth.

A number of pieces of domestic silver such as teapots, waiters and sauce boats are recorded during the eighteenth century, but, apart from the considerable production of quaichs mentioned above, there is little else besides flatware. In the last two decades, however, betrothal brooches, which in Edinburgh became known as Luckenbooth brooches, made their appearance in increasing numbers, with a great variety of single and double heart designs, usually in silver but occasionally also in gold. The Royal Museum of Scotland has a simple gold one by Alexander Stewart of Inverness, made around 1800. It is probably fair to say that whereas

[1] H. Fothringham: *Small Inverness Quaichs, c.1760–c.1840 (The Antique Collector, April, 1973).*

Inverness adopted the quaich from the Lowlands, Edinburgh assimiliated the idea of the betrothal or Luckenbooth brooch from the Highlands. Edinburgh examples are dealt with in Chapter XIV, but I mention the subject here in order to draw attention to their earlier existence in Inverness, and also because they lead us into the particular peculiarity of nineteenth-century Inverness work, Highland jewellery and accoutrements: plaid brooches, buckles, sporran-mounts, dirks, skean-dubhs, kiltpins and doublet buttons, dress snuff horns and powder horns. Inverness Museum and Art Gallery has a fine representative collection of all types, and a visit there to see them is better than any number of photographs or words. Almost every Highlander in the nineteenth century, however poor he might be, had some precious personal ornament for the Sabbath, or for weddings and wakes; while the lairds and chiefs and their families wore such things every day as a matter of course.

The usual town mark of Inverness is I N S, used from the beginning through to the mid-nineteenth century, after which some makers used I N V S instead. A Camel seems to have been used first by Robert Anderson, 1755, and in the nineteenth century a Cornucopia is adopted by several makers. Both devices are featured in the armorial bearings of the burgh, the Cornucopia as crest and the Camel as dexter supporter. In addition Robert Naughton, John MacRae and Thomas Stewart, among others, occasionally use a thistle. The maker's mark, though usually his initials can be complicated in the early eighteenth century by the prevalence of names beginning with 'Mc' or 'Mac'. William MacLean uses ML conjoined and Simon MacKenzie uses MK conjoined with no initial of their Christian names appearing at all. Later 'Mac' goldsmiths generally give us the benefit of a full set of initials, as John MacRae, elder, who uses J.Mc.R. in the 1820s and 1830s.

The presence of date letters has already been mentioned, and a word of warning is needed about this: Not all letter punches are necessarily date letters. While Simon MacKenzie's letters all appear to be date letters, those of William MacLean nearly all are, and those of Robert Elphinstone probably less often signify a definite date. In the latter case, two or three letters seem to turn up too often, and others never. It is likely that he began a cycle of letters at one time and then let the same letter run meaninglessly on from year to year until the punch wore out. Many of the predicted date letters have not been seen on the work of any maker.

Lastly must be mentioned these marks once thought to be Inverness which are not. Mr. Finlay pointed out in the first edition of this book that:

> . . . neither Hamilton & Co. nor 'T. & Co.' can be accepted as Inverness firms. Their names do not appear in any of the records and their town-marks — elephant and urn, in the case of the first, and an unknown quadruped for the second — have no connection with Inverness. The elephant and urn were part of the Calcutta mark, as Jackson was aware, and Hamilton & Co. were goldsmiths of that city. This disposes of a considerable number of small pieces hitherto thought to be characteristic of the northern town.

This matter was further explored in 1960 by L. J. Cardew-Wood[1] and by W. Wilkinson[2] in 1973.

ELGIN

Elgin, in the fertile and prosperous Laigh of Moray, is a handsome eighteenth-century town built around the ruins of its medieval cathedral, and it is not surprising that it produced some elegant silverware. The most important single event in the town's history was the founding of the cathedral in 1224. The church, as was usual in the Middle Ages, was among the chief patrons of the goldsmiths' art, and Elgin Cathedral possessed all the plenishings usual for such an establishment. The early records of the burgh contain the names of many men whose callings are never stated, and it is quite possible that some of them were goldsmiths. By the sixteenth century, several goldsmiths are mentioned, among whom the most colourful character is Walter Hay, whose frequent misdemeanours span some fifty years in the records of both town and kirk. For example, in 1551, while he was still in his wild youth, he was fined half a stone of wax 'for selling of wyne within the college of Moray'.[3] In 1597 he was hauled before the Kirk Session 'for playing at the boulis and golff upoun Sondaye in the tym

---

[1] L. J. Cardew-Wood: *Calcutta Silver* (in *the Proceedings of the Society of Silver Collectors*, No. 2., 1960).

[2] W. R. T. Wilkinson: *Indian Colonial Silver*, pp. 49 and 137.

[3] Wm Crammond: *The Records of Elgin*, Vol. I, p. 114.

of the sermon',[1] while in 1600, by which date he must have been over seventy years old, he set upon his unfortunate fellow goldsmith, Andro Stalker, 'with a drawin sword in his hand, speciallie apoun a nicht befoir the celebration of the Lord's Supper',[2] for which he was committed to the stool of repentance.

Andro Stalker is apparently the same man as the Andrew Stalker who had been admitted to the freedom of the Edinburgh's Goldsmiths' Incorporation on 6 July 1597. He must have moved to Elgin almost at once, for we find him ratifying a promise of marriage there in the following year. After being attacked by the troublesome Walter Hay, as recounted above, the records have little to say about him until 18 July 1642 when the council minutes record that 'the council orderit Andro Annand (their treasurer) to giff out puir folkis mondy tua croce dollouris, being v lib 6s.8d., to Andro Stalker, goldsmith, to help him in his necessitie, being depauparat'. Two years later he is mentioned for the last time in the books of the Kirk Session on 26 March 1744: 'To Andro Stalker, half one dollor for mending the Communion Cupes'.

The Incorporation of Hammermen existed in the sixteenth century. It received a new Sett, or code of rules and regulations, along with the other trades of the town in 1657, at which date there were no goldsmiths working in the Burgh. In a town council minute of 5 October that year, the Sett is signed by each of the deacons of the several crafts 'with our hands at the pen, led by Alex. Hay, notary, at our command specialle required hereto, because we cannot write of ourselves'. The sole exception to this illiteracy was James Dick, deacon of the Wrights and Masons.

Unfortunately, the Incorporation's records are missing until 1812 and so we have to rely on the town register and other municipal archives for information about earlier times. There is very little information available concerning seventeenth-century goldsmiths, and interest only picks up again when the William Scotts, father and son, were admitted as burgesses in 1700 and as freemen in 1701, having come from Aberdeen via Banff. In the town register we find:

'23 September 1700. To ane treat given by the magistrats to the goldsmith William Scott, elder and his son, when they got their burges

[1] Ibid, Vol. II, p. 46.   [2] Ibid, Vol. II, p. 79.

ticketts, being eight choppin Claret wyne, thre punt sack posset and ane chopin and tobacco pyps, in all 14 lib 9s. 2d. Scots'.

The fine pair of communion beakers made for the parish church of Elgin are by the elder William Scott dating from 1681, nineteen years before he became free of the burgh, and were made in Aberdeen. They are inscribed 'This cupp is dedicat for the church of Elgin by William Cummen of Achry, late provost of Elgin Anno Domini 1681'. The donor's arms are engraved on the bottoms, the outline of these cups is most unusual, being much more flared-out at the rim than any other beakers of Scottish origin. The silver mount of the Huntly sporran, now in a private collection, is by the younger William Scott, and is marked with what is probably the date-letter D for 1708–9, and the town's name in full.

James Guthry, an Edinburgh journeyman was admitted to the craft in 1712 but no work of his has yet been identified. The same is true of Alexander Innes, who was admitted in 1715.

William Livingstone gained his freedom in 1729, having served his apprenticeship in Edinburgh with James Tait, for seven years from 2 February 1714. He is the maker of the beautiful Communion Beakers of Boharm and Rothes, dated 1728, from which it may be seen that he was already working in Elgin before his admission to the craft.

James Humphrey became a burgess in 1753 and took two apprentices the following year, John McBeath and John P. Cruickshank. The latter became a freeman in about 1760 and is the maker of a beautiful coffee pot with stand and lamp, lent by Mr. R. J. Mackenzie to the Glasgow Exhibition of 1938. The pot is of simple cylindrical form and must date to the early 1760's. The stand with its lamp, suspended by silver chains, has a classical look which accords well with the quietly classical air of the town itself.

Charles Fowler, perhaps the most prolific Elgin goldsmith, must have been in business by about 1790. He was still excercising his craft in 1820 when he was a town councillor. Besides flatware in old English and fiddle pattern styles, he also made small domestic pieces such as snuff boxes, and a very elegant and attractive wine funnel which was in the Morris Collection.

John Keith, the same man who had working in Banff since c.1794, was admitted in Elgin in 1808, on condition that he paid the usual dues and presented an essay-piece for examination; he immediately produced from his pocket a watch-chain by way of an essay-piece, and was admitted. It is probable that his becoming a freeman was in order to allow him to retail his work in Elgin, and not so that he might work there himself; consequently, unless there is an obvious Elgin-type mark beside his initials, his work should be assumed to have been made in Banff.

Thomas Stewart appears to have been admitted in 1813. Besides flatware, which is consistently of excellent quality and weight, he made small items of a domestic nature.

With William Steven Ferguson we meet a case of someone working in the burgh as a burgess and guildbrother without ever becoming a member of the Hammermen. The Incorporation considered his case in 1843, as to whether it could compel him to join the craft. This comes only three years before the Act of Parliament which abolished exclusive privileges of trade. Although he never became a freeman, he continued to work in the burgh until at least 1867. He is the maker of a quantity of flatware of good quality, and also of a famous snuff box in the town's museum, with a presentation inscription to John Shanks, a local 'character' and keeper of the ruined cathedral

> 'for discovering on the 23 September 1833 four steps in front of the Grand Entrance, which had been hid by rubbish for centuries, and have now restored this noble part of the Building to its just proportions'.

The box turned up in an Edinburgh antique shop in about 1890, having been pawned in Canada, and then found its way to the Edinburgh shop via a dealer in Liverpool.

During the remainder of the nineteenth century a number of goldsmiths, silversmiths and jewellers worked in the burgh, some of them merely as retailers. Marks have been identified for John Sellar, who had his shop at 81, High Street from at least 1837 till 1852 (though he is absent from the 1844 directory). In 1847 there was a James Sim, jeweller, in business, also in the High Street, who could be responsible for Elgin marks with the same initials, but this seems unlikely.

Joseph Pozzi was working on his own in 1825 but was in partnership with Robert Stewart in 1837, and was on his own once more by 1844 until at least

1847. John R. Mackay, goldsmith, 165 High Street, appears in the directory for 1863, but seems to have worked only a short time in the burgh. There are several other workers to whom no marks have yet been ascribed.

The town mark of Elgin is variable as each marker used his own set of punches. William Scott, younger, used ELGIN in full (with the N reversed) on the mount of the Huntly Sporran, together with the letter D, apparently the date-letter for 1708–9, in parallel with the second Edinburgh cycle. During the middle years of the eighteenth century the town name is often contracted to ELG or ELN, and Charles Fowler uses the name in full once more. James Humphrey, on the other hand, uses his own initials, ingeniously combined with the letters ELN to form a complex monogram. A virgin-and-child, the west front of the cathedral and the figure of St. Giles are all used as accompanying marks in the late eighteenth and early nineteenth centuries. The marks of John Sellar defy explanation. His punches for the letters E, L and N are straightforward enough, but he sometimes uses a tree and a series of odd marks unique to himself. For the mark ELL^N, see Ellon.[1] (pages 228-229)

BANFF

Banff is a county town and seaport and lies about forty-five miles from Aberdeen and rather more from Inverness. Although a royal burgh by the reign of William I, the Lion (1165–1214) it remained little more than a fishing village until the mid-eighteenth century. Its population by 1782 was 2,380 and a century later this had almost doubled. Most, but not all, of the goldsmiths, silversmiths and jewellers who worked in the burgh were members of the Hammermen's Incorporation. Marks have been identified for about a dozen goldsmiths working in the burgh between the 1690s and the 1890s and there are one or two apparent Banff makers of the early to middle eighteenth century who remain unidentified.

Surprisingly little new information has emerged concerning Banff goldsmiths, despite the efforts of myself and others, which is a disappointment to the enthusiast who finds Banff silver one of the more rewarding subjects for collection and study. Since the Hammermen's records which were discovered in 1888 have once again disappeared, it has

[1] p. 205.

not been possible to do any original research on them, and I have had to rely on the work of William Cramond, who was the school-master at nearby Cullen, who extracted information from them in that year. To complicate matters, one or two people have written on the subject with insufficient knowledge and have thus perpetrated errors and inaccuracies which the reader naturally believes to be true. I was myself guilty of this in 1970, when I based an article on someone else's work (which turned out to be as much imagination as anything else) which was very muddled indeed. Regrettably this has since been quoted as an authority. Until the Hammermen's minutes come to light again there is little future in pursuing the subject. A certain amount remains to be gleaned from the town and presbytery records, etc., and it is hoped that this will be achieved in the near future.

The first Banff goldsmith to whom marks are ascribed is William Scott, elder, who was admitted to the Hammermen of Aberdeen in 1666. He did not move to Banff until about 1690 but was already a member of the Hammermen's Incorporation there by 1688. He made the communion beakers for Forglen in 1692 and for Banff itself in 1698. In 1701 he was admitted to the Hammermen of Elgin and died very shortly afterwards. He made a number of thistle cups and other small pieces of hollow-ware during his Banff period as well as the usual spoons etc.

William Scott, younger, came from Aberdeen to Banff probably in 1699, in which year he is mentioned in the Banff register of sasines. He and his father were both admitted to the Hammermen of Elgin in 1701 in order to allow them to trade in that burgh. He continued to live and work in Banff until his death in 1748. The rumour that he was appointed assay master is quite untrue and needs clarification. There was never an assay office or assay master in Banff and the reference is to his being chosen to oversee the *essay* of Patrick Gordon in 1732.

Patrick Scott, the son of William Scott, younger, was apprenticed to Robert Sharp, goldsmith in Aberdeen, in about 1691 and came to Banff on the completion of his apprenticeship, together with his father, in *c*.1699. He remained in the burgh until at least 1731. He made the communion beakers for the Banffshire parish of Auchterless and also tableware. A teapot by him has been recorded and also a superb hash spoon in a private collection.

Patrick Gordon was admitted as a gold and silversmith in 1732; his essay, of which the younger William Scott was one of the overseers, was 'a silver outer case of a watch, a spoon and a gold stoned ring'. He made the excellent and beautiful sugar bowl and milk jug which were stolen a number of years ago from the late Mr. Noble of Ardkinglas. He is last mentioned in 1741.

Alexander Shirass (or Shirreff) was apparently not a member of the Hammermen's Incorporation. He is mentioned in the town's records from 1750 until his death in 1761. His marks are found on well-made flatware of the 1750s, including a particularly fine and heavy marrow scoop whose marks include the letter S (back to front) in an engrailed punch. [Pickford 1989, p.591, line 7].

John Argo was admitted as a silversmith in 1771 although he did not become a burgess until 1785. He is last mentioned in 1806. A small amount of flatware by him is keenly sought after by collectors.

William Byres was apprenticed to James Wildgoose of Aberdeen for seven years from 3 August 1767 and presumably served him as a journeyman thereafter until 1778 when he was admitted to the Hammermen's Incorporation of Banff. He was deacon there in 1781 and continued to work in Banff until 1792 when he returned to Aberdeen, where he died in 1811. During his fourteen years in Banff he made a quantity of excellent flatware and also some larger pieces of domestic silver, most notably a beautiful two-handled cup and cover which is now in the Royal Museum of Scotland. It is quite exceptional as a large piece of provincial hollow ware made by a goldsmith most of whose known output consists of teaspoons and toddy-ladles.

In David Izat we meet yet another goldsmith with Aberdeen connections. He was apprenticed to James Gordon and Co., goldsmiths in Aberdeen, for seven years from 3 June, 1786. He is mentioned in Banff between 1794 and 1799. He made flatware, including serving pieces and, like John Argo, he used a thistle as one of his marks. He returned to Aberdeen in 1799 or 1800 and is thought to have worked thereafter as journeyman for George Roger, who was by that time the sole proprietor of Gordon and Co. Roger died in 1824 and Izat in 1836. It seems that the firm of Gordon & Co. was merged with the business of William Jamieson at Roger's death in 1825, and David Izat, who was only about 50 at the time, may therefore have worked for Jamieson for some years before he retired.

John Keith, the most prolific of Banff's goldsmiths, although his output is almost wholly flatware, was admitted to the Hammermen in about 1789.

He was elected a master of the craft between 1798 and 1801, was boxmaster in 1802–3 and deacon in 1804–5. He became free of the Elgin Hammermen in 1808 but that was only to allow him to retail his work there. It appears that he continued to live and work in Banff until his death in 1823.

John MacQueen is mentioned between 1816 and 1839, but was not apparently a member of the Hammermen's Incorporation. Pigot's 1825 directory lists him as a silversmith with premises in Bridge Street.

George Elder appears in the Hammermen's records from 1819 to 1843. In the directories we find him in Low Street in 1825, High Shore in 1837 and back to Low Street (at No 6) by 1852.

William Simpson, elder, is mentioned between 1825 and 1855. In the 1837 directory he is classified as a jeweller and silversmith, in Carmelite Street.

William Simpson, younger, the son of the above, is given in Slater's 1852 directory as a working jeweller, with his premises at 53 High Street. His maker's mark is found with local marks and has also been seen with the Glasgow Assay Office marks for 1874–5. He was still in business in 1888 when William Cramond was conducting his researches.

I have omitted to mention in the above entries several goldsmiths who have no work or marks ascribed to them and about whom very little is known.

The marks used by Banff goldsmiths form a subject of great interest for collectors. Various contractions of the town's name are the most usual town marks, and the younger William Scott used a fish. None of the random letters of the alphabet appear to be date letters, not even those used by the William Scotts. The ABC mark used by the elder William Scott on the pair of communion beakers at Cullen is not a Banff mark, but relates to the maker's Aberdeen period: its possible significance is discussed in the end-notes to Chapter X (Page 112). A thistle mark is used by John Argo and also by David Izat and later ones by John McQueen and George Elder. John Keith occasionally used a rare and much sought-after fish punch and various letters of the alphabet. George Elder uses a two-handled vase and a Virgin and Child punch based on the seal of the burgh.

MONTROSE

Montrose is a seaport and ancient royal burgh in Angus, about twenty-one miles up the coast from Arbroath and about thirty miles north-east of Dundee. The town has a history supposedly going back over a thousand years, and Hector Boece tells us that the inhabitants were massacred by the Danes in the year 980. By 1357 Montrose has become the ninth town in Scotland in point of population and trade, but the people were almost wiped out by plague in 1566 and again in 1648–9. During the risings of 1715 and 1745 Montrose was predominantly Jacobite and it suffered considerably thereby. Thomas Pennant went there on his second tour of Scotland in 1772 and stated that the town had increased by one third since 1745. He also observed that 'numbers of genteel families, independant of any trade, reside here as a place of agreeable retreat, and numbers keep their carriages'.[1] The following year Dr. Samuel Johnson thought the town well-built, airy and clean, but Boswell remarked that many of the houses were built with their ends to the street, which he felt looked awkward. During the eighteenth century the wealth of the burgh derived principally from the manufacture of linen yarn and thread. Flax spinning began here in 1805 and continued throughout the nineteenth century.

Against this background we might expect to find more goldsmiths than are known at present. Only three appear before 1700, five in the eighteenth century and ten or so in the nineteenth, including retail jewellers. Thomas Johnston, 1743, and Benjamin Lumsden, 1788, are the only eighteenth century makers with work ascribed to them. Both men used a rose as their town mark and Thomas Johnston used letters of the alphabet in addition, which probably started out as a private cycle of date letters which was not continued. He made the pair of Communion Cups which were presented by the Rev. William Thomson to the parish church of nearby Marykirk, probably in the 1750s. They stand almost 8 inches high and the bowls are 4 inches in diameter. The presentation inscription on the cups is not original, but was added by a subsequent minister of the parish more than a century later.

Benjamin Lumsden was the son of Benjamin Lumsden, goldsmith of Aberdeen, and was apprenticed to James Gordon and Co., goldsmiths of that city, in 1782 for the space of four years. His most famous and interesting work is an oval gold snuff box which appeared at auction in Glasgow in 1985. Some 3½ inches across, it has bright-cut borders and the

[1] Thomas Pennant: *A Tour in Scotland. 1772.* Vol. III, p. 142.

lid is engraved with the complete armorial bearings of the royal burgh of Montrose. The lid has a very attractive double scroll thumb-piece and inside it is engraved '*A Token of Gratitude from the Town of Montrose to Sec^ty Henry Dundas for the Abolition of the Tax on Coals in Scotland.*' Dundas was Home Secretary from 1791 until 1794 and the box was presumably made during that time, but the *Public General Statutes affecting Scotland* are silent about the abolition of the tax referred to, and so I am unable to date the box more accurately at present.

The three goldsmiths of the nineteenth century whose work is sometimes met with are William Mill or Mills, 1811, Peter Lambert, 1833, and James Sturrock, 1860. The first two used the rose for a town mark, but Lambert also used a thistle as well as some anomalous marks unique to himself. He was admitted to the Aberdeen Hammermen's Incorporation on 11 June 1804. Sometime before 1820 he left Aberdeen, but whether he moved straight to Montrose or worked somewhere else in between for a while is unknown. Between 1833 and 1838 he sent small amounts of flatware to Edinburgh for assay, and in the latter year he, or another of the same name, did so from Berwick-upon-Tweed, where a Peter Lambert, Jeweller and dentist, is listed in directories as being at Hide Hill, Berwick, between 1820 and 1852.

James Sturrock, usually listed as a watchmaker and jeweller, is apparently the author of the J.S. punch seen with a Montrose rose and also with a mitre or bell mark, usually on fiddle pattern teaspoons or flimsy construction.

TAIN

Tain is a royal burgh on the southern shore of the Dornoch Firth, some forty-four miles north of Inverness. The town enjoyed modest prosperity during the eighteenth and nineteenth centuries. As early as 1659 the stent roll of the burgh reveals the presence of a goldsmith, unfortunately un-named.

In 1717, Robert Innes, goldsmith in Inverness, took one Hugh Ross as an apprentice for five years. Whether this was the same man as is found working in Tain from about 1730 onwards is not proven, but seems very probable. If apprenticed at the usual age of thirteen, he was probably born in about 1704. Since he died in about 1782, he was long-lived for those days. The earliest piece of his which I have seen is a wavy-end tablespoon marked with his maker's mark only. Although it looks distinctly Queen Anne in style it could have been made somewhat later as a replacement for one missing from a set. From at least 1730 until about 1750 he used a cycle of date letters along with his other marks. There are quite a number of references to him in the town records, none of them adding much of importance to our knowledge. In the roup of his belongings in 1787 after his death were three pairs of silver buckles for £1.8s.6d., nine silver tablespoons weighing 21½ ounces for £5.1s., forty-seven silver hearts (presumably bethrothal or Luckenbooth brooches) for £3.5s.6d. and one gold heart for 11s.6d., eleven silver rings, nine teaspoons, two sugar spoons, five gold rings, two candlesticks, a caster, two coffee-pots, three nutmeg graters and a punch-ladle. The Royal Museum of Scotland has a dish ring by Hugh Ross *c*.1760, bought from the Morris Collection, and two teapots have been noted.

The next goldsmith to consider is Alexander Stewart, who had business premises in Tain in 1825–6, according to Pigot's directory.[2] He is the same man as Alexander Stewart, goldsmith and jeweller in Inverness, but it is entirely wrong to suppose that he was an itinerant tinker, as Jackson and others have assumed him to be. On the contrary, he was a prosperous and eminent burgess of Inverness and a member of the Hammermen's Incorporation there. He had business premises for work and retail purposes, he resided permanently in the burgh and he paid all the dues and local taxes. Exactly how long he kept his retail premises in Tain is uncertain.

The only other goldsmiths so far identified with marks arc Walter Innes, 1820–35, and Richard Maxwell Wilkie, 1860–70.

The town mark of Tain as used by Hugh Ross is the figure of St. Duthac with the letters S and D, one either side of him for "Sanctus Duthacus". The similar mark often illustrated as having a 'B' for the second letter instead of a 'D' is a mistaken interpretation of a rubbed 'D'. Later, the word TAIN was used in addition to the Saint Duthac mark. Subsequent makers dropped St. Duthac and used TAIN by itself. Alexander Stewart in addition used the letter C and sometimes a 'wheat sheaf' or 'shuttle mark'; these were also used with his "INS" punch for Inverness and cannot therefore be taken to

[2] Pigot & Co: *New Commercial Directory of Scotland*, p. 641.

indicate a Tain origin by themselves; indeed, none of Stewart's silver was made in Tain, as far as one can tell, but was merely marked with the town's name if it was to be retailed there. Wilkie often added a thistle.

PAISLEY

Paisley grew up as a sleepy village around the abbey which Walter the High Steward had founded there in 1163. It became a burgh of barony in 1488, at which date its craftsmen gained independence from those of Renfrew. The magistrates and council of Paisley granted a charter in favour of the Society of Hammermen and Clockmakers of Paisley on 15 May, 1761, and their minute book dates from that time. Not many goldsmiths or jewellers joined the society, however, so the researcher needs to seek elsewhere for most of his information. Paisley began a programme of modernisation and of laying out new streets in 1779, and from then on the town's prosperity increased dramatically. By 1786 the annual value of Paisley pattern cotton, etc., produced by the numerous mills in the town amounted to £165,000, so there was enough money in circulation to justify the presence of more than one goldsmith at any one time.

So far, only three eighteenth-century goldsmiths have been positively identified as working in Paisley, though the unascribed maker's initials PH appear to come from there in the last decade of that century. The first is Malcolm Gillies, who was admitted to the Hammermen's Society on 20th September 1783, though he may already have been in business some years before his admission. He appears in the directory for that year, described as a silversmith, with premises in High Street. His mark has not yet been identified.

John Allan was admitted as a clockmaker on 13 September 1790, and is probably the author of the maker's mark J·A found with an anchor and also with the animal mark discussed below.

The third and most prolific maker was William Hannay, who was booked journeyman to James Wyllie of Glasgow on 26 August 1791, and established himself back in Paisley in 1794. Although he sometimes used to mark his work himself and sell it unassayed, he also sent a fair proportion of it to the Edinburgh Assay Office from then until the opening of the Glasgow Office twenty-five years later. It consisted almost entirely of flatware and serving pieces, including sugar tongs. He sent work there in sixty-two out of the seventy-one months covered by the earliest surviving King's Duty Book, the same number, as it happens, as Robert Keay, senior, from Perth. He was a founder member of the Glasgow Goldsmiths' Company in 1819, Paisley falling within the limits "forty miles west and south" of Glasgow, after which his name is not found again in the Edinburgh records. His work is of excellent quality and often a cut above most other provincial workers, as one might expect from one who had learned and perfected his trade in Glasgow. The pointed ends he sometimes gives to his spoons and ladles are particularly pleasing, and his sugar tongs, of which there were a good many, are exceptionally elegant.

As an example of his output, I have condensed his entries in the King's Duty Book for the period covered by the date letter U for the assay-year 1800–1801, as being more or less representative of his whole work. During that time, he submitted seventeen parcels of plate weighing a total of 502 oz. 10 dwt.

William Hannay: 1800–01, letter U.

Teaspoons	191	Tureen-spoons	9
Tablespoons	78	Salt-spoons	8
Dessert-spoons	74	Caddy-spoons	6
Sugar-tongs	19	"Tumlers"	4
Sauce-spoons	12	Mustard pots	2

The nomenclature varies according to who is filling up the book, but "tureen-spoon" means soup-ladle, "sauce-spoon", means gravy-spoon and "tumlers" means tumbler cups.

About fifteen more names are found mentioned in the directories and elsewhere during the nineteenth century, excluding watch and clock makers, but many of them were probably only retailers. By 1812 we find William Hannay with a shop in High Street and his house in Sneddon Street, while Andrew Mercer, jeweller, was in Smith-hills. Mercer is not mentioned again in the directories, but Hannay continues until at least 1825. The 1828 directory does not mention him, but gives us the name of Allan Stewart, watchmaker and jeweller, at 212 High Street. James Hannay is mentioned between 1830 and 1852 and became a member of the Glasgow

Goldsmiths' Company 1848. In 1838 we find Robert Donald, working goldsmith and lapidary, at 9 St. Mirren Street. The year 1852 brings a crop of three new names, all classified as jewellers and silversmiths, Alexander Harris, William Harris and James Newlands. Three more names appear in 1860, Duff and Millar, Robert Harris and John B. Newlands; these are followed by James Wilson in 1867, and by Mungo Guthrie and James Duncan in 1880. Duncan, Duff and Millar, and Guthrie all registered maker's punches with the Glasgow Goldsmith's Company in that order, but the dates of registration have not been recorded.

Some of the accompanying marks of Paisley are extremely similar to those of Greenock, with which they are easily confused if the maker's mark is not ascribed. Usually they consist of a plain anchor and the letter S. The mark representing an animal, variously suggested as a mouse, rat, fox or kangaroo (in descending order of probability) is found used sometimes by John Allan, William Hannay and the as yet unidentified partnership I & G. H. Before 1819 William Hannay's mark is often found with Edinburgh Assay Office marks, while after that date he used the Glasgow Office. All local Paisley marks appear to cease in 1819, from which date its goldsmiths sent their work to be assayed and marked in Glasgow.

GREENOCK

Greenock is a seaport and manufacturing town and lies on the southern shore of the Firth of Clyde twenty-one miles downstream from Glasgow. It became a burgh of barony in 1635, by virtue of a charter which also prohibited it from engaging in foreign trade, which was the exclusive privilege of royal burghs. This was remedied in 1670, from which time the town began to prosper. This prosperity was based principally on herring fishing, some three hundred fishing boats operating out of Greenock at that period. In 1674, over 20,000 barrels of herring were exported to La Rochelle alone, besides quantities to others parts of France, to Dantzig and to the Baltic ports. Throughout the eighteenth and nineteenth centuries, Greenock grew in wealth and size and by 1900 had become the seventh largest town in Scotland largely due to ship buildings, which eventually took over from fishing as the chief industry of the place along with factories such as Tate and

Lyle. The population in 1735 stood at 4,100 and by 1851 it had reached over 36,000. The goldsmiths and jewellers who worked in the town do not appear ever to have belonged to any trade incorporation or society and so information about them is rather scattered and still very incomplete.

Although one or two unascribed Greenock-looking marks have been noted in the earlier part of the eighteenth century, no names of goldsmiths have been discovered before 1775 when John Taylor, goldsmith, is mentioned. His will is registered in the commissariat records of Edinburgh on 18 November 1785, where he is described as 'some-time goldsmith in Greenock, theresafter in the Island of St. Eustatius'. His initials are found on flatware of c.1775–80, together with the marks of an anchor and the letter S.

John Campbell appears in 1776 and is the maker of a delightful cream-jug engraved with tulips and the inscription '*Presentation to Mr. John Gardner by Greenock Florist Society for first Prize of Tulips 21 May 1796*'.

In the directory for 1783 appears the name of John McFarlane, Jeweller in New Street.

John Clark, watchmaker, became a member of the Glasgow Goldsmith's Company on 1 July, 1822. He may be the author of the J C punch used at about this time. His son, Alexander M. Clark, became a member of the same body on 3 July 1848. By this time he had joined his father in the business and by 1852 they are called John Clark and Son. Pigot lists the father under Goldsmiths and jewellers as well as under watch and clock makers from 1820 onwards. The 1815 directory lists eight workers as goldsmiths, silversmiths, or jewellers, of whom three combined their craft with that of watchmaker, and James Davie is called 'silversmith and Vintner'. The other four are: James Burrell, working jeweller; Thomas Davie, working silversmith; John McLeod, goldsmith and jeweller; and Robert Scott, silversmith.

In 1820 appear the names of John McLeod, John Heron and William McMaster, while in 1836 we find George Buchanan, who is presumably the author of the G B maker's mark which appears around that time. Several other names occur in directories but no marks have as yet been found for them.

The accompanying marks found on Greenock silver vary from maker to maker, the earliest being an anchor, always plain and never wreathed with a rope, together with the letter S, the latter being not unlike the S punches found in Paisley and mid-eighteenth-century Glasgow. John Heron and Thomas Davie use a ship in full sail in addition to the anchor, in allusion to Greenock's position as an independent port and ship-building centre, a ship under sail also featuring on the seal of the burgh. Heron and others use a tree mark, supposed to be a rebus for a 'green oak', punning upon the town's name, although the true derivation is quite different. A number of other marks, including some random letters of the alphabet which are not date-letters, remain unexplained.

Two marks in particular, which were once thought to be Greenock on account of the presence of an anchor, turn out not even to be Scottish. One of the marks carries the initials J H, but may usually be distinguished from that of John Heron by the presence of tally marks typical of the British working in India. It is the mark of John Hunt of Calcutta, while W H T is the mark of William Henry Twentyman, also of Calcutta.[1] The latter's anchor is invariably wreathed.

Greenock fell within the loosely defined limits of jurisdiction of the Glasgow Goldsmith's Company, and from 1819 its goldsmiths presumably sent much of their work to Glasgow to be assayed and marked, although locally marked Greenock silver continued to be made, probably for another twenty years or so.

The reader may feel, disappointed, as I do, that so little new information has come to light concerning Greenock goldsmiths and their marks, especially since much of what was once thought to have been Greenock silver is now shown to have been made in Calcutta. It seems at first sight rather strange that the craft was not more developed there, but on reflection perhaps it is not so surprising. It was probably a natural consequence of Greenock's close proximity to Glasgow which caused her goldsmiths' activities to be overshadowed by those of her larger neighbour.

CUPAR

Cupar was a royal burgh before its earliest surviving charter in 1356. It is also the county town of Fife and stands upon the river Eden, some twelve

---

[1] W. R. T. Wilkinson: *Indian Colonial Silver*, pp. 74 and 118.

miles south by road of Dundee. The principal trading centre for farm produce for the whole of central Fife, Cupar also had a number of light industries which flourished there during the eighteenth and nineteenth centuries, including the weaving of linen and the manufacture of bricks, tiles and earthenware. There were eight incorporated trades, led by the Hammermen, to which some of the goldsmiths belonged.

Up to ten goldsmiths have so far been recognised as working in the burgh, some of them doubtless as retailers, between 1740 and the early years of the present century. Of these, marks have been positively ascribed to three: Robert Robertson, 1815, David Duncan, 1834–66, and Thomas Lumsden Brown, 1887. Robertson was the son of a tinsmith and was born in Cupar in 1793. He served his apprenticeship with his maternal uncle, William Duncan, in London, and in 1815 bought out the business of George Constable, 1800–15. In 1857 he took his son George Brunton Robertson into partnership and, as R. & G. B. Robertson; the firm lasted until 1917. Robert had been appointed officer for weights and measures for Fife in 1834 and his maker's marks are on his brass weights which he used. He died of bronchitis on 14 May 1877.

I only know of flatware made by Robertson, though he may have been capable of more ambitious work. Dundee Museum has a punch ladle by him with a twisted whalebone handle, the deep circular bowl attached to the handle by a curious flat section. Robertson's mark, besides his initials, is a *fleur-de-lis* and sometimes an additional letter R. Note, however, that the marks of a *fleur-de-lis* accompanied by a cockerel are not Cupar and remain unascribed at present. I rather doubt if they are Scottish.

David Duncan registered a punch at the Edinburgh Assay Office and sent some work there for assay in the 1830s and 1840s. Much later, Thomas Lumsden Brown registered a punch at Edinburgh and sent mostly goldwork and masonic medals there for assay.

LEITH

Leith is the port for Edinburgh, and the goldsmiths who worked there in the eighteenth and nineteenth centuries had, with one exception, no distinctive local marks. From 1784 onwards they were obliged to send all their work to Goldsmiths Hall in Parliament Close to be assayed and marked, as did their fellow craftsmen in Canongate, since they were too close to the mother city to escape detection if they did otherwise.

People have attempted to ascribe various anomalous silver marks to Leith, but I cannot accept that there were ever any local marks stuck there, apart from the perfectly straightforward one of John Hay, whose 'LEITH' punch is nearly always accompanied by Edinburgh Assay Office marks. All Leith makers used the Assay Office, as far as anyone can show, and for all practical purposes may be regarded as Edinburgh goldsmiths, in the same way as one thinks of workers in other suburbs of the City such as Portsburgh, Canonmills or Newhaven. Thus the series of Star and Thistle punches associated with the initials EW, CW, PC and R·N are positively not Leith marks.

John Hay is first mentioned in the Leith directories in 1810, when his business is described as 'jeweller and silver-plate warehouse' and was at 13, Barnard Street. He is called simply 'jeweller' in 1816 and by the next year he moved to Waterloo Street. He had a house in Constitution Street by 1821 and by the following year is working at 1, Waterloo Buildings, described as 'jeweller, lottery and tea agent', a rather curious combination. He continued in business until 1829. He used his surname in full instead of his initials as his maker's mark and it is found with Assay Office marks; he only sometimes used the 'LEITH' mark in addition. He appears sometimes to have added his maker's mark and 'LEITH' mark to the work of other goldsmiths when acting as retailer.

Besides John Hay, a few other goldsmiths and jewellers are to be found in the directories. David Marshall, goldsmith, previously by the Council Chamber door in Edinburgh, moved to the foot of Tollbooth Wynd, Leith, in 1793 and remained there three years. Charles Galli, jeweller, was at the Wet Dock from 1818 until 1821. Robert Smeaton (sometimes called Smiton), jeweller, had premises at 78 Kirkgate, Leith, from 1819 to 1824. He then moved to 101 Kirkgate and appears to have died in 1826 or early in 1827, for the directories give Mrs. Robert Smeaton at this address, also classified as a jeweller, for the next three years. In 1830 George Barclay, jeweller, is given at the Smeatons' old address.

FORRES

The royal burgh of Forres was anciently the principal town of the province of Moray until 1224, when the seat of the bishopric was moved to Elgin. It was a royal burgh by the end of the fifteenth century but has always been overshadowed by Elgin in point of population and trade. The town blossomed modestly in the nineteenth century as a spa resort because of its good climate and low rainfall, and it is in that century that goldsmiths are found working in the burgh.

The principal maker in the town was Patrick Riach who learned the business of silversmith with Charles Fowler in Elgin; then 'for a time he was in the south acquiring greater proficiency in his trade'.[1] He set up in Forres in 1817, in financial partnership with his brother John, who was not a silversmith. This lasted until the brothers married two sisters from Elgin in 1823. Patrick continued on his own under the name of J. and P. Riach until 1841, in which year he appears to have given up business in order to devote himself to local politics, became a councillor and was provost of the burgh from 1855 to 1858. He retired from the council because of failing health and died on 30 August, 1864. The Riachs first mark consisted of their initials, IPR, and a punch representing the Nelson Tower, a local landmark. The second mark is I & P.R. FOR^S, all contained in a single punch, which, because of its length, is often poorly struck. The date of the change-over from one mark to the other may have been as early as 1823, although it could have been made at any time up to 1836, the year of John Riach's early death.

Two other workers from the middle years of the century deserve a brief mention, Robert Stewart and Robert Hendrie. The former is apparently the same man who briefly partnered Joseph Pozzie in Elgin; his Forres dates are roughly 1844–67. Hendry worked from 1850 and is last mentioned in the directories in 1867. Both men used their respective initials either side of the letter F. Their F punches appear to be identical, which leads one to suspect that they had some sort of partnership arrangement. Their work is very rare and I have only ever seen fiddle pattern flatware of moderate quality by them. My attention has recently been drawn to a fiddle pattern teaspoon

---

[1] Robert Douglas: *Annals of the Royal Burgh of Forres*, p. 227.

marked with the same Nelson Tower punch used by the Riachs, together with a gothic m and the initials of the unidentified maker, W·A.

ARBROATH

Arbroath, like Paisley, owes its existence to its abbey, in this case founded by William, the Lion in 1178. He dedicated it to Our Lady and to his friend, Saint Thomas of Canterbury, who had been murdered only seven years before. The town became a Royal Burgh in 1599, from which time it had seven incorporated trades, of which the Hammermen are placed first. Prosperity was only moderate, despite the catching and smoking of haddock and herring, until the last years of the eighteenth century, and took off in a much bigger way with the coming of flax weaving in 1806.

Only two of Arbroath's possible goldsmiths have marks ascribed to them, the first being George Ritchie, 1823–66. His initials are found with the same Portcullis punch as was used by Andrew Davidson. He appears to have been a retailer of Davidson's work, and may or may not have produced work of his own as well. Andrew Davidson was in business by 1825 and seems to have worked for some thirty years in the burgh. Besides fiddle pattern flatware, and very rarely old English pattern also, he produced wine-labels and cowrie shell snuff-boxes. He sent a small amount of work to the Edinburgh Assay Office for assaying and marking from time to time. Jackson records an instance of this in the assay year 1838–9. Note that his christian name is definitely Andrew and not Alexander, as some would have it.

Besides the two names already mentioned, the following appear in the directories as jewellers rather than watchmakers: Alexander Glenney and Cornelius Davidson both in 1852, Alexander Glenny and Co, George Black, and Messrs. Christie and Barrie in 1860. The usual marks used as town marks by Andrew Davidson are a portcullis, based on the arms of the burgh, and another mark the nature of which it is difficult to be certain about, owing to its always being found in a worn state without any details visible; it possibly represents a bell.

PETERHEAD

Peterhead, the chief port of the Buchan district of Aberdeenshire, became a burgh of barony in 1593, when it is thought that there were only between fifty and sixty inhabitants. The harbour was constructed in 1773 which marks the beginning of the town's prosperity, and around 1800 it enjoyed a short-lived reputation as a healthy watering-place. The real wealth of the town has always derived from the sea, and fishing and foreign trade continued while unsuccessful land-based ventures came and went.

The trade directories name three watch and clock makers in the town in 1825, one of whom, Alexander King in Rose Street, has silver marks ascribed to him. His initials are found on fiddle-pattern flatware, together with the letters P, H, D, each in a separate punch. In the same directory is George Angus, silversmith, Jamaica Street, but no marks have yet been ascribed to him. Another maker's mark of about this date has not yet been assigned to any maker. It consists of the initials W F either in a plain rectangular shield or, later, in a shaped one, accompanied by the letters P H D in a separate punch to match. The plain W F and P H D marks have been seen together with Edinburgh marks for 1826–7. The shaped punches probably date anything up to ten years later. There is no known evidence to support the theory that these marks pertain to William Ferguson of Elgin, as some people seem to think. The initials W S are also unascribed and are found with a PH^d punch and a wreathed anchor mark, noted by Jackson erroneously under Greenock, as being on fiddle pattern teaspoons belonging to Lord Breadalbane. They probably date from *c*.1840. The mark of a key, found with various initials, can by no stretch of the imagination be construed as coming from Peterhead, and there is no shred of evidence to support such an impossible theory. Pieces marked in this way do not even appear to be Scottish.

STONEHAVEN

Stonehaven became the county town of Kincardineshire in 1607, by which date it was already a burgh of barony. It lies sixteen miles South of Aberdeen where the rivers Carron and Cowie flow into the North Sea. The town's economic life centred around the fishing fleet and the curing of herring and haddock, while a tannery and a net and rope works flourished in the town during the nineteenth century. The place experienced a considerable increase in prosperity and trade in 1826 when the huge rock which partially blocked the harbour entrance, and incidentally gave the place its name, was blasted away. The population in 1841 stood at 3,012 souls, and one of the names which appear in the census of that year is Alexander Glenny, jeweller, aged thirty-five. He lived and worked in the High Street with his wife, Elizabeth, who was ten years his senior, and two children, Christina aged thirteen and David aged ten. He had no journeyman or apprentice working with him at that time. Glenny's maker's mark, A·G, is found on a fiddle pattern teaspoon of that period, accompanied by the letters S, T, O, N, H, N, each in a separate punch. This teaspoon is the only piece of his of which I have ever seen, and his work must be among the rarest of all nineteenth century provincial silversmiths.

WICK

Wick is a royal burgh, a seaport and the county town of Caithness. It is a hundred-and-sixty miles north of Inverness and only eighteen miles from John O'Groats. It has the distinction of being mentioned in a Nose *Saga* of about the year 1140 when 'Earl Rögnvald went over to Caithness and was entertained at Vik by a man named Harold'.[1] Throughout its long existence it has owed its being to the catching and curing of herring, but this was not put on a regular commercial basis until 1768, and no proper harbour existed until 1810. Pigot's directory for 1825 includes the name of John Sellar, watchmaker and jeweller in Bridge Street, to whom I ascribe the J.S. punch, hitherto usually said to pertain to James Sinclair. Sinclair does not appear in the directories until 1860, and was a watch and clock maker with a shop in Market Place; I think it unlikely that he ever worked in silver.

ELLON

Ellon is a village some eighteen miles north of Aberdeen, and was anciently

[1] *Jack's Ordnance Gazetteer of Scotland* (1901), p. 1617, ii.

the centre of jurisdiction for the Earldom of Buchan. There is no evidence of any goldsmith working in the village until the second quarter of the nineteenth century. In the census for 1841 is the name of John Mackie, jeweller, aged thirty-five. To him I ascribe the initials J.M. accompanied by four separate punches E, L, L, N, found on a very few pieces of fiddle pattern flatware.

NAIRN

Nairn is a royal burgh and seaport at the mouth of the river Nairn, lying some fifteen miles east of Inverness and twenty-one miles west of Elgin. In the early years of the nineteenth century it was a considerable spa and was popularly known for a time as 'The Brighton of the North'. In 1851 the population numbered 2,977 and this rose ten years later to 3,435. In Slater's directories for 1852 and 1860 is to be found the name of Daniel Ferguson, classified as a watch and clock maker, with premises at 74 High Street. He is apparently the maker of the betrothal brooch in the Royal Museum of Scotland, marked with the initials DF and the name NAIRN. It has been represented to me that these marks actually pertain to Donald Frazer, silversmith in Inverness, but this appears to be an error as there is no known evidence of his ever having worked or retailed in Nairn. It is probable that this Daniel Ferguson is identical with the man of the same name who appears in Inverness.

FOCHABERS

Fochabers is the chief town of the parish of Bellie in Morayshire, on the River Spey, a few miles from Elgin, and dates only from the last decade of the eighteenth century. However, it does possess the distinction of harbouring an unidentified silversmith with the initials J.McI. These initials are found with the letters FOCHRS on a fiddle pattern teaspoon, probably from the third quarter of the nineteenth century.

KEITH

The town of Keith in Banffshire has no known history of goldsmithing, nevertheless, the mark J, C, K, E, I, T, H has been seen on a very few poorly made fiddle pattern teaspoons of the middle of the nineteenth century. There is no-one of these initials to whom the mark may be ascribed, and so they remain anonymous. There is always the possibility that they are not Scottish at all, and may pertain to one of the Keiths in Australia or Canada.

In addition to the burghs dealt with in this chapter, there is positive proof of goldsmiths working elsewhere in Scotland, for example in Stirling, Huntly and Kilmarnock. They are omitted here, even though they are part of the history of Scottish silverwork, because they have no work or marks ascribed to them, and much research still remains to be done. Much more detail might also have been given, especially when dealing with the larger towns, but space does not permit it.

I cannot leave the subject of Scottish silver, and particularly of provincial work, without alluding to one or two further matters. Many silver marks which may be Scottish remain unascribed or have been misascribed in the past. It is fruitless and misleading to base ascriptions on guesswork or second-hand information, or upon the ideas of people who have not done their own research into the subject, and it is irresponsible to publish an unjustified or unresearched ascription. Auction catalogues are frequently guilty of perpetuating misascriptions quite needlessly, as are numerous articles written in the lesser magazines, purporting to be saying something new but in fact only recycling misinformation and misunderstandings, often with new errors added. A truly horrendous example of this type of article appeared in the spring of 1989 in a certain magazine, written by someone who obviously had no grasp of the subject whatever. In the space of a few hundred words the writer of that article committed an unbelievable number of errors and misunderstandings. To correct them all would be the work of several pages. I mention this particularly blatant instance of unscholarly ignorance in order to draw attention to the dangers of believing everything one reads in such articles, and as a warning to those who intend to write about Scottish silver to check their facts before going into print. The writer asserted, for example, that 'items for assay' were being marked in provincial centres, as if there were assay offices in those places, which there were not. Dingwall is claimed as one of these places, but there is no evidence that any silver was ever made there; nor is it true that Arbroath, Forres, Peterhead, St. Andrews, Stonehaven or Wick produced silver 'by the Eighteenth Century'. All these places (except St. Andrews) produced silver in the nineteenth century, but not any earlier, and there is no evidence that the mark of St. Andrew standing behind his cross actually comes from St. Andrews. There then occurs the most astonishing piece of nonsense I have come across for years. The writer seriously believes that journeymen were so called from their journeying about from place to place plying their craft, and equates them with tinkers. A number of eminent burgesses of Aberdeen are, who held considerable property in the City, are then accused of being tinkers, including John Leslie and William Jamieson! A further example of ineptitude is furnished by a reference to the pair of recusant candlesticks by Coline Allan of Aberdeen (see p.189)[1] as being typical of Scottish work, when they are in fact very exceptional, or even possibly unique.

I have said enough to show that it is necessary to be thoroughly conversant with the subject and to sift all the evidence before committing oneself to print, and I plead with all would-be experts on Scottish silver not to go on repeating all the old *mumpsimi*, but to replace them with their corresponding *sumpsimi*, and to do their own research for themselves.

Even two or three articles which I have cited in this chapter for the useful information which they contain also include errors and misunderstandings which I have foreborn to mention. These mostly concern silvermarks and hallmarks in law and in practice. What the law required and what actually happened were not always the same thing, and no assumptions should ever be made on what the situation was *supposed* to be. For instance, the Act of Parliament which came into force in 1720, requiring sterling standard as the minimum and imposing plate duty, *did* apply to Scotland. The goldsmiths of Edinburgh *did* pay the duty (*vide* John Rollo's account book, etc.), though they fought the Inland Revenue over it, but they continued to use the old Scots standard of eleven penny-weights fine until September 1759. The change of mark from the assay master's initials to a thistle was intended to denote this change from the old standard to Sterling, which was done

[1] See pp. 168-9 & plate.

voluntarily by the Edinburgh Goldsmiths' Incorporation on their own initiative and for their own convenience, since the easiest and cheapest source of bullion at that time was London, and that bullion was of sterling standard. However, a few years later it appears that the old Scots standard was again in use, and the situation was not finally resolved until the nineteenth century.

Another trap to be avoided is the describing of any piece of silver with Edinburgh marks upon it as being made in Edinburgh, even though the maker's mark is unidentified or even pertains to an identifiable goldsmith working elsewhere. Catalogue descriptions such as 'Edinburgh 1812, by Robert Gray & Son of Glasgow' are still frequently met with and do not actually make sense. Virtually *all* silver made in Glasgow between 1784 and 1819 was sent to the Edinburgh Assay Office to be assayed and marked, and the description would more accurately read 'by Robert Gray & Son, Glasgow, with Edinburgh marks for 1812–13'. A small percentage of work from other towns such as Aberdeen and Perth was also sent to the Edinburgh Assay Office after 1784. A description such as 'Edinburgh 1839, by R. Keay of Perth' should read 'by Robert Keay, jnr. of Perth, with Edinburgh marks for 1839–40'.

There is still much more to be discovered about Scottish silver and its marks and makers, both from Edinburgh and the provinces, that has not yet come to light or which is waiting to appear in print. Passing references to goldsmiths and their work are scattered through a wide range of manuscripts and printed sources, some of them quite unexpected. Gathering them all together and drawing satisfactory conclusions is a lifetime's work for several people. Mr. J. H. Sanderson began the process of discovery in 1860. Mr. A. J. S. Brook, Sir Charles James Jackson and Commander G. E. P. How have all greatly expanded the horizons. The first edition of the present work was a great landmark in the study of the subject and it has stood the test of time, while Mr. Ian Finlay's many articles, some of which are to be found in the bibliography (p.233), have added further to our store of knowledge. At the present time Mrs. G. E. P. How, Mr. Stuart Maxwell (formerly deputy-keeper of the National Museum of Antiquities of Scotland), Mr. George Dalgleish (of the Royal Museum of Scotland), myself and others are all engaged in further research which it is to be hoped will one day see publication.

SELECT BIBLIOGRAPHY AND REFERENCES

by

Henry Fothringham

This bibliography is arranged in three parts, each of them selective. Part One gives printed books, including catalogues of sales and exhibitions. Part Two covers fifty-two articles in *The Proceedings of the Society of Antiquaries of Scotland*. Part Three comprises articles in other journals, magazines, etc. In each section works by any one author are arranged chronologically. Works more easily or logically referred to by title than by author or editor are arranged alphabetically, sometimes by the principal or most obvious key-word of the title, *e.g.*: *The Chartulary of Lindores* appears as *Lindores, Chartulary of.* Articles of a derivative or unoriginal nature that add little or nothing to the subject in hand, or which contain too many serious errors, have been omitted.

PART ONE: PRINTED BOOKS

Aberdeen, Commissariot Records of. Scottish Record Society, Edinburgh 1899.

Acts of The Parliaments of Scotland (1124–1707), 12 Vols. Edinburgh 1844–75.

Anderson, Joseph: *Scotland in Early Christian Times*, 2 Vols. Edinburgh 1881.

Anderson, Joseph: *Scotland in Pagan Times: The Iron Age*. Edinburgh 1883.

Anderson, Joseph: *Scotland in Pagan Times: The Bronze and Stone Ages*. Edinburgh 1886.

Arnot, Hugo: *The History of Edinburgh*. Edinburgh 1788.

Atkinson, Stephen: *The Discoverie and Historie of the Gold Mynes in Scotland, Written in The Year M.DC.XIX.* (1619). *Bannatyne Club*, Edinburgh 1825.

Balfour-Paul, Sir James: *The Scots Peerage*. 9 Vols. Edinburgh 1904–14.

Bannatyne Miscellany, The. 3 Vols. *Bannatyne Club*, Edinburgh 1827, 1836 and 1855.

Boece, Hector: *The History and Chronicles of Scotland* (Translated by John Bellenden), 2 Vols. Edinburgh 1821.

Breadalbane Collection of Silversmith's Work, The. Dowell's Ltd. Sale Catalogue, 30 and 31 May 1935. Edinburgh 1935.

Buccleuch and Hopetown Silver: *Catalogue of Highly Important English, Scottish and Continental Silver, the property of His Grace the Duke of Buccleuch . . . and The Hopetoun Estates Company*. Sotheby's Sale Catalogue 25 June 1953.

Buchanan, John Lane: *Travels in The Western Hebrides 1782–90*. London 1793.

Burns, Rev. Thomas: *Old Scottish Communion Plate*. Edinburgh 1892.

Canongate, Book of the Records of the Ancient Privileges of the. Scottish Record Society, Edinburgh.

Catalogue of the Exhibition of Scottish Silver, Royal Scottish Museum, Aug.–Sept. 1948. Edinburgh, 1948.

Catalogue of a Loan Exhibition of Scottish Art and Antiquities. London 1931.

Childe, Gordon: *The Prehistory of Scotland*. London 1935.

Clarke, D.V., and others: *Symbols of Power at the Time of Stonehenge*. Exhibition Catalogue, Edinburgh 1985.

Close-Brooks, Joanna: *St. Ninian's Isle Treasure*. Edinburgh 1981.

Cochran-Patrick, R. W: *Early Records Relating to Mining in Scotland*. Edinburgh 1878.

Cochran-Patrick, R. W: *Catalogue of The Medals of Scotland*. Edinburgh 1884.

Colston, James: *The Incorporated Trades of Edinburgh*. Edinburgh 1891.

Coupar-Angus, Register of the Abbey of. (Edited by Charles Rogers). Edinburgh 1872.

Cramond, William: *The Annals of Banff*. 2 Vols. *New Spalding Club*, Aberdeen 1891–3.

Cramond, William: *The Records of Elgin*. 2 Vols. *New Spalding Club*, Aberdeen 1908.

Curle, A. O: *The Treasure of Traprain*.

Dalgleish, George: *Silver and Pewter* in Hugh Cheape and George Dalgleish, etc: *At Home: Ten Years Collecting from Historic Scotland*. Edinburgh 1984.

Dalgleish, George, and D. Mechan: *'I Am Come Home'. Treasures of Prince Charles Edward Stuart*. Edinburgh 1985.

Dalgleish, George, and Stuart Maxwell: *The Lovable Craft, 1687–1987*. Exhibition Catalogue. Edinburgh 1987.

Dalgleish, George: *The Silver Travelling Canteen of Prince Charles Edward Stewart*. In Fenton and Myrdal [Eds.] *Food and Drink and Travelling Accessories*, pp. 168-184. Edinburgh 1988.

Dobie, Kirkpatrick H: *Dumfries Silversmiths*. Dumfries n.d.

Douglas, Robert: *Annals of The Royal Burgh of Forres*. Elgin 1934.

Emery, John: *European Spoons before 1700*. Edinburgh 1976.

Empire Exhibition, Glasgow, May to October 1938: Old Scottish Silver, Catalogue of Loan Collection in Scottish Historical Pavilion. Glasgow 1938.

English and Scottish Silver. (Royal Scottish Museum) Edinburgh 1954.

Eogan, George: *Royal Torcs in Britain and Ireland*. In O'Connor & Clarke (q.v.) 1983.

Fallow, T. M. and H. B. McCall: *Yorkshire Church Plate*. 2 Vols. Leeds 1912 and 1915.

Finlay, Ian: *Art in Scotland*. Oxford 1948.

Finlay, Ian: *Scottish Crafts*. London 1948.

Finlay, Ian: *Celtic Art*. London 1973.

Finlay, Ian: *Columba*. London 1979.

Fordun, John of: *Scotichronicon, or Chronica Gentis Scotorum*. (Wm. Skene Edition) Edinburgh 1871.

Four Centuries of Scottish Silver. Exhibition at the Royal Scottish Museum, Edinburgh 19??.

Foster, Joseph: *Members of Parliament, Scotland, 1357–1882*. London 1882.

Foulis, Sir John of Ravelston: *Account Book 1671–1707*. Scottish History Society. 1st Series. Vol 16. Edinburgh 1894.

Franklin, T. Bedford: *A History of Scottish Farming*. Edinburgh 1952.

French Connections: Scotland and the Arts of France. Exhibition Catalogue, Edinburgh 1985.

Graham-Campbell, James: *Some Viking-Age Penannular Brooches from Scotland and the Origins of the 'Thistle Brooch'*. In O'Connor & Clarke (q.v.) 1983.

Grant, James: *Cassell's Old and New Edinburgh*. 3 Vols. London n.d.

Henry, Françoise: *Irish Art in the Early Christian Period*. 1st Edition, London 1940; 2nd Edition 1965.

Henry, Françoise: *Early Christian Irish Art*. (Translated by Mairie MacDermott.) Dublin 1954.

How. G. E. P.: *How of Edinburgh Ltd., Silver Exhibition at 15 Stratton Street, London, W1, 1936*.

How. G. E. P.: *How of Edinburgh Ltd., Silver Exhibition at 15 Stratton Street, London, W1, 1937*.

How. G. E. P.: *A Coconut Cup by Thomas Lindsay of Dundee, circa 1600*. London 1947.

How. G. E. P. and Jane P. How: *English and Scottish Silver Spoons*. 3 Vols. 1952-7.

How, Jane: *The Huntly Race and its Trophies*. In O'Connor & Clarke (q.v.) 1983.

Hunt, Colin A: *The Perth Hammermen Book (1518–1568)*. Perth 1889.

Imlach, James: *History of Banff*. Banff 1868.

Jack, T. C. and E. C: *Ordnance Gazetteer of Scotland*. 'New Edition' Edinburgh 1901.

Jackson, Sir Charles James: *English Goldsmiths and their Marks*. 1st Edition, London 1905; 2nd Edition 1921. 3rd Edition (re-written) 1989.

Jackson, Sir Charles James: *An Illustrated History of English Plate*. 2 Vols. 1st Edition, London 1911; New Edition 1967.

James, Dr. I. E: *The Goldsmiths of Aberdeen, 1450–1850*. Aberdeen 1981.

Kendrick, Thomas Downing: *Late Saxon and Viking Art*.

Kinloss, Records of the Monastery of, Edinburgh 1872.

Lee, Georgina E. and Ronald A: *British Silver Monteith Bowls*. Byfleet, Surrey, 1978.

Lindores, Chartulary of. Scottish History Society. 1st Series, Vol. 42. Edinburgh 1903.

List of Persons Concerned in The Rebellion (1745). *Scottish History Society*. 1st Series, Vol 8. Edinburgh 1890.

Loan Exhibition of Scottish Art and Antiquities, at 27 Grosvenor Square, London. February 5th–March 1st 1931, Catalogue of.

Lumsden, Harry, and P. Henderson Aitken: *History of The Hammermen of Glasgow*. 2nd Edition, Paisley, 1915.

McClenachan, Richard. L: *Some Scottish Quaichs*. 2 Vols. Skokie, Illinois 1955 and 1968.

MacDougall, Margaret O: *Inverness Silversmiths*. Inverness n.d.

Macintosh, Herbert B: *Elgin Past and Present*. Elgin 1914.

Mackay, John: *History of The Burgh of Canongate*. Edinburgh 1886.

Mahr, Adolf: *Ancient Irish Handicraft*.

Maitland, William: *The History of Edinburgh*. Edinburgh 1753.

Maxwell, Stuart: *Letters from Walter Allan, Armourer in Stirling, to Colin Mitchell, Goldsmith in Canongate, 1741-1750*. In David H. Caldwell [Ed.]: *Scottish Weapons and Fortifications 1100-1800*. Edinburgh 1981, pp. 408-18.

Maxwell, Stuart: *Quaichs*. In O'Connor & Clarke (q.v.) 1983.

Morris Collection: *Scottish Provincial Silver from the David Morris Collection, 3 July 1984*. Christie's Sale Catalogue 1984.

Morris Collection: *Scottish Provincial Silver from the David Morris Collection, 9 October 1984*. Christie's Scotland Sale Catalogue.

Munro, Alexander M: *Records of Old Aberdeen*. 2 Vols. *New Spalding Club*. Aberdeen 1899 and 1909.

Noble, John: *Exhibition of Scottish Silver from the Collection of John Noble, Chairman of the Scottish Craft Centre, 24 August–12 September, 1959*.

O'Connor, Anne, and D. V. Clarke (Editors): *From The Stone Age to The 'Forty-Five. Studies Presented To R. B. K. Stevenson . . .* Edinburgh 1983.

Oman, Charles C: *English Domestic Silver*. 1st Edition London 1934; 6th Edition 1968.

Palace of History: Scottish Exhibition of National History, Arts & Industry, Glasgow (1911) 2 Vols. Glasgow n.d (1911).

Paton, James (Editor): *Scottish National Memorials*. Glasgow 1890.

Paton, James (Editor): *Scottish History and Life*. Glasgow 1902.

Pennant, Thomas: *A Tour in Scotland 1769 and 1772*. 3 Vols, London etc. 1774–6.

Perth City Art Gallery and Museum: *A History of Perth Silver*. Perth 1980.

Porteous, J. Moir: *God's Treasure House in Scotland*.

Public General Statutes Affecting Scotland, 1707–1847. 3 Vols, Edinburgh 1876.

Quig, Rev. Gordon: *The Romantic Adventures of Two Old Monifeith Communion Cups*.

Register of The Privy Council of Scotland (1545–1689). 36 Vols. Edinburgh 1877–1933.

Renaissance Decorative Arts in Scotland, 1480–1650. Exhibition Catalogue, Edinburgh 1959.

Report of the Departmental Committee on Hallmarking. H.M.S.O. 1959.

Scottish Silver, A Loan Exhibition in Huntly House Museum, Canongate, August–September 1960.

Shaw Collection of Important Scottish Silver and Pistols, The. 29th March 1983. Christie's Sale Catalogue.

Silver Teapots from The John Bell of Aberdeen Collection, 20th November–16th December 1961, at the Ceylon Tea Centre, Glasgow. Exhibition Catalogue, 1961.

Small, Alan, & others: *St. Ninian's Isle and its Treasure*. 2 Vols. Aberdeen University Studies Series, No 152. Oxford 1973.

Smith, John: *The Hammermen of Edinburgh and their Altar in St. Giles Church*. Edinburgh 1906.

Statistical Account of Scotland, The. 1st Edition, 21 Vols., Edinburgh 1791–99; Reprinted, 20 Vols, 1978.

Statutes of The Scottish Church. Scottish History Society, 1st Series Vol. 54. Edinburgh 1907.

Stevenson, R. B. K: *Pictish Art*. In F. T. Wainwright (Editor) *The Problem of The Picts*. Edinburgh 1955.

Stevenson, R. B. K and Stuart Maxwell: *Brooches in Scotland*. Edinburgh 1958.

Taylor, Joan J.: *Bronze-Age Goldwork of the British Isles*. Cambridge 1980.

Taylor, Joan J.: *An Unlocated Scottish Gold Ore Source or An Experiment in Alloying?* In O'Connor and Clarke (q.v.) 1983.

Watts, W. W.: *Old English Silver*. London 1924.

Wilkinson, W. R. T: *Indian Colonial Silver*. London 1973.

Wilson, Sir Daniel: *Prehistoric Annals of Scotland*. 2 Vols. Edinburgh 1st Edition 1851. 2nd Edition 1863.

Wood, L. Ingleby: *Scottish Pewter-ware and Pewterers*. Edinburgh n.d. (c.1904.)

Wood, Marguerite: *Court Book of The Regality of Broughton and The Burgh of The Canongate 1569–1573*. Edinburgh 1937.

Young, Robert: *Annals of the Parish of Elgin*. Elgin 1879.

PART TWO: PROCEEDINGS OF THE SOCIETY OF ANTIQUARIES OF SCOTLAND (P.S.A.S.)
(Selected articles. Some titles have been slightly shortened.)

Anonymous: *Notice of an Ancient Celtic Brooch the property of William Rose Campbell . . . of Ballochyle*. Vol. I, p. 170. 1852-3.

Anderson, Joseph: *Notes on the Relics of the Viking Period of the Northmen in Scotland . . .* Vol. X, pp. 536–594. 1873–4.

Anderson, Joseph: *Notice of an Ancient Reliquary exhibited to the Society by Sir Archibald Grant, Bart., of Monymusk*. Vol. XIV, pp. 431–5. 1879–80.

Anderson, Joseph: *Notice of a Fragment of a Silver Penannular Brooch . . . found at Achavrole, Dunbeath . . .* Vol. XIV, pp 445–52. 1879–80.

Anderson, Joseph: *Notice of the Gold Ornaments found at Lower Largo, and of the Silver Ornaments, etc. found at Norrie's Law*. Vol. XVIII, pp. 233–47. 1883–4.

Anderson, Joseph: *Notice of a Highland Brooch in Silver, ornamented with Niello . . . and of other Highland Brooches in Silver and Brass*. Vol. XXXIII, pp. 57–67. 1898-9.

Anderson, Joseph: *The Architecturally Shaped shrines and other Reliquaries of the Early Celtic Church in Scotland and Ireland*. Vol. XLIV, pp. 259–281. 1909–10.

Brook, Alexander J. S.: *Notice of a Silver Brooch with Blackletter Inscription and Ornamentation in Niello . . .* Vol. XXIII pp. 192–9. 1888–9.

Brook, Alexander J. S.: *Additional Notes on the Silver Chain called 'Midside Maggie's Girdle'.* Vol. XXIII, pp. 445–52. 1888–9. pp. 49–141. 1889–90.

Brook, Alexander J. S.: *Technical Description of the Regalia of Scotland.* Vol. XXIV, pp. 49–141. 1889–90.

Brook, Alexander J. S.: *Notice of the Silver Bell of Lanark, a Horse Racing Trophy of the Seventeenth Century . . .* Vol. XXV, pp. 174–188. 1890–1.

Brook, Alexander J. S.: *An Account of the Maces of the Universities of St. Andrews, Glasgow, Aberdeen and Edinburgh, the College of Justice, the City of Edinburgh, etc.* Vol. XXVI, pp. 440–514. 1891–2.

Brook, Alexander J. S.: *An Account of the Archery Medals belonging to the University of St. Andrews and the Grammar School of Aberdeen.* Vol. XXVIII, pp. 343–469. 1893–4.

Brook, William: *Note on the Boss of the Bute Mazer.* Vol. LXV, pp. 252–3. 1930–1.

Callander, J. Graham: *Scottish Bronze Age Hoards.* Vol. LVII, pp. 123–166. 1922–3.

Callander, J. Graham: *Fourteenth Century Brooches and other Ornaments in The National Museum of Antiquities of Scotland.* Vol. LVIII, pp. 160–184. 1923–4.

Callander, J. Graham: *A Hoard of Coins, Two Spoons and a Cane Top of Silver from Irvine and a spoon of the same Metal from Haddington.* Vol. LIX, pp. 120–127. 1924–5.

Coles, John M.: *Scottish Early Bronze Age Metalwork.* Vol. 101, pp. 1–110. 1968–9.

Craw, J. Hewat: *Gold in Scotland and Ireland.* Vol. LXIII, p. 188. 1928–9.

Crichton, Lionel A; *On the Provenance of the Bute Mazer.* Vol. LXV, pp. 251–2. 1930-1.

Curle, Alexander O.: *Report of the Excavation on Traprain Law in the Summer of 1919.* Vol. LIV, pp. 54–124. 1919–20.

Curle, Alexander O.: *A Note on Four Silver Spoons and a Fillet of Gold found in the Nunnery at Iona;* . . . Vol. LVIII, pp. 102–111. 1923–4.

Cursiter, James W.: *Notes on a Hoard of Silver Ornaments and Coins, Discovered in the Island of Burray, Orkney,* Vol. XXIII, pp. 318–322. 1888–9.

Denaro, Victor F.: *The Canongate, Edinburgh, and Maltese Silver.* Vol. 102, pp. 237–40, Pls. 19–21, 1969–70.

Dowden, John: *The Inventory of Ornaments, Jewels, Relics . . . belonging to the Cathedral Church of Glasgow in 1432.* Vol. XXXIII, pp. 280–329. 1898–9.

Dunglas, Lord: *Notice of The Discovery of a Massive Silver Chain of Plain Double Rings or Links at Hordwell, Berwickshire.* Vol. XV, p. 64. 1880–1.

Edwards, A. J. H.: *The Mary Queen of Scots Pendant.* Vol. LXXIV, pp. 137–8, and Pl. LIV. 1939–40.

Eeles, Francis C.: *The Methven Cup: A Piece of Sixteenth Century Scottish Plate.* Vol. LV, pp. 285–289. 1920–1.

Eeles, Francis C.: *The Guthrie Bell and its Shrine.* Vol. LX, pp. 409–419. 1925–6.

How, G. E. P.: *Scottish Standing Mazers.* Vol. XVIII, pp. 394–411. 1933–4.

How, G. E. P.: *Early Scottish Spoons.* Vol. LXIX. pp. 138–157. 1934–5.

McKerrell, Hugh: *Chemical Analysis of the Cadbol Cup and Watson Mazer.* Vol. 104, pp. 309–15. 1971–2. [See Stevenson, R. B. K., 1971–2.]

Macpherson, Norman: *Notice of Communion Cups from Duirnish, Skye, with notes of Other Sets of Scottish Church Plate.* Vol. XX, pp. 399–446. 1885–6.

Macpherson, Norman: *Notice of a finely ornamented Chalice of Silver, parcel-gilt. The Property of R. B. Ae. Macleod, Esq. of Cadbol.* Vol. XXII, pp. 423–32. 1887–8.

Maxwell, Stuart: *The Galloway Mazer.* Vol. LXXXVIII, pp. 227–8 and Pl. XLV. 1954–5.

Maxwell, Stuart: *The Queen Mary Jewel.* Vol. XCIII, pp. 244–5 and Pl. XIV. 1959–60.

Maxwell, Stuart: *An Embossed Silver Standing Dish of 1667–9.* Vol. XCVIII, p. 325 and Pl. XLV. 1964-6.

Maxwell, Stuart: *A Silver Coffee Pot and Hot Milk Jug by Colin McKenzie, 1713.* Vol. 100, pp. 199–200 and Pl. 24. 1967–8.

Richardson, A. B.: *Notice of a Hoard of Broken Silver Ornaments and Anglo-Saxon and Oriental Coins found in Skye.* Vol. XXVI, pp. 225–240. 1891–2.

Sanderson, James H: *An Account of the Plate Marks used in Scotland Since the year 1457, and Chronological list of those of Edinburgh since 1681; to which is added a Note of Those Used in Glasgow.* Vol. IV, pp. 541–8 and Pls. XIX and XX. 1861–2.

Simpson, J. Y.: *Notes on some Scottish Magical Charmstones or Curing—Stones.* Vol. IV, pp. 211–224. 1860–1.

Simpson, W. Douglas: *Excavations at the Doune of Invernochty.* Vol. LXX, pp. 170–81. 1935–6.

Smith, John Alexander: *Notice of a Silver chain or Girdle . . . and of Other Ancient Scottish Silver Chains.* Vol. X, pp. 321–347. 1872–3.

Smith, John Alexander: *Notes of . . . Silver Chains found in Scotland.* Vol. XV, pp. 64–70. 1880–1.

Stevenson, J. H.: *The Bannatyne or Bute Mazer and its Carved Bone Cover.* [With five appendices by other writers.] Vol. LXV, pp. 217–55. 1930–1.

Stevenson, R. B. K.: *Charles I's Coronation Ampulla.* Vol. LXXXII. pp. 237–41. 1947–8.

Stevenson, R. B. K.: *Pictish Chain, Roman Silver and Bauxite Beads.* Vol. LXXXVIII, pp. 228–30. 1954–6.

Stevenson, R. B. K.: *The Kames Brooch.* Vol. XCV. pp. 308–9 and Pl. LIX. 1961–2.

Stevenson, R. B. K.: *The Cadboll Cup.* Vol. 104, pp. 306–8. 1971–2. [See McKerrell.]

Struthers, J.: *Note of a Gold Brooch of the 13th or 14th Century, found in the Water of Ardoch, near Doune Castle.* Vol. VIII, pp. 330–3. 1869–70.

Stuart, John: *Historical Notices of St. Fillan's Crosier, and of the Devotion of King Robert Bruce to St. Fillan.* Vol. XII, pp. 134–182. 1876–7.

Tulloch, Very Rev: *Notice of Three Silver Vessels Belonging to St. Mary's College, St. Andrews.* Vol. XVII, pp. 141–4. 1882–3.

PART THREE: ARTICLES

Auld, A. A: *Silver—Some Recent Acquisitions* [by Glasgow City Art Galleries and Museums] in *Scottish Arts Review,* Vol. XI, no. 3, pp. 22–3. Glasgow 1968.

Baker, Malcolm: *Quiet Splendour of Kirk Silver.* In *Country Life,* Vol. CXLVIII, pp. 386–7. 13 August 1970.

Baker, Malcolm: *Patrick Robertson's Tea Urn and the Late Eighteenth Century Edinburgh Silver Trade.* In *Coinnoisseur* Vol. CLXXXIII, pp. 89–94. August 1973.

Beard, Charles R: *The Monymusk Reliquary.* In *Coinnoisseur* Vol. XCII, pp. 182–3. November 1933.

Bryden, D. J: *Three Edinburgh Microscope Makers: John Finlayson, William Robertson and John Clark.* In *The Book of Old Edinburgh Club.* Vol. XXXIII, pp. 165–76. Edinburgh 1969.

Comstock, H.: *Edinburgh Teapot of 1726.* In *Connoisseur* Vol. CIV, pp. 298–9. December 1939.

Cumming, Victor J: *Old Scottish Silver.* In *Apollo* Vol. XXVIII, pp. 10–12. July 1938.

Cardew-Wood, L. T: *Calcutta Silver.* In *Proceedings of The Society of Silver Collectors* No. 2, pp. 6–8 and 2 plates. London 1960.

Clayton, Michael D. G: *Archery Prizes and Medals.* In *Proceedings of The Society of Silver Collectors.* No. 11, pp. 17–21. Autumn 1968.

Coles, John M.: *The 1857 Law Farm Hoard.* In *Antiquities Journal* XLVIII, pp. 163–74. 1968.

[Cramond, William]: *Clockmaker, Watchmakers, Gold and Silversmiths and Jewellers . . . in the City of Elgin . . . 1697 until . . .1838.* In *The Scottish Antiquary,* Vol. III, pp. 48–9. Edinburgh 1889.

Cuthbert, Alexander: *Scottish Wine Labels and Scottish Provincial Marks*. In *The Wine Label Journal*, pp. 141–6. n.d. [*c*.1960].

Dalgleish, George: *Prince Charlie's Canteen*. In *The Antique Collector*, October 1985, pp. 66–71.

Drysdale, William: *Notice of an Ancient Gold Seal in the Possession of J. W. Williamson Esq. of Kinross*. In *Archaelogia Scotia* Vol. IV, pp. 420–1. Edinburgh 1857.

Eogen, George: *The Associated Finds of Gold Bar Torcs*. In *Journal of The Royal Society of Antiquaries of Ireland*. Vol. 104, pp. 74–119. 1974.

Fell, H.G: *Scottish Silver at Stratton Street* [Messrs. How of Edinburgh] in *Connoisseur*. Vol. CIII, pp. 107 & 109. February 1939.

Finlay, Ian: *Old Scottish Silver In Scottish Churches*. In *Connoisseur* Vol. CIV, pp. 64–70. August 1939.

Finlay, Ian: *Scottish Silver*. In *Apollo*. Vol. XLIV, pp. 145–148. December 1946.

Finlay, Ian: *Scottish Silver*. In *Apollo*. Vol. XLV, pp. 31–34. February 1947.

Finlay, Ian: *Scottish Silver*. In *Apollo*. Vol. XLV, pp. 67–70. March 1947.

Finlay, Ian: *The Watson Mazer*. In *Apollo*. Vol. XLVIII, pp. 101–2. November 1948.

Finlay, Ian: *Scottish Silver in Edinburgh*. In *Connoisseur*. Vol. 122, pp. 88–93. December 1948.

Finlay, Ian: *Scottish Silver*. In *Antiques*. Vol. LVI, pp. 271–3. October 1949.

Finlay, Ian: *Some Silver and Gold Work recently acquired by The Royal Scottish Museum*. In *Apollo* Vol. LIII, pp. 69–72. March 1951.

Finlay, Ian: *Highland Pistols*. In *Antiques*, September 1951, pp. 198–9.

Finlay, Ian: *The Milne Davidson Collection*. In *Connoisseur* Vol. CXXXV, pp. 173–7, May 1955.

Finlay, Ian: *Old Scottish Sporting Plate*. In *Country Life*, 12 January 1956, pp. 68–9.

Finlay, Ian: *Scottish Ceremonial Plate*, Part I. In *Apollo*. Vol. LXIII, pp. 6–8. January 1956.

Finlay, Ian: *Scottish Ceremonial Plate*, Part II. In *Apollo*. Vol. LXIII, pp. 48–50. February 1956.

Finlay, Ian: *Silver in The Royal Scottish Museum*. In *Connoisseur* Vol. CXLIII, pp 9–13. June 1959.

Finlay, Ian: *The Finest Age in Scottish Silver*. In *Country Life*, 27 August 1959, pp. 130–133.

Finlay, Ian: *Silver Seal Case of The Earl of Montrose*. In *Burlington Magazine*. Vol. CI, pp. 404–7. November 1959.

Finlay, Ian: *Masterpieces of Scottish Silver*. In *Country Life*, 22 August 1963, pp. 443–4.

Fothringham, H. S.: *Scottish Silver: Marks Are Not Everything*. In *Antique Finder*, December 1972, pp. 14–15.

Fothringham, H. S.: *Small Inverness Quaichs c.1760–c.1840*. In *Antique Collector*, April 1973, pp. 73–6.

Grimwade, A. G.: *A New List of Old English Gold Plate*, Part I. In *Connoisseur*. Vol. CXXVIII, pp. 10–16. 1951.

Grimwade, A. G.: *A New List of Old English Gold Plate*, Part II. In *Connoisseur*. Vol. CXXVIII, pp. 83–89. 1951.

Hallen, A. W. Cornelius: *Silver Mines at Alva, Stirlingshire*. In *The Scottish Antiquary*. Vol I, pp. 53–5. Edinburgh 1888.

Hallen, A. W. Cornelius: *Scottish Pearls*. In *The Scottish Antiquary*, Vol. IV, p. 82. Edinburgh 1890.

Harbison, P.: *Hartmann's Gold Analyses: A Comment*. In *Journal of The Royal Society of Antiquaries of Ireland*. Vol. 101, pp. 159–60. 1971.

Hawkes, C. F. C.: *Gold Earrings of the Bronze Age, East and West*. In *Folklore* Vol. 72, pp. 438–74. 1961.

How, G. E. P.: *Scottish Teaspoons*. In *Connoisseur*. Vol. XCII, Supplement p. 30. November 1933.

How, G. E. P.: *Scottish Standing Mazers*. In *Connoisseur*. Vol. XCIII, pp. 313–9, and p. 340. May 1934.

How, G. E. P.: *Early Scottish Spoons*. In *Connoisseur*. Vol. XCVIII, pp. 341–6. December 1936.

239

How, G. E. P.: *Scottish Silver Teapots.* In *The Antique Collector.* May 1939. pp. 108–11.

How. G. E. P.: *Canongate Goldsmiths and Jewellers.* In *Burlington Magazine* Vol. LXXIV, pp. 283–88 and 2 plates. June 1939.

How. G. E. P.: *Scottish Silver* In *Notes on Antique Silver.* No. 1, pp. 19–23. 1941.

How. G. E. P.: *Sentiment for Sale.* In *Notes on Antique Silver.* No. 2, pp. 7–11. 1942.

How. G. E. P.: *The Watson Mazer, A Criticism.* In *Apollo.* Vol. XLIX, pp. 16–17, 1949.

Hutcheson, A.: *Old Communion Plate, Dundee.* In *The Scottish Antiquary,* Vol. VII, pp. 6–9. Edinburgh 1893.

Jones, E. Alfred: *Collection of Sir J. H. B. Noble: Old English, Scottish and Irish Silver.* In *International Studio.* Vol. XCVI, pp. 48–52, May 1930; and pp. 20–4, June 1930.

Jones, E. Alfred: *Some Old Scottish and English Plate of The Marquess of Linlithgow, K.T.* In *Apollo.* Vol. XVIII, pp. 153–161. September 1933.

Jones, E. Alfred: *Binning Collection of Old English and Scottish Plate.* In *Burlington Magazine.* Vol. LXVIII, pp. 118–125. March 1936.

Jones, E. Alfred: *Collection of Plate of Sir John Stirling Maxwell, Bart. K.T.* In *Apollo,* Vol. XXIII, pp. 96, 99–104, February 1936; and pp. 207–14, April 1936.

Jones, E. Alfred: *Some Scottish and English Plate at Castlemilk.* In *Burlington Magazine.* Vol. LXXI, pp. 278–83. December 1937.

Jones, E. Alfred: *Old Silver in Scottish Churches.* In *Connoisseur.* Vol. CI, pp. 316–20. June 1938.

Jones, E. Alfred: *Silver at the Exhibition of Scottish Art.* In *Burlington Magazine,* Vol. LXXIV, pp. 71–2 and plate. 1939.

MacRoberts, David: *Some Post-Reformation Chalices.* In *The Innes Review.* Vol. XVIII, Part 2, pp. 144–6. Autumn 1967.

MacRoberts, David and Charles Oman: *Plate Made by James II & VII for the Chapel Royal of Holyrood in 1686.* In *The Antiquaries Journal,* Vol. XLVIII, Part 2, pp. 285–295. 1968.

Murdoch, A. D.: *Reply to Query about Old Scottish Church Plate.* In *The Scottish Antiquary,* Vol. I, pp. 30–2. Edinburgh 1888.

Norman-Wilcox, G.: *The Methven Cup.* In *Los Angeles Museum of Art Bulletin,* Vol. 13, No. 3, pp. 10–15. 1961.

Norman-Wilcox, G.: *Some Jacobite Silver.* In *Los Angeles Museum of Art Bulletin,* Vol. 17, No. 4, pp. 13–15. 1965.

O'Dell, A. C. and others: *St. Ninian's Isle Silver Hoard.* In *Antiquity* Vol. XXXIII, pp. 241–268, December 1959.

Oman, Charles C.: *Scottish Silver at the Royal Academy.* In *Connoisseur* Vol. CIII, pp. 70–75. February 1939.

Penzer, N. M.: *The Tree, The Bird, The Fish and The Bell.* In *The Wine Label Journal,* pp. 92–5. n.d.

Robinson, F. W.: *Eight Examples of Prehistoric Irish Gold.* In *Detroit Institute of Art Bulletin* Vol. 33, No. 3, pp. 64–5; and No. 4, pp. 53–4.

Scott, Jack G.: *Scotland's Ancient Treasures.* In *Scottish Arts Review* Vol. III, No. 4, pp. 8–10 and colour plate. 1951.

Scott, Jack G: *Gold Ornaments of the Bronze Age.* In *Scottish Arts Review.* Vol. VI, No. 3, pp. 15–17. 1957.

Stevenson, J. H.: *The Usher of The White Rod.* In *The Scottish Antiquary.* Vol. XI, pp. 158–70. Edinburgh 1897.

Stevenson, R. B. K.: *Pins and The Chronology of The Brooch.* In *Proceedings of The Prehistoric Society,* Vol. XXI, pp. 282–94. 1955.

Stevenson, R. B. K.: *The Hunterson Brooch and its Significance.* In *Medieval Archaeology,* Vol. XVIII, pp. 16–42. 1974.

BIBLIOGRAPHY

Victor Cumming Collection of Silver, The. In *Scottish Arts Review.* Vol. I, No. 3, pp. 24–5, 1946.

Watt, Rosemary: *Ten Years of Silver Purchases for Kelvingrove.* In *Scottish Arts Review.* Vol. XV, No. 2, pp. 16–21. n.d.

Whyte, Joy Scott: *Scottish Silver Teaspoons.* In *Scottish Arts Review.* Vol. X, No. 4, pp. 8–13 and 29–30. 1966.

Whyte, Joy Scott: *Scottish Silver Tablespoons.* In *Scottish Arts Review.* Vol. XI, No. 2, pp. 12–17 and 27–9. 1967.

Wood, Marguerite: *The Hammermen of Canongate* (Part I) In *The Book of The Old Edinburgh Club.* Vol. XIX, pp. 1–30. 1933.

TABLE OF PLATES AND OWNERS

NOTE:

An asterisk (★) before a plate number indicates that the item was not illustrated in the first edition of this work. The page numbers in the column on the right refer to entries in the text. There are a few instances of objects whose present whereabouts and ownership are not known for certain. These have usually passed through the hands of dealers and are probably all now in private collections.

CHAPTER 8: EARLY COMMUNION PLATE

CHAPTER 9: SECULAR PLATE, EARLY SEVENTEENTH CENTURY

CHAPTER 10: SEVENTEENTH CENTURY PROVINCIAL WORK

CHAPTER 11: THE LATER SEVENTEENTH CENTURY

CHAPTER 14: EDINBURGH – THE LATER EIGHTEENTH CENTURY

CHAPTER 15: THE BURGH CRAFTSMEN, 18th and 19th CENTURIES

Cruickshank. *Private.* p.209

PLATE 120,i: Sugar Bowl and Cream Jug. Banff, *c.*1735, by Patrick Gordon. *Stolen from the late Mr. John Noble.* pp.212–213

★PLATE 120,ii: Oval Sugar Basket with Swing Handle. Canongate, *c.*1780–84, by John Robertson. *Edinburgh City Museum, Huntly House.*
p.178

★ ★ ★ ★ ★ ★

INDEX

Seal-case of 3rd Earl of Montrose, Canongate, 1604, by George Cunningham senior.